RULING CLASS, RULING CULTURE

RULING CLASS
RULING CULTURE

Studies of conflict, power and hegemony
in Australian life

R. W. CONNELL

CAMBRIDGE UNIVERSITY PRESS
Cambridge
London · New York · Melbourne

Published by the Syndics of the Cambridge University Press
The Pitt Building, Trumpington Street, Cambridge CB2 1RP
Bentley House, 200 Euston Road, London NW1 2DB
32 East 57th Street, New York, NY 10022, USA
296 Beaconsfield Parade, Middle Park, Melbourne 3206,
Australia

Library of Congress catalogue card number: 76-22981

ISBN 0 521 21392 4 hard covers
ISBN 0 521 29133 X paperback

First published 1977

Printed in Great Britain
at the
University Printing House, Cambridge

CONTENTS

TABLES AND FIGURES

TABLES

FIGURES

Note: Sums of money are expressed throughout in Australian dollars, unless otherwise specified.

If there remained any lingering doubt about the class nature of Australian politics, the events of late 1975 must have resolved it. There is hardly a clearer case, in the recent history of the 'western democracies', of the way a threatened ruling class is able to mobilize fragments of state power, business connections, financial resources, and the legitimacy given them by the dominant culture, in a campaign to remove an offending government.

The Labor leadership itself immediately interpreted the coup of October–November as the product of a personal lust for power in the Liberal parliamentary leadership. This was an understandable reaction, but it is far from being an adequate analysis. The stock market, a sensitive if oblique indicator of the state of mind of capitalists, jumped 17 points on the day Whitlam was dismissed, and had previously twitched upwards at every rumour of trouble in the government. Fraser's parliamentary manoeuvre had only been made possible by the intransigence of conservative state governments in refusing to replace Senate vacancies with Labor nominees; Kerr's dismissal of Whitlam was made possible by the banks' refusal to extend temporary finance. As the essays in this book show, the moves of late 1975 were only the last in a series of attempts to mobilize ruling-class forces since the fragmentation of the early 1970s. This time, with the aid of the Governor-General appointed by Whitlam himself because of his respectability and moderation, they succeeded.

That says a lot for respectability and moderation. In fact the Whitlam government had been distinguished for just these traits. For all the ranting that was heard from the right about 'Canberra socialism', it had a most circumspect and modest programme of reform. Only a few redistributive measures had squeezed through the parliament, and nothing radical was in train. The government had managed to impose a partial wage freeze on the union movement, and was moving towards accommodations with mining and manufacturing capital. Within the spectrum of constitutional reformers in the Labor leadership, the more radical had been defeated or discredited in the year before the conservative constitutional coup. The threat of Labor was, by most standards, not a very terrifying one. But it seems that even the Whitlam brand of reform, committed to making capitalism a little more just and a good deal more efficient, is something that powerful sections of the Australian ruling class cannot stand for long.

The essays in this book will, I hope, go some way towards making these bizarre events intelligible by filling in their structural and cultural context. With the exception of Chapter 7, they have all been written over the last three years as products of a larger project that has attempted to grasp and analyse the class patterning of Australian society. In *Class Structure in Australian History* Terry Irving and I have given an account of the processes of class formation and class interaction in the past, and developed a theoretical framework to analyse it. The essays in this book take that history and theory as their point of departure for the analysis of contemporary politics and culture. They are written in the conviction that class analysis is fundamentally historical, that the present is intelligible as history and only in that light. They are also written in the conviction that theory is best developed in concrete analyses. A definite theory of class underlies the analyses presented here, but apart from the short introductory sketch it is not expounded separately.

The first part of this book sets out briefly the logic of class analysis, and explores the ways in which class questions have been treated in Australian social science. The second part brings together a number of studies of the ruling class in Australia, focussing on the recent history of its dual leadership. The third part steps back from politics and big business to examine consciousness and cultural processes, ending with a speculative chapter on the general pattern of hegemony in Australian life. This is the most important, and the most tentative, of these essays; for breaking through hegemony is both the most difficult and the least understood of the problems confronting Australian socialism.

This is a collection of studies, not a comprehensive account of the class structure. Most obviously it does not tackle the relationship between sexual oppression and class structure, or the dynamics of the labour movement. Yet there is a consistency in its problems and approach. The collection is offered in the belief that an analysis of this kind is badly needed, both in constructing a sociology of Australian life and in working out plans for political and cultural action. The modest successes, hesitations, and defeats of reformism in the first half of the 1970s must not be dismissed, or bewailed, but studied and learned from. There is a lot of history still to come; we have only begun to fight.

11 November 1975   R. W. Connell

ACKNOWLEDGEMENTS

Pam Connell, Terry Irving and Murray Goot have worked over these issues with me for a number of years, and their ideas, criticisms, and researches have shaped a great deal of this argument. Research by Martin Indyk was the inspiration for Chapter 5, as explained there. For critical comments on various chapters at different stages I am indebted to Ron Witton, Henry Mayer, George Munster, Tim Rowse, and the participants in a number of conferences listed below. For source material I am indebted to the secretaries of many of the companies discussed in Chapter 4, and the children and teenagers who took part in the surveys analysed in Chapters 7–9. Mary Pollard did the transcription of interviews in Chapter 7; Rebecca Jackson and Heather Williams did the typing and layout of the manuscript.

Some of these chapters have seen print in earlier versions: Chapter 3 as 'Structure and structural change in the Australian ruling class' in E. L. Wheelwright and K. Buckley, ed., *Essays in the Political Economy of Australian Capitalism*, vol. 1, Sydney, ANZ Book, 1975, 227–41; Chapter 5 as 'Conflict in the Australian ruling class, 1970–1972' in M. Richards and R. Witton, *The American Connexion*, Melbourne, Macmillan, 1976; Chapter 7 as 'Class consciousness in childhood' in the *Australian and New Zealand Journal of Sociology*, 1970, vol. 6, 87–99; Chapter 8 as 'Class structure and personal socialisation' in F. J. Hunt, ed., *Socialisation in Australia*, Sydney, Angus and Robertson, 1972, 38–66; Chapter 9 as 'Myths media and the middle-class', *New Journalist*, March–April 1974, no. 13, 16–20. For permission to reproduce material I am indebted to the publishers and editors of these publications. (All papers have however been rewritten, some extensively, for this book.) Chapters 3, 6 and 10 are based on papers given to the

Sociological Association of Australia and New Zealand in 1973, 1974 and 1975; 2, to a seminar at the Australian National University in 1975; 4, to the Sydney class analysis conference in 1975; 5, to the ANZAAS congress in 1973; and 9, to the Media and Society conference in Adelaide in 1974.

Approach to Class Analysis

In 1973 there was a long strike at the Ford car-assembly plant at Broadmeadows near Melbourne. During the late 1960s and early 1970s Ford Australia, a subsidiary of the American multi-national, had expanded rapidly with a strategy of producing large, flashy, fast saloons, which turned out to be immensely popular. In early 1973 it was on the point of displacing General Motors-Holden from its leading position in the Australian car market. At the same time the motor industry unions, spurred by a rising rate of inflation, were about to launch a campaign for increased over-award payments to employees, one of the more flexible parts of the wage structure. They intended to put pressure first on GMH, as the company in the most vulnerable position.

But the Ford workers took the issue away from their officials. At a mass meeting on 18 May, where union officials were ex-plaining their tactics, they insisted that demands be more actively pressed on Ford, and stopped work. After some weeks' strike Ford management offered a modest wage rise, and at a mass meeting of workers on 11 June a vote was taken to return to work. But the vote was close; many of the workers did not speak English and had not understood what was being voted on; there remained bitter opposition to a return without more concessions from the company. On 13 June, the day scheduled, some went back to work but others, perhaps 2000 strong, gathered outside the plant to picket it. The Ford management decided to close the gates, and a violent demonstration erupted, with the workers attacking the buildings, smashing windows, and clashing with the police who had been sent in by the state government. The company refused to negotiate further until the unions were able to 'control' their members; the union officials, badly shaken, moved to a more militant position in support of their members; and the strike resumed. The Federal Minister for Labor weighed in with an attack on the multinational company and its control of industrial issues from New York. In early July GMH arrived at an agreement with the unions for higher over-award payments, but Ford remained intransigent on this issue, while offering concessions about working conditions on the assembly line. After nine weeks' strike the position of the workers had deteriorated. The deadlock ended with a proposal for an enquiry on the wage issue by an Arbitration Commission judge; at a mass meeting on 23 July, carefully organized by the unions with interpreters, the assembly workers voted by a large majority to go back to work. A month later the arbitrator recommended a small rise in over-award payments and a relaxation of the company's penalties for late attendance. Both sides accepted the solution.

How can an event like this be understood? At one level, simply as an industrial episode: a squabble over pay which happened to turn nasty; which cost, as the newspapers duly calculated, $60 million worth of car production and $3 million in wages. Yet in every way the industrial dispute points beyond itself, to a larger structure of relationships. The fact of a largely migrant workforce points to the way the expansion of industrial capitalism in Australia has depended on an inflow of relatively cheap labour from Europe; and their unexpected militancy challenges the common assumption that migrants make a docile labour force. The unions' tactics depended on the oligopolistic structure of the motor industry, and the pressure that a threat to profit or market share can place on the management of capitalist enterprises. The company's determined resistance is one illustration of the financial strength of multinational companies, even when employer solidarity within an industry, the traditional basis of the industrial strength of local capital, is lacking. The intervention of the two governments – one to protect the company's property, the other to criticize multinational control – and the Arbitration Commission, raise the question of the relationship of the state to the system of industrial production, and the connections of the major parties with industrial interests.

And at a deeper level again, the Broadmeadows strike relates to some basic features of the social order in which it occurred. If one asks what the strike was 'about', the immediate answer is over-award payments; if one asks why the sums involved were important to workers, the answer relates mainly to their positions in families and the dependence of domestic life on wage income. Wages, moreover, were only one of the issues in the strike. Others related to the nature of work and social control on an assembly line, penalties for lateness, getting an afternoon tea break, getting a relief worker for those who wanted to go to the toilet. The last point is not meant to be humorous – it is rather a striking illustration of the physical humiliation imposed on workers by social control in the work-place under industrial capitalism. The dramatic shift of a section of the Broadmeadows workers, well beyond the position taken by a union leadership that was actually quite mili-tant – even the Communist officials in the unions concerned were left flat-footed – points to a level of anger and a potential for radicalization in the workforce that is normally completely concealed. And the context in which the whole thing happened, as the immigrant origins of both the workers and the company illustrate, was not simply the outskirts of Melbourne in a particular winter, but a pattern of relationships that extends across the world and back through decades of history.

To understand the strike in depth, then, demands more than an account of industrial relations. It demands an analysis of politics, of the structure of business, of the nature of industrial production and private life; and in particular it demands a way of accounting for the relationships among all these things. This is essentially what class analysis attempts to do. The theory of class is a theory of the organization of social relationships on the very large scale, which is concerned above all to establish the connections between disparate facts, and apparently separ-ate spheres of life. An event like the Broadmeadows strike can then be understood as a crystallization of patterns, and a realization of possibilities, that can be traced through many other places and times.

'Class analysis' is not a single pattern itself. On the contrary, there is an enormous range of theory and speculation about class. This is to be expected from its importance, complexity, and opacity, not to mention the struggles of classes and their intellectuals to define the social world in ways that are friendly to their own interests. To begin to cut through the mighty jungle of modern literature on class and stratification, it is useful to make some logical distinctions. I would suggest that the most important, in terms of what a theory is good for, is between two types of approach which may be called respectively 'categorical' and 'generative'.

A categorical theory is one whose basic move is to find a systematic way of sorting people. All societies, a familiar argument runs, are 'stratified', that is to say divided into groups or sections which are hierarchically ordered in some way. The task of theory is to discover and formulate the bases of this division and ordering in various societies, and the task of research is to trace out their correlates and consequences. The underlying notion of class is that of a kind of map-maker's grid, on which people (or in some versions, families) can be located. Spatial metaphors – 'social mobility', 'social distance', 'dimensions' of differentiation, even 'stratification' itself – are so fundamental to it that their non-metaphorical meaning is normally taken for granted. The characteristic research problems that arise are matters of technique: identifying the dimensions, measuring the distances, and correlating other things with them.

This is the conception of class that underlies most of the modern sociology of stratification, including survey research on mobility and the various dimensions of differentiation, some American functionalist theories of social hierarchy, and neo-Weberian stratification theories. But it is by no means confined to the universities, nor to bourgeois theory. A lot of left-wing thinking about class is also in the 'categorical' style: notably versions of marxism which take a bourgeois–proletarian distinction as a fixed framework and devote themselves to fitting particular groups into it, or interpreting events, particularly political events, as signifying the presence of this framework.

Marx's own theory was not of that type; the systematic exposition of class categories was of such minor importance to him that he left it an unfinished fragment at his death. *Capital* begins with something quite different, a discussion of the nature of commodities and the transactions that make up a labour market; and from this foundation Marx's massive analysis of the history and dynamics of capitalism is developed. Here is a theory of class as a structure generated by the operation of some fundamental and highly general processes, whose effects ramify from the labour market into all other spheres of life.

4

We may call this type of theory 'generative' (on the analogy of linguistics) to stress its most distinctive feature, the way in which elementary structures and processes are seen to generate a huge and complex historical reality. The stress here is on the processes producing social groupings, rather than the categories they produce; and on the activity of people, not merely their location in social space. There have been other attempts to develop this kind of theory, such as Dahrendorf's attempt to make authority relations (rather than property relations) the basis of class theory; and, in some regards, Parsons' sophisticated functionalism. Marxism of Marx's kind remains the most important and fully developed instance of generative theory.

Its importance lies, as his work shows, in the possibility of offering an account of the historical dynamics of societies. If class is, as Thompson roundly declared, an event, rather than a category – and that idea, however formulated, underlies all socialist politics – then we need an approach to class that makes it possible to reveal its historical emergence and analyse it as a causal pattern. It is generative theory that is needed to give an account of the linkages that become apparent in analysing an episode like the Broadmeadows strike; and this type of theory underlies the analyses in this book.

The basic ideas used, briefly, are these. The system of power that we call private property or private ownership defines a labour market, in which employer–employee relationships are formed. The system of property means that the employer keeps control of the product of the work. This makes possible the gaining of profit and the accumulation of capital, a basic dynamic of the system. Rights of property are transferable, and the system has been modified to allow a partial transfer of rights, which allows the combination of capitals and the formation of companies, now the main form in which private ownership of industry is organized.

Capitalist society, characterized by these processes, develops a class structure, and it is the structure as a whole that is primary – classes develop in interaction (both conflict and alliance) with each other. The class structure develops by the extension of the labour market to engulf other forms of economic organization, and the economic, social and political mobilization of the groups who appear in the labour market. Mobilization typically occurs under the influence of smaller groups, who may find their positions solidifying as the leadership of a class. It is conditioned by the consciousness of class membership, and the possibilities of class action, that have been developed by the members of emergent classes. Mobilization is never total, and can be reversed. Working-class mobilization is always undertaken against odds, not only the economic but also the political and cultural strength of the owners of capital. Where the mobilization is weak and the indirect controls effective, we speak of a hegemonic situation.

A vital means by which direct and indirect controls are imposed is the activity of the state. The state is understood as the sphere of direct enforcible social relationships (as against the indirect relationships of markets), which underlie markets and also provide the basis for the construction of the state organizations such as courts, parliaments and government departments. One of the characteristic forms of class mobilization is a struggle for control of these organizations. A major form of working-class politics devotes itself to this struggle in order to use the state organizations to improve the lot of the underprivileged without changing the basic character of the state or the labour market. Following a convenient though tendentious left-wing tradition, we may call this 'reformism', and contrast it with anarchist and socialist politics which imply an abolition of the state and the labour market.

The state organizations are typically confined within the boundaries of 'nation-states'; but the growth of capitalism has seen a spread of property relations across the world and the development of imperialist systems where the labour and raw materials of one region are exploited by the capitalists of another. There is a tendency for a reproduction of the entire capitalist system wherever its basic structures are introduced. But in much of the world this is checked by the overwhelming economic strength of the major capitalist powers. In recognition of this we speak of the world system of capitalism as 'imperialism' while acknowledging its polycentric character.

This is a very bald outline; some suggestions about how it can be filled in in the analysis of specific problems, will be made in later chapters. The ideas derive, as will be obvious, from the socialist tradition of class analysis. Within that tradition they are eclectic, though not, I think, inconsistent. I depart from the marxist system on some crucial points, such as the postulates in the analysis of the labour market from which such conclusions as the declining rate of profit are deduced; but have found a great deal of value in Marx's work as a model of method, and his modern followers' in the analysis of consciousness and culture.

A generative theory, however convincing or unconvincing in the abstract, is only validated by yielding an intelligible account of historical reality. And a schematized history is of no value. The detail of events must be examined, and at times rather more than detail; facts, as Norman Mailer remarked at the trial of the Chicago Seven, are nothing without their nuances. Here I have tried to get some of the nuances, as well as the brutal outlines, of Australian capitalism, and to show how all can be used in building an interpretation of the whole.

2

The idea of class in Australian social science

Both of the great upswings in class conflict in twentieth-century Australia, in the 1910s and the 1940s, produced a burst of socialist argument about class relations and political change, and both produced an outstanding critic, researcher, and analyst. The first, Vere Gordon Childe, served an apprenticeship in the NSW Labor Party, and out of the depth of his anger produced what is still the most informed, sustained, and biting critique of Australian labour politics. But his anger also drove him from the country, and so the most brilliant intellectual Australia has produced never gave a full-scale analysis of his own society – though it drew him back to a strange death in the end.[1] The task was taken up by Brian Fitzpatrick, in a series of books and pamphlets produced in the years 1939 to 1946. Sharing with most socialists a conviction of the importance of economic process, Fitzpatrick produced a detailed economic history of Australia as the product and field of British imperial expansion. From this base he moved to a history of the Australian people and of the labour movement, reading this partly as the bearer of democracy and partly as a means of social integration in the interests of capital. As a radical activist he produced a vivid analysis of power and ownership in Australian business, and fought a sustained battle against censorship and repression by successive governments.[2]

No one will deny that there were flaws in Fitzpatrick's arguments. They were, as Irving and Berzins have argued, strongly tinted with the populism common in Australian radicalism; he often simplified the analysis of the ruling class to an attack on 'monopoly', and hence among other things missed the rise of the new groups of capitalists involved in industrial diversification that were gathering strength in the 1940s. Looking back into history, he, like other contemporary intellectuals such as H. V. Evatt, was prone to discover classes wherever he discovered oppression.[3] Both tendencies perhaps flowed from the lack of any formal theory of class, an impatience with what George Orwell in 1940 called 'the smelly little orthodoxies' that dominated political thinking at the time, but which happened to include, in marxism, the strongest line of socialist theory about class. Fitzpatrick also, by focussing on the place of the Australian colonies in the trading economy of the British empire, underplayed the formation and growth of cities, whose economic weight has been shown by later technical research, and whose significance as the matrix of class formation has also become increasingly clear.[4]

But such criticisms of the details of Fitzpatrick's formulations pale beside the intellectual and moral scale of his project. Here, produced under difficulties (he was not cushioned by university lectureships) in the heat of political struggle, was an attempt to grasp the whole process of formation of the social structure, not as an object of literary contemplation but as a guide to the transformation of an oppressive society. Here was an attempt to show the interconnections of the structure of economic power, the life of ordinary people, the emergence of resistance movements, and the place of the country in a world context. It was a remarkable achievement; and however corrected by later research, it remains the most impressive model in Australian writing of what class analysis is about.

But to say that, is to say that Fitzpatrick produced no successors – at least, none who attempted to do the same kind of thing. The period of class struggle in the 1940s ended, not with a break-out towards socialism, but with a ruling class victory. The next generation saw a conservative hegemony in politics and the completion of industrialization under firm capitalist control. In intellectual life, a corresponding movement occurred. Fitzpatrick's flawed synthesis broke up and was replaced with specialisms. In the universities, sociology emerged with a claim to give a scientific account of social structure independent of historical method; while history became more technical, and itself divided into specialisms like economic history, labour history, and the history of politics. In tracing the accounts of class given by both disciplines, we are in effect studying, at the most rarefied level, the emergence of a new hegemony: a slow, complex, but very definite retreat from the radical implications of Fitzpatrick's intellectual position.

Class and the historians

In the 1950s and 1960s academic studies in Australian history multiplied. As Rowse has argued, there was an attempt by many intellectuals to re-think the character of Australian civilisation and society from the new vantage-point of an advanced industrial capitalism.[5] In academic history this mainly took the form of a monographic exploration of political and economic developments. Class processes of course come into most of the problems that were written about. This is particularly clear in regional studies: thus we find treatments of class differentiation and economic relationships in regional histories of pastoralism and its transformation such as Kiddle on the Western District and Waterson on the Darling Downs, and we find a sketch of 'class relations and the rise of Labour' in Serle's history of Victoria in the 1880s.[6] So a full analysis of the treatment of class would require a complete historiography. Since my concern is with the underlying conception of class and its relationship to methods of analysis, I will concentrate on the work of a smaller number of historians where the approach to class is relatively explicit or fully worked out.

The banner of class analysis since Fitzpatrick's day has been most prominently carried by historians of the labour movement.

Labour history is history of a new kind: it introduces the concept of masses rather than *élites* as the moving forces in the historical process ...The labour movement is the institutional method by which the masses transform themselves from passive to active elements in society, from weights to be pushed around to social levers in their own right.[7]

So Turner in 1965, in what remains the most complete statement and illustration of the project of labour history: history written by the left, for the left, and – by virtue of the second sentence – mostly about the left. What theory of class, and what method of analysis, are contained in its practice?

Gollan's *Radical and Working Class Politics*, which appeared in 1960, is a useful point of departure. The book announced a class framework in its title, and its author had no inhibitions about talking of classes. His usage is in fact remarkably uninhibited. There is a 'privileged class', a 'propertied class', an 'employing class', an 'upper class' and a class of squatters [but not anywhere, I think, a ruling class]; a 'middle class', a 'middle class of small scale producers', a class of independent farmers, 'professional classes', and at one point a Legislative Assembly 'drawn mainly from the professional, small landowning, manufacturing, and trading classes'; a 'working class', 'poorer classes', a 'wage- and salary-earning class', a class of bushworkers, a class of employees, etc.[8] Plainly, 'class' is not being used as a consistent theoretical category.

What then is the theoretical basis of the book? At first reading one might think it was a methodological idealism. Gollan takes as primary certain democratic ideas and aspirations, and enquires into how these were realised in politics. The Land Acts, for instance, are presented as 'the culmination of a political struggle between two opposed concepts of society', in which democratic political ideas 'were confirmed as the ruling ideas in Australian society during the second half of the nineteenth century'.[9] The book thus becomes a history of ideas, more exactly a history of ideas-in-social-context; the context being provided by a theory of interests, and these in turn being identified by the statements of men who became active in politics.

But on closer examination, this is not an adequate analysis of what Gollan is doing. There is certainly an idealist programme in the book; but the meat of it is an analysis of political and to a lesser extent economic organization, and the details of a series of parliamentary and organizational struggles. The categories in which this analysis is conducted – with one important exception, where Gollan describes the 'new unionism' of the 1880s as the process of a class becoming conscious of itself[10] – are essentially those of the actors themselves. Hence the diverse usages of 'class' in the book, which reflect the language of class in the period itself. Classes themselves are taken as unproblematic facts.

The basis of the book, then, is a methodological empiricism of a fairly thoroughgoing kind. Class *is* what the documents say it is. Regardless of the political intentions of the author, class history is assimilated to the mainstream of academic historiography, whose characteristic approach – as illustrated in the journal *Historical Studies* as well as in the teaching programmes of Australian history schools – had developed by the 1960s into an empiricism characterized by technical virtuosity and very little else.

In *Industrial Labour and Politics* a few years later, Turner formulated a more systematic definition of the 'working class':

It is used here to describe an objective social category: the class of men and women who work for wages, as distinct from the employers of labour and the self-employed.[11]

His usage is consistent with the definition. But the kind of history he writes in the book is very like that of Gollan: it is a history of the organizations of the labour movement, their factional conflicts and their involvement in politics. The working class is present essentially as background to this analysis. In the first chapter of the book Turner discusses the economic context, and describes the working class in an economic-demographic sketch of major categories of employees; he even develops some account of the character of work. But apart from some discussions of wage movements and the trade cycle, the social relations of the workplace (let alone those surrounding it) drop out of sight in the body of the book. And when he comes back in the last chapter to describe 'The Working Class in 1921', politics is all – the chapter is in effect an account of the state of play in the unions, parties, and socialist sects.

This focus on organizational politics is characteristic of most writing on labour history. Combined with the empirical methodology that gives much of this writing its technical strength, we get a result that is really very curious for the intellectuals of a labour movement. For we find that class exists in these histories *by allusion* – either as a statistical category that provides an abstract backdrop to the drama of the political actors, or through the shadows it casts in the minds of the actors themselves.

The latter becomes very clear in Gollan's most recent book, *Revolutionaries and Reformists*, which traces the Communist Party from the early twenties to the mid fifties – i.e. through some large-scale changes in the class structure. The working class, in this book about the 'party of the working class', is hardly ever referred to, except when the political actors are talking about it; and then only in their terms. The logic of Gollan's first book is here carried to an extreme. In conse-

quence his important conclusion about the failure of the revolutionaries to be revolutionary[12] is left without explanation –
except the implicit one that this happened to be the current
outcome of tactical battles in the unions. There is no theory
of hegemony; indeed there is no theory of resistance. One is
left without any particular explanation of why so many people
should have joined and struggled in the way the book
describes, of how such a party was possible.

Plainly, something very important has been lost by the
methods that produce this kind of history. The social context
of politics has been lost, or at best rendered abstractly. The
experience of the process of production – whose importance
Gollan notes right at the end of his first book[13] – the way such
experience generates a politics; the cultural struggle to define
the experience; the social structure and characteristic interactions of working-class life – all of these are missing, and with
them, more than half the working class. Women appear in these
books, and until very recently in the pages of *Labour History*,
only in rare irruptions into union and public-political affairs. At
one point Turner explains that domestic servants and shop
assistants are 'not relevant to a study of the labour movement
since they gave rise to no significant trade unions '[14] – as if that
were the only way they could be 'relevant'. Children, and the
process of child-rearing, character and attitude formation,
appear not at all.

The most important extension of labour history towards a
history of the working class comes in works of a narrower
focus, on the history of particular unions or strikes. Gollan has
written one of the best of these, *The Coalminers of New South
Wales*. The book is principally a history of industrial relations
in the coal industry and the politics surrounding it, and this
takes it beyond a history of the miners as it requires also an
analysis of the employers and the interaction between the two.
Particularly in his discussion of the nineteenth century, where
he is able to draw on the records of the Australian Agricultural
Company (the leading miner, despite its name), Gollan is able
to give an illuminating account of the relationship between
working-class and ruling-class economic organisation –
showing *inter alia* the importance of the union in promoting
employer organisation. But the analysis of this interaction is
limited to industrial relations and pressure-group politics. And

apart from a few gestures towards the idea of the miners' settlements as isolated communities, the explanation of their radicalism rests on an account of the technical conditions of their work.

This, again, is characteristic of much labour history; but there have since been some interesting attempts to extend the approach. Dixson's work on the coal lockout of 1929–30 has shown the role of extra-union activity, particularly by women, in sustaining industrial militancy; and Cochrane's study of a Victorian coal town on the other side of the Depression has shown the bases of a union victory in the mobilization of the social and economic resources of an entire town. Richardson's analysis of the background of the Port Kembla 'pig iron' strike is another notable example of how the roots of industrial action can be traced back into the experience, social structure, and economic history of a district.[15] All three, of course, are studies of relatively isolated settlements, and it no doubt easier to grasp the totality of the problem at this level than when discussing events in Sydney or Melbourne.

Labour history is, as Turner remarks, 'almost necessarily partisan'; and it seems that this affects in a very general way the notion of historical process as well as the identification of goodies and baddies. Labour history is characteristically written within a framework of social progress, 'assuming that in Australia the labour movement has been the principal initiator of social change'.[16] Organization, struggle and triumph against difficulty are the springs of the story. In such a framework it is difficult to think of ideology as anything but the ideas of the movement, or the rhetoric of its opponents. The concept of a dominant ideology serving the interests of the powerful through a structure of social control is difficult to formulate. But the problem cannot be escaped; and if not formulated explicitly, its influence is felt indirectly. All four of the books just discussed, end in a minor key: one with the Labor leadership losing touch with its roots, one with the miners in retreat before mechanization, one with the emasculation of the One Big Union and the socialization objective, and the last with the Communist Party discredited and splitting. In the conclusion of the last book Gollan has retreated a long way indeed from the democratic character he gave the 'ruling ideas' in the nineteenth century; now characterizing the scene of the communists' labours as 'a community whose predominant values were reactionary and obscurantist'.[17] Strong words, and a big change – if it was a change. Only a direct analysis of the problem of ideology can tell.

Ward's *Australian Legend* (1958) was precisely that: an attempt to analyse the dominant ideology in Australian history – quaintly hung on the peg of national character – and trace its sources in the social structure. Stepping back from formal politics, Ward addresses himself to the question of social relations and the social attitudes– explicitly distinguished from political attitudes – that grew out of them. In the tedious dispute over national character, this level of Ward's history has been somewhat neglected. He is for instance one of the few Australian writers of any kind, not only historians, to recognise (in Erikson's words) 'that all people start as children and that all peoples begin in their nurseries'; and to recognise that sexuality is an important dimension of social life, needing analysis rather than derision.[18]

If there is an idealist programme implicit in Gollan's work, it is explicitly stated and argued for by Ward:

> The dreams of nations, as of individuals, are important, because they not only reflect, as in a distorting mirror, the real world, but may sometimes react upon and influence it.[19]

The tone is defensive, even apologetic, but the position is clear. Yet the claims for the influence of ideology remain vague, because in fact Ward is focussing upon another problem. Where Gollan presupposed ideology and enquired into its realisation in politics and union organisation, Ward takes the ideology as problematic and enquires into the way it was produced. The basic concept is that there is a social base for the ideology, a key group out of whose experiences it arose and by whose social practices it was shaped. From this base it was conveyed to much wider groups:

> From the beginning, then, outback manners and *mores*, working upwards from the lowest strata of society and outwards from the interior, subtly influenced those of the whole population.[20]

Ward devotes a good deal of attention to the processes by which this osmosis is supposed to have occurred.

For all its importance, the social base is a curiously nomad category: the more closely one tries to approach it, the more it seems to retreat. The creators and bearers of the ideology are first convicts and the sons of convicts, then the Australian-born generally; workers in the bush, then bushworkers west of the Dividing Range, and especially in New South Wales; then cattlemen more than sheepmen. The retreat finally ends at the idea that there is a kind of 'élite' ('anti-élite' might be better) of overlanders who are the purest of the lot.[21] The general intention is clear, but the categories used in pursuing it are hardly models of consistency. Ward is if anything more exuberant than Gollan in his use of class terms – 'lower orders', 'working people', 'working men', 'labouring classes', 'pastoral proletariat', 'working class', 'bushmen', all at various times seem to cover the same people.

That this is not simply a matter of giving variety to the writing, that Ward is in fact uneasy with class concepts, is shown by a trick of style. His much-quoted statistical argument about the weakness of the middle class in the mid nineteenth century is curiously undermined by the fact that the phrase 'middle class' in his own text is in inverted commas – as, within a few pages, are the 'upper class' and the 'gentry'.[22] He seems much more certain about the existence of the workers. The unease, and the inconsistency of language, are symptomatic. Ward is able, as a sensitive analyst of situations, to trace the relations between workers and owners in the pastoral industry, not only their conflicts but also their solidarity and shared attitudes. But there is no theory of class formation or theory of ideology to give shape to his research.

In consequence, faced with the fundamental problem of explaining the ideology he traces, Ward falls back on that great standby of colonial social analysis, environmental determinism.

Such ideas as they [bushmen] held in common were practical rules of conduct, or habitual modes of thought and action, springing directly from the conditions of their life or from their traditions which, as we have seen, were themselves largely a response to the material environment.[23]

At a later point he suggests the mediating role of social relations, in adopting the suggestion that the environment made the Australian outback a big man's frontier; but in most of the book the effect of environment is direct. And in this Ward has decisively abandoned class analysis. One is not surprised at ending the book in the grip of a faded nationalism where '. . . today's task might well be to develop those features of the Australian legend which still seem valid in modern conditions.'

The task of McQueen's *A New Britannia* (1970) is to demolish this line of argument, and he sets about it with great vigour and – in the early part of the book – similar methods. The argument is about the common assumptions of political and social attitudes and familiar literature, refuting the idea that they are fundamentally radical. Ideas are loosely tied to social bases identified by the familiar smorgasbord of class and quasi-class terms: 'workers', 'labouring classes', 'lower class', 'middle classes', etc. Indeed at times McQueen outstrips the vagueness of ideas like 'national character' and 'Australian legend' to speak of 'Australia' as an actor in its own right.[24]

But as he moves on from demonstrating the full nastiness of the national tradition to an account of the social groups involved in its creation, the outlines of a very different approach to class emerge: a much more coherent and systematic approach indeed. The crucial step is to query the applicability of class concepts, as understood in formal socialist theory, to Australian society in the nineteenth century. As he remarks on the earliest period,

It is misleading to clothe the convicts in the aura of class struggle since for its first fifty years at least, Australia did not have a class structure, but only a deformed stratification which had been vomited up by the maelstrom which was redefining class in England.[25]

One might take issue with the implications of 'deformed' – what is a well-formed class structure in colonial conditions? But this should not obscure the major theoretical advance implied in the assumption that the concept of a *class structure* is the basis of the application of class terminology, and that this is a special kind of social order. It is not equivalent to any system of stratification, or any system of exploitation or oppression, as Fitzpatrick and Evatt, as well as more recent writers, had been inclined to assume. It arises, as McQueen develops the argument later, only at a fairly advanced stage of economic development (by implication, with the dominance of industrial capitalism); and a working class (or a proletariat, if one wants to speak Latin) is present only where there is a body of wage

17

labourers created by this development whose interests commit them to the destruction of capitalism. Plainly, in Australian history, that can only be a twentieth-century affair.

This theoretical framework immediately poses the problem of class formation as the crucial historical question; and McQueen's main line of argument is developed around this issue. He gives an account of the way the political and economic (not natural) environment of the early labour movement and the 'labouring classes' (it is admittedly difficult to write about it without some kind of shorthand) shaped their social theory and political practices as the radical wing of a widespread liberalism rather than in opposition to it. So far Gollan could agree; but McQueen formulates the dynamics of the development very differently, as a case of hegemony where the cultural and political initiative came from owners of property, and the labour movement was contained with *their* ideological framework.[26]

McQueen's position is not derived from an accumulation of new facts that place old interpretations in doubt; as he notes himself, *A New Britannia* relies largely on the 'old left' historians for its data. It arises from a conscious break with empiricist method; what he is doing is comparing the materials of Australian historiography with the categories of a pre-existing model of class, which are given to him by the European marxist tradition. His theory of class does not arise from the study of Australian history, it is confronted with it – and one has the sense that Australian history does pretty badly out of the confrontation. The obvious danger in this, apart from any objections one might have to that particular theory of class, is that the argument may become teleological. Thus McQueen speaks of the 'immaturity' of the labouring classes in the movement for land reform (his own analysis suggests their responses were quite appropriate to the actual situation), and of the emergence of a 'genuine' working class (as if there were something inauthentic about what went before).[27]

It is difficult to quarrel with an author who disarmingly discovers five major weaknesses in his argument while reading the page proofs;[28] but there are two limitations in his treatment of class that should be noted. The first concerns the problems of hegemony and class alliance. With the important exception of the exploration of literary racism, these are treated essentially in terms of political ideas and practices. In this, Mc-Queen's work is narrower than Ward's, which attempted to grapple with the question of the social relations of production and at least some of the social relations extending out from it. McQueen is here closer to the focus of Gollan and Turner. The second is that the implications of the idea of class structure and the idea of hegemony itself are worked out only on one side – the side of the subordinate groups. If one takes the idea of hegemony seriously, it is the *hegemonic* groups that must provide the focus of an account of the situation. In the roll-call of groups whose part in the ideological origins of the Labor Party provides the structure of McQueen's book – emigrants, convicts, diggers, selectors, etc. – there is one echoing absence: capitalists.

The missing material is provided, in full measure and running over, by Clark, in a massive research project that has been going since the 1940s. In his books of documents (1950–7), *Short History of Australia* (1963), and the three volumes so far of *A History of Australia* (1962–73), we have an attempt to grasp and represent the meaning of Australian history on a scale even grander than Fitzpatrick's. Clark is not only a comprehensive but also a complex and subtle historian, whose methods and concepts are not always immediately obvious. His treatment of class is on the whole indirect – a chapter called 'Towards a Colonial Gentry', for instance, is mostly about high politics and passion at the end of Darling's administration, and contains no discussion of class formation – and has to be extracted from an analysis of his general method.[29]

This may well start with his explicit idealism. Clark's great work is announced as a study of the coming of civilization to Australia, and 'civilization' has the meaning above all of systems of ideas – a much more traditional concept than that developed by Childe.[30] The plot of his drama is that of the clash of great systems of thought, and in due course the emergence of new visions of man and the world. As with Ward, then, we might expect to find social groups, including classes, treated essentially as the bases or bearers of ideologies, and this is to some extent true. The commercial bourgeoisie of the 1840s, for instance, emerges in Clark's treatment as the carriers of a 'British philistinism' which is to sweep all (or most) before it; the labour movement of the twentieth century is the carrier (though not the only one) of a social optimism which gets more and more battered by fate. Once again, however, this is not a complete methodological idealism. At least in his treatment of the nineteenth century, Clark has a sharp eye for material interests and economic constraints. He gives a brilliant short sketch of the political economy of the Hobart bourgeoisie, for instance, and knows that the Rum Rebellion was not a product of class conflict.[31] It is rather that Clark, while aware of power structure and economic process, interprets their significance in terms of ideology.

Clark sees the bearers of ideology (if one can reduce his 'visions' and 'faiths' to that prosaic term) more often as persons than as social groups. He announced early the importance of character and the small details that betray it:

Parkes, for example, appears quite often *as a name* in this collection, but consider how much he *begins* to come alive if we put in the illuminating detail that his hand-shake was as cold as that of the proverbial fish.[32]

His later narrative is developed as a series of character-sketches and chronicles of personal action. The society the characters move in, and create, often seems to be an afterthought:

While the actors in the centre of the stage were creating all this sound and fury from the day Phillip landed till Bligh sailed out on the high seas in May 1810, other developments were occurring in the colony of New South Wales and its dependencies. The settlement gradually spread: population increased: a convict system was created: the natural wealth was exploited: the rudiments of a civilization began to take shape.[33]

The impression, however, is misleading. Clark is often talking about social groups and processes by a technique of personification. Thus for instance he takes Riley and Hume as exemplars of the early settlers and their vicissitudes in the chapter whose opening was just quoted; a pseudonymous letter-writer, 'Betsey Bandicoot', as a symbol of the brash native-born populace; and in the *Short History*, Hughes, Lang and Curtin as illustrations of the perspectives generated by the labour movement. At its best, this technique produces a social history that is not only more vivid than a discussion of groups *per se*, but also solves one of the most difficult problems of historical exposition by achieving a synthesis of economics, ideas, and daily life within the basic unit of writing, the narrative episode.

At its worst, it falls back into the bad old practices of history before Namier, before the Webbs, indeed before Ranke. In Clark's account of the twentieth century, not only do we find a primacy of parliamentary politics, but we find that parliamentary politics is the rise, decay, and fall of great men: an utterly conventional moral tale. And when it is simply being applied in a routine fashion, the effect is repetitive without being cumulative. The long discussion of 'country gentlemen' in the 1840s amounts to a series of homestead histories that repeatedly approaches, but repeatedly evades, the problem of class formation. Similarly Clark escapes the problem of talking about the industrial working class by talking about parliamentarians, militants, optimism, etc.; when the working class does appear, it is simply as followers of the leaders.[34]

The top-down perspective that is obvious here can be found, in a more subtle but very pervasive form, in most of his work. He writes a lot about the convicts, the pastoral workers, the currency lads and lasses; but he writes about them very largely as the lower orders, from the perspective of their social superiors. This follows from a basic feature of his method. Though opposed in feeling and intention to the bland empiricism of mainstream academic history, he embraces a radical empiricism in the course of writing. His prose can very often be found, when compared with the documents on which it is based, to be constructed of extracts from documents, woven into paragraphs by Clark, but reproducing sentences, phrases, even cadences, from the originals. It is, in Collingwood's term, scissors-and-paste history;[35] raised to a high art, but scissors-and-paste nonetheless. The point of Collingwood's comments on this method is that it prevents one from criticising the documents themselves, and extracting knowledge of a new order from the process of critique. It is symptomatic that Clark's notes normally consist of bare citations, not analyses of the sources, and the text rarely has analyses either. Clark then is committed, apart from his editorial comments on character and fate, to the perspectives on events available to him in his material. And this perspective is normally, naturally, that of the literate, propertied, respectable and male – those who have produced the overwhelming mass of the surviving documentation of Australian history. For lack of a method and theory that would allow him to grapple with the problem of hegemony in the evidence itself, Clark has produced, in the final analysis, a phenomenology of Australian society as seen by its rulers.[36]

The combined effect of an idealist purpose, a technique of personification, and a phenomenological approach to social reality is to work a suppression of social process. If one asks of Clark's history 'how do things happen?', the answer very often is, 'by chance' – different things just happen together. One of his favourite phrases is 'by an odd irony . . .'. By odd ironies, in various contexts, Wentworth does not approach the colonial office – John Macarthur crushes a small landholder – an immigrant writes of Australia as a land of hope – the mighty in London contribute to the destruction of the aborigines – the critics of the Pastoral Association seek help in London – the Petrov affair brings ALP faction fighting to a head. 'Life, as John Macarthur was fond of saying, was a fearful lottery – and not without its odd ironies.'[37] No doubt one can satirize any style. The point is that Clark's history really is heavily dependent on contingency and chance, for it is juxtaposition which allows him to bring out the spiritual significance of events and people. At times it is good dramatic technique, at times it becomes bathetic: 'At the same time over in New South Wales public men went on talking about those things which touched them most deeply . . .'[38] Either way, it pushes out to the fringes of attention the connections between events which make history intelligible from the perspective of social process. Clark is capable of analysing process, as a couple of instances already cited show; and he does have a general outline of the history of dominant classes and class relations in Australia, which is actually quite like McQueen's.[39] But in the body of his work, class is present only as the understanding of class held by his characters, or as part of the stage machinery which makes their moral drama more poignant.

In these historians, then, we can see the erosion of the class framework for history that had sustained an earlier generation, affecting even history written from a consciously radical standpoint. The erosion occurs under the influence of an empiricist methodology (distinguishing empirical methods, which are of course used in class analysis, from a methodology that constitutes the immediately given as the unique object of study), and the emergence of new problematics, which can be seen most highly developed in Clark. Class does not disappear from history, but it is transformed; it moves from centre stage to backdrop, and changes from a dynamic process to a system of categories or social perceptions. McQueen is able to separate himself from this only by an act of intellectual violence. But in doing so he stakes the claim of class theory on this territory, and in the last few years the claim has begun to be worked. We may now examine the course of events in sociology. It turns out to be rather similar.

Class and the sociologists

The emergence of a self-conscious discipline of sociology in the 1960s is one of the more interesting, even curious, developments in recent Australian intellectual life, and there is already some discussion of its causes and its meaning.[40] The approach to class that characterized university sociology in the late 1960s, however, began rather earlier; it came out of other academic contexts, notably anthropology and psychology, and was soon practiced in departments of politics, education, and social work. A large body of research accumulated – a bibliography covering Australian studies on stratification in the period 1946–67, certainly incomplete, listed nearly a thousand books, articles, and pamphlets[41] – though it was characteristic that there were very few attempts to draw the findings together and extract their message. The passion of the sociologists was description and measurement, not analysis and synthesis. As with the historians, a complete account of this literature would be an enormous, and unfruitful, task. I will concentrate on the more notable pieces, those which seem to be diagnostic of the sociology of class as an intellectual enterprise.

The main outlines were drawn in the volumes on *Social Structure and Personality in a City* and *Social Structure and Personality in a Rural Community* published by the Melbourne University psychology school in the early 1950s, reporting a series of surveys and observations in a suburban district of Melbourne and in a small town in the Mallee. The inspiration for these studies had nothing to do with class, coming rather from field theory in social psychology and the post-war concern with the origins of prejudice – the main funding came from an international research programme on this topic. But because the problem was posed in terms of a study of 'social tensions' and tensions in the late 1940s patently had a lot to do with class, both books deal quite extensively with the subject. They deal with it from several perspectives, as they were written by committees whose members obviously had conflicting ideas. There are three rather different approaches to class that can be disentangled from the texts.

The first is an approach to class in terms of economic conflict, in several sections evidently written by Sharp, the group's field research organizer. His approach is plainly marxist, though it is very much more sophisticated than the crude historical determinism that passed for theory in the Communist Party at the time. There is for instance an excellent discussion of the linkages between economic conflict and social hostility, an attempt to link economic processes with the categories of ortho-dox survey research via an account of control in the work situation, and a discussion of the division of labour in the rural economy.[42] This must rank as one of the most interesting and original pieces of analysis to come out of Australian socialism. But is has remained unsung, and appears to have had little influence on the other authors of these volumes. For their main discussion is carried on in a very different manner, where 'class' exists essentially as a grid for the classification of other things: attitudes, family structures, childrearing practices, and so on. The focus is not on the interaction of classes, the issue central to marxist theory, but on their similarities and differences. The technique is the descriptive survey; and the implied role of class analysis is to provide a useful scale of social categories that can be entered in the survey plan as an independent variable. The scale chosen – a choice that has become nearly universal in later survey research – is a scale of occupations; which in much of the *City* volume is called 'class' *tout court*.[43] The third approach, developed in the *Rural Com-munity* volume, attempts to extract from intensive observation of a relatively small settlement an account of the main social groups that are differentiated in the habitual face-to-face inter-actions of the inhabitants: class, in effect, as people do it. This yields a vivid portrait of the local élites, particularly the somewhat philistine Methodist farmers who were carried by the rural boom to dominance of the town; and piquant descriptions of the isolation of the poor in old age and the plight of single labourers stuck on the farms where they were employed.

Here are two approaches to class that break sharply from the conceptions of Fitzpatrick's work a few years earlier. Neither is argued for theoretically as an alternative, but one can sense the movement. Indeed at one point one can see it, where a draft of Sharp's was rewritten by Hammond, and the class concepts are eroded (rather than directly criticized) in a cautious discussion of 'factors that cut across and obscure this relationship between class position and social tensions'.[44] The effect of the psychological theory and tradition of measurement was not to give an alternative account of class processes, but to displace them. The focus, in the *City* volume particularly, moves from class as social structure to class as a problem in a theory of attitudes. Class consciousness which is explored in detail by survey technique, is thought of as the attitudinal consequence of position in a taken-for-granted framework of social categories. Indeed with the development of the occupational grid, class itself can be classified on it; and thus we get the problem of 'social mobility', understood as the statistical question of the relationship of the father's position on the grid to the child's.

The approach used in the second of the Melbourne studies had already been developed, in a rather more systematic way, in the anthropology department at Sydney University under Elkin. Sociology to Elkin was the application of scientific method to illuminate the problems of contemporary society – the problems then being handled unscientifically by politicians, social workers, etc.[45] The main method available was the protracted field observation familiar in ethnography; and since it is hard to observe a city, the product tended to be an intimate account of a country town. This poses the problem of how to move to an analysis of the whole society. The Mallee Town study made the link by pointing to economics and government, stressing the dependence of the district on the international wheat market and the involvement of local white-collar workers in city-based bureaucracies; but had not attempted to generalize except to other farming towns. A different solution was offered in an article summing up the Sydney research by Martin, called 'Marriage, the family and class' (1957).

The solution involved a generalization of the idea of class as a grid, a system of classification of persons:

Whatever embellishments may be attached to class differences, a class structure in any society must be based ultimately on the differentiation of the total population, whereby some sections enjoy greater access to 'social values' – the most highly valued goods, services, positions and activities – than do other sections. The members of the society are ranked according to their positions on certain commonly recognized scales. There have existed societies where a single criterion such as land ownership virtually determined social status. The class structure is much more difficult to conceptualize when it is based on several scales of ranking, as in our own complex society. Wealth, occupation, education, and family membership are the important scales in this country...

The differentiation of the Australian people in wealth, occupation, education, and family membership provides the raw material out of which the class structure is built, for such distinctions become the basis for the objective ranking of people into higher and lower grades and for the individual's subjective judgment of his own position.[46]

Three features of this position are important. As is suggested in the argument about 'any society', the aspiration of this kind of theory is to refer to all possible societies; it is not based on an understanding of the dynamics of any particular type. Its logical basis is necessarily extremely abstract. The intellectual affiliations are not with socialist class analysis but with the sociology of stratification that had developed as an answer to marxist theory in European and American universities, and had been given classic formulation by Parsons in the 1940s.[47] Martin however does not adopt the functionalism of Parsons' version – nor have most of her local successors – and hence is left in some difficulties in explaining why things should be thus.

The second point is that class is understood to consist of a system of grades, whose members constitute 'strata'; it is an instance of the categorical models of class discussed in Chapter 1. In much local writing since, class has simply been reduced to the scales of income, occupation, etc., themselves. Martin takes a more subtle, and more defensible, position: that these scales form the bases of social evaluations which have their consequences in the interactions of daily life. Here the material from the descriptive community studies comes into its own, as education, family prestige, etc., are shown to affect the details of interpersonal relations. This leads to an interesting argument about the role of women in the maintenance of the class structure which has received all too little attention. Even so, an intractable problem remains: how are the 'grades' to be defined on the implied dimension of status; indeed how many of them are there? Ultimately, there could be as many as the most subtle distinctions of status made in daily life; or as few as the observer chose to regard as vital. This indeterminacy is common to all stratification models, and will be encountered again and again in local empirical research.

The third point is the stress on the 'complexity' of Australian society, in particular the argument that there are a number of 'scales of ranking', or in the terminology that has become more common, 'dimensions' of stratification. Martin argues that they form 'an interrelated system, one factor strongly influencing another',[48] and offers illustrations of the links. They remain, however, conceptually distinct at the most fundamental level; the connections between them are empirical and contingent. (Nor is any reason given why these four should be thought the vital ones in Australia.) Again, this has been characteristic of much later sociological writing; the existence of a number of measurable dimensions has served as an argument against unified accounts of class, and indeed seems to have become something of a barrier to causal argument of any kind.

Nonetheless Martin is able to pose the question of class formation. Within the stratificationist framework this becomes a question, not of how the major dimensions of differentiation are formed, but of how the strata (as abstract categories) defined on them, or on a scale of status derived from them, become 'cohesive units which are class groups in the fullest sense of the phrase'.[49] The main case analysed here is the pastoral élite, whose social solidarity is in large part a matter of kinship ties. This is a matter of crystallization of networks within a social category, not a matter of the dynamics of the whole system. Dynamics, in fact, are treated only through the problem of social mobility, which is used to point out the 'flexibility' of the structure. In a curious argument, Martin objects to Barcan's commonsense observation that Australia has a 'large working class with middle-class standards of living' (commonsense if one reads this as meaning that real income from wages in the 1950s widely approached what were traditionally thought of as middle-class levels) on the grounds that this obscures both the re-evaluation of standards (thus the framework of differentiation is preserved) and the way higher incomes stimulate individual mobility (odd, if the first point is correct).[50] For a moment the argument has touched on the question of hegemony and the formation of a labour aristocracy; but the stratificationist assumptions insistently pull it away.

I have dwelt on this paper (without exhausting it) not only because it has the best description of Australian class relations produced in two decades of local sociology, but principally because it states in a particularly clear and persuasive way the method of thinking about class that, with variations more of technique than of ideas, became dominant in Australian sociology. The largest body of work has developed the idea of scales of differentiation through the application of survey methods, and it is necessary to say something about the general logic of this technique. Surveys of one kind or another have been done in Australia at least since 1845, when Caroline Chisholm toured the back blocks of NSW collecting life histories of immigrants by 'placing in the hands of the individual a folio sheet of paper containing a column of printed questions, and a blank column for written answers'.[51] The modern style of survey, with a definite theory of sampling and refined techniques of analysis, got under way in the 1930s in the universities, commercially in the 1940s and in the 1950s was very widely used; by 1965 Davies and Encel could even define sociology as 'an academic discipline seeking to illuminate the results of social surveys'.[52] There are of course infinite variations on survey methods. Most, however, have been built on two foundations: what Lafitte in an early and penetrating critique called 'categorical abstraction',[53] by which social reality is sliced, in the process of collecting and organizing information, into a few distinct categories of 'facts' (e.g. in the answers to forced-choice questions); and the technique of cross-classification, with statistical refinements such as correlation and factor analysis, as the basic method of analysing the results. The close correspondence of these features of survey method with the logic of a stratificationist approach to class practically guaranteed their marriage.

The first problem of stratification research is the care and maintenance of the dimensions of stratification themselves. Survey research takes nothing (except its own method) on trust; the supposed dimensions had to be shown to exist by being measured, and methods devised for classifying people on them. A good deal of effort went into this in the late 1950s and the

1960s, in which the rough scales used in the Melbourne studies and in public opinion polling were refined and extended. The logic of the research can best be seen in the studies of the status of suburbs and occupations by Congalton, published in a series of small monographs in 1961–3 and reprinted in 1969 in a book called *Status and Prestige in Australia.*

The method is superb in its simplicity. Congalton took a list of suburbs from a street directory of Sydney, and printed each name on cards. Interviewers (evidently mostly students) were then sent out into the world with collections of the cards. 'Each person to be questioned was to be asked to indicate the amount of prestige associated with a particular suburb by ranking it on a 7-point scale.'[54] That is, the cards are sorted into seven piles, from those with 'the highest social standing' to those with 'the lowest social standing'. Since people do not always agree on the right pile, an average is taken; the seven piles are declared equivalent to the numbers 1 to 7, and averages across all respondents are calculated arithmetically. Measures of the extent of disagreement can be calculated, as well as averages for particular groups in the sample (which is done for a sub-sample of real-estate agents!). An exactly similar method is applied to get a scale of the prestige of occupations, using 135 job names in the place of names of suburbs.

The results of these surveys have been widely used in research (and widely reprinted in popular magazines). They have come in for a certain amount of technical criticism: the sampling is rotten, the measures of average values are arguable, etc. But these points can in principle be cleaned up, and have been in later research that has used essentially similar methods to generate status maps of cities.[55] The important point is what is common to all these studies: that the set of statistical averages is taken as the meaning of the term 'status'. No matter if the subjects are not very clear about what they are doing in sorting the little cards into piles (as some of them complained),[56] if one can show statistically that there is a certain measure of agreement in the piles produced. Status has been successfully measured, and the *measure* in effect becomes the *thing*.

With an abstract method of stratification research established, the ambition grew to make it more systematic. Prestige is after all, only one of the dimensions of which stratification theory speaks. The drive towards systematization, which developed in the 1960s mainly in the work of sociologists in Canberra, has taken two main forms. The first was an attempt to organize statistical material already available, mainly in the census. One branch of this has been a re-classification of census job-categories into a composite occupational scale (drawing on studies of prestige, income, etc.), on which all sections of the workforce can be represented; this can be applied for instance, to tracing the expansion and contraction of occupational groups over time, by reclassifying the material from each successive census onto the common scale.[57] Another branch is 'social area analysis', in which census figures about jobs, households, nationality, etc. are taken for each of the collectors' districts (a few blocks each) of a city, and correlated with each other. Factor analysis can then be applied to summarize the sets of intercorrelations as a small set of principal dimensions, and scores on these dimensions can be calculated for each collector's district, yielding ultimately a map of the patterns of differentiation in the city – which is taken to be an account of dimensions of 'urban social structure', or more modestly, a 'social ranking' of suburbs.[58]

What can be got this way is of course limited to what is in the census, and that is very limited. To get closer to the model of multidimensional stratification theory, it was necessary to mount new surveys, and this was done by Broom, Jones and Zubrzycki (more exactly by a market research company under their instructions) in 1965. They announced this, rather boldly, as 'a nationwide survey designed to provide a first approximation to delineating the social stratification of Australia';[59] and as it is a centrepiece of local stratification research, more sophisticated and systematic than most other survey studies, it is worth examining in a little detail. The basic idea was to collect, from each of the 2000-odd members of their sample, information about 'five measures of social rank', and a variety of other things such as voting, religion, etc., that could be correlated with them. The five measures – it is interesting that in the main reports of the study there is no initial explanation of why these five were chosen, apart from the fact that they are 'widely used', nor of the nature of the thing they were supposed to be 'measures' of – were 'subjective social class identification' (i.e. what class the respondent said he or she was a member of), interviewer's assessment of the respondent's 'economic class' (a standard item in the polls done by the firm employed), and three 'objective attributes of the respondent' – income, occupation, and education. These were made into five scales. In the case of education there appeared to be 'natural breaks' defining 'functionally pertinent categories' (primary, secondary, etc.), but in the others the usual stratificationist problem of where to locate cut-off points had to be solved in the usual way, arbitrary definition.

The intellectual problem that was then posed, and whose solution to Broom, Jones and Zubrzycki constituted 'a first statement of the social stratification of Australia's population', was what the relationships among these five scales were. The relationships were conceived (in contrast to Martin's approach to the problem) as purely statistical: it was a problem of finding the correlations, which is of course a straightforward piece of arithmetic. The correlations turned out to be all positive, and to cluster around 0.4. The next move was very striking:

The pattern of intercorrelations...indicates that all five measures of social rank throw significant light on Australia's stratification system. Yet no single measure is sufficiently discriminating to warrant treatment as a criterion variable...

A more useful approach to the analysis of Australia's system of social stratification is to regard each of these five measures of social rank as contributing *some* information about a given individual's position in the national stratification system, and to treat them as a set of interdependent variables whose joint effect determines an individual's social rank position.[60]

This is done by a principal components analysis, a technique that summarizes the relationships among the correlations (themselves summaries of the statistical relationships between the original variables). The first principal component is taken to represent 'social rank': it becomes a scale, on which individuals can be given scores by a combination of the original variables; and clusterings of scores on it (identified statistically) are taken as defining 'strata'. Here, finally, is the empiricist apotheosis of class, class by the bootstraps; for what, in the final analysis, the five 'measures of social rank' are measuring is – themselves.

Broom, Jones and Zubrzycki went on from this rather startling position, not to reconsider the notion of 'social rank', but to explore in other articles the connections between their main variables and pieces of information such as voting, father's occupation, ethnicity, etc. The most recent stage of their research, as outlined by Jones, seems to have dropped the index of social rank in order to concentrate on occupation. It is still very firmly within the stratificationist framework, taking the existence of a system of 'statuses' as unproblematic, and enquiring into the ways people are distributed among them.[61]

In the substantial body of survey research, from many hands, that has looked at the connections among occupation, voting, nationality, attitude, etc., and that has been accumulating since the 1950s, class normally appears as a kind of pigeon-hole, along with age, sex, etc., for the classification of respondents. The question typically posed is whether there are differences in attitudes, intelligence, or whatever the subject of the survey is, between groups defined in such ways; and if there are, there is sometimes a little speculation about the economic or cultural reasons.[62]

Cross-classification studies in political science, however, have led in rather more interesting directions so far as the concept of class is concerned. Correlations between occupation, scaled in the usual way, and party preference have regularly appeared in surveys since the 1940s. This is hardly news; but the repetition of such polls has made it possible to trace changes in the strength of the relationship. A North American survey analyst who undertook this study roundly declared that 'the Australian parties have distinctive class bases', but found that the level of 'class voting' (class being understood as the difference between manual and non-manual workers) declined in the 1950s and 1960s. He was able to draw some interesting inferences about the political effects of shifts in the general level of occupational polarization. (Not surprisingly, this was taken to refute Marx.)[63] This at least gave a high-level structural interpretation of the relationship. Other political scientists who included questions about class consciousness in the survey package, and found it correlated with the vote, read off the link in subjective terms and made out both things to be expressions of a 'general social stance'. In the mid 1960s Davies pushed this to its logical conclusion in some fascinating surveys of class images. He escaped the rigidities of scalar models and the difficulties of definition, but did it by dissolving class almost entirely into class consciousness, understood in essentially psychological terms.[64]

The bulk of survey research on class, however, has been of the kind sketched before. It developed largely under North American influences, some of the studies actually being carried out by visiting academics and many others being attempts to replicate locally the findings of overseas research; a number indeed have been published overseas. The understanding of class, and the problems about it that were tackled, arose more from these sources than from local political needs. This is not to say, however, that local stratification studies lacked political and ideological significance. They had it, in two ways. If practical conclusions are drawn from them, they are necessarily couched in terms of 'inequalities' rather than oppression or exploitation (not that these are incapable of empirical analysis, but they are concepts impossible to formulate within the framework of 'dimensions of stratification'), and the implications drawn are for administrative action rather than class mobilization. The stratification framework is peculiarly compatible with an administrative view of the world, which wishes to classify and order the subject population and learn how to manipulate it. The consequences can be seen, for instance, in urban studies, where these research techniques have now been widely used. Class becomes one of the variables in an élitist planning approach to the city; the characteristic problem to which it is applied is how to make the city less boring for the well-to-do without changing its power structure. Stretton's advocacy of mixed income levels in residential areas is a well-known example of this. A more recent case is the Urban Systems Corporation's City of Adelaide Planning Study, which states as an objective '...to retain a broad social mix of different types of households, age and income groups within the City'.[65] Not, be it noted, to *do* anything about the existence of different income groups; just to make sure that they mix – broadly.

The second effect, of a more general ideological kind, is to emasculate the concept of class itself. This research makes a claim to empirical knowledge; but it is a peculiarly bloodless empiricism, where the lived reality of class is reduced to an abstraction for the purpose of statistical treatment. And this abstract empiricism expands its claims to occupy the entire field; it claims to offer the first empirical (scientific, realistic) account of the system. The Broom *et al.* article which makes this claim is called, simply, 'Social stratification in Australia'; though it consists purely of extracts from the 1965 survey and says nothing about the processes involved or the nature of Australia as a stratified society. Congalton's book is called *Status and Prestige in Australia*; though it, too, is purely a statistical summary, saying nothing about the nature of prestige or the processes that produce it. So far has this gone that a critique has now emerged from within the stratification framework itself. Wild has pointed out that the original concept of stratification involved the idea of a system of relations between people of an entirely different kind from the abstract 'relation' of being higher or lower on a survey-taker's scale. He argues for the importance of status as a system of deference relationships, thus returning towards Martin's conception of it. It is interesting that this has come out of a new attempt to apply an ethnographic method (as before, to a country town); but a similar criticism has also come from urban research by Hiller under the influence of phenomenology.[66]

As the studies of country towns have shown, some forms of stratification theory lead readily to studies of local élites; but it proved difficult to move from that to a sociology of élites on a national scale. Such an enterprise was plainly required in a sociology that accepted anything but the most abstract notions of what a class structure was. Its roots in Australia go back to a flourishing literature of pamphlets in the 1930s and 1940s sketching the leading companies and the shareholdings of the richest families, with titles such as *Wealthy Men* (communist), *The Rich Get Richer* (Fitzpatrick's, and the best), and *The Money Monopoly in Australia* (social credit). The tradition has continued, with a solid volume on *The 60 Rich Families Who Own Australia* (1963) and *Australia Taken Over* (1974).[67] Not all of these have been produced by the left, but they usually assume a rough marxist model of the economy and try to show how it is dominated by a small group of inter-linked monopolists – an enterprise actually more populist than marxist in inspiration. More careful and sophisticated, but still essentially atheoretical, accounts of company ownership and the personnel of business, bureaucratic and political élites were produced in the 1950s and 1960s by Wheelwright and Playford.[68]

The attempt to weld this material into a sociology was undertaken almost single-handed by Encel, in a long series of papers whose results were brought together in 1970 in *Equality and Authority*. The enormous mass of material in this book defies easy analysis; its mixture of perspectives has been pointed out by critics,[69] and in some ways it is better regarded as a source-book than as the synthetic sociology of Australian stratification systems it set out to be. But it is possible to suggest that there are two principal models in it, and that the theoretical uncertainties of the book largely arise from the difficulty of combining them. One is a fairly straightforward mass-élite model of society, in which attention is concentrated almost wholly upon the élite and the mass remains as undifferentiated background. Encel offers a very detailed account of the personnel of the élite, divided into political and bureaucratic, economic and military sectors. This brings together the evidence from the ownership studies, from Encel's own surveys of social backgrounds, from family histories, and so on, tracing out kinship networks and political alliances, and the role of private schools in giving social solidarity to these groups, etc. Their power, in the sense of relationships with subordinate groups, is very much taken for granted; the main analysis is internal to the élite.

The other model, developed in the first section of the book, speaks directly of differentiation in the whole of the population. It is in fact a pure stratificationist theory, derived from Weber via Runciman, which argues that there are three basic dimensions of stratification, class, status, and power. These are understood as meaning economic, social and political inequality:

The relation between class, status and power may be summarised for analytical purposes as follows:

class refers to superior/inferior access to and control over the processes of production and distribution of material goods;

status refers to superior/inferior position in an accepted or established hierarchy of social roles and functions;

power refers to superior/inferior access to and control over the political, legal and coercive mechanisms of influence and authority.

The way in which class, status, and power are related to each other will vary considerably from one society to another...[70]

Rather confusingly, Encel does not address himself to the logic of measuring these theoretical dimensions, but moves immediately to a discussion of some 'social relationships' that are to be taken as 'relevant' to them or 'important' or 'significant' in understanding them. These in fact are not 'social relationships' in the ordinary sense of the phrase, but are scales of income, occupation, education, etc.: i.e. the familiar classifying variables of empiricist stratification research. Thus, when he comes to formulate a 'model' (i.e. summary description) of the Australian class system, he is operating with two frameworks at once; both dimensional, but very loosely linked by comments about the 'probable order of importance' of the latter for the former.[71]

Onto this rather wobbly construction Encel nails the élites that are his real concern. There is no way of doing it except by regarding them as occupying the top bits of the theoretical dimensions. As usual in the stratificationist approach, the cut-off points are entirely arbitrary, and here there is the added difficulty that there is nothing very tangible to cut. In practice, when formulating his account of the class dimension ('the most important axis'), Encel falls back on a conventional six-point occupational scale; and the whole business is forgotten when he comes to the detailed analyses of élites already discussed.

Though the theoretical enterprise failed, it was extremely significant that it was attempted. As with academic history the development of post-war sociology traced a curve through empiricism that moved further and further away from a structural analysis of class. And as with history, there came a reversal; though its character and effects were somewhat different. Here, it was a continuing awareness of the facts of power and privilege that provoked the attempt; but the attempt, when made, was contained within the logical framework of the stratification theory that had become predominant in local as in Anglo-American sociology.

A very similar observation can be made of the approach to some distinctly non-élite groups that was emerging at the same time, the study of 'poverty'. This too came out of a particular form of practical consciousness, the consciousness of social workers engaged in administering the welfare system; and it showed in mirror-image the assumption of a relatively homogeneous, affluent society from which the object of study was differentiated.[72] The problem of poverty was then formulated as a question of inequality. The major research on the problem, in typical fashion, tackled it with a battery of objective measures of welfare, with the aim of identifying, for remedial effort, those groups which scored lowest.[73] Poverty was understood as an anomaly, to be handled by administrative action, not as a structural feature of the system.

The revival of class analysis

If this paper had been written five years ago, there would have been little more to add, apart from some stirrings of a novel theory in the socialist magazine *Arena* that had attracted little attention at the time. In the last few years, however, there has been an important revival both of theory and empirical research on the left. The *Arena* group broached the problem of the relationship of culture, particularly higher education, to the processes underlying the class structure; proposing that a change was occurring in advanced capitalism that made cultural and technical workers central to the productive process and thus increasingly the locus of its fundamental conflict and the source of change.[74] In the 1970s *Arena* has also been the forum for a sustained argument over the class character of the Labor Party, and for some attempts at an analysis of culture and ideology that had been very rare in Australian socialist thought.

Perhaps the most sustained effort has been given to a new analysis of the history of class relations. In one form, notably in the work of Rowley, this has meant an attempt to re-think Australian development from the perspective of political economy, and thus arrive at a theoretical understanding of the evolution of the class structure.[75] There has also been a shift of labour history towards the history of the working class, still mostly focussing on crises but at least beginning to incorporate women into the story.[76] The history of the ruling class as a class is still underdeveloped – there is no journal for it – but some beginnings have been made.[77]

Class analysis has also been extended to novel problems, such as the shaping of Australian cities. In Sandercock's work on this there is a recognition of the role of classes as historical agents that has hardly been present in any field outside of the Australian legend and party politics; her work demonstrates some of the possibilities of explanation through class dynamics.[78] The impact of the women's movement on socialist groups and labour organisations has provoked theoretical work along two (related) lines, one trying to understand the relationship of housework and family processes to the class system, the other reconsidering concepts in class theory (such as productive labour) in the light of feminist critique.[79]

The list certainly does not exhaust the new work – in the wake of the Vietnam war, for instance, there have been more systematic attempts to grasp the position of Australia within imperialism – but it is enough to indicate that there is a real ferment going on, and an intellectual movement in a direction substantially different from the mainstream history and sociology of the 1950s and 1960s.

THE RULING CLASS

3. The structure of the ruling class

The idea of a 'ruling class' is itself a structural concept, embodying claims about the way relations extending through the whole society are ordered. It is a logical step from analysing the structure of relations between classes to analyse the structure of relations within them. If some of the same principles can be shown to apply, the original theorizing will be greatly strengthened. An account of the internal structure of classes is necessary if class analysis is to be properly historical, if the formation and conflict of classes is to be understood in anything but the most abstract way. Classes are never homogeneous, and the situation faced by any person or group within a class is in large part made up of relationships with others in the same class. An analysis of the structure of these relationships is required both to make the reasons for their actions intelligible, and to understand their consequences.

The basic hypothesis of socialist analyses of capitalism is that its ruling class is defined by the private ownership of productive resources, and this can be taken as the starting point for an analysis of ruling class structure. Private ownership of productive resources takes a number of forms. Some of them involve ownership on quite a modest scale, such as the family ownership of a farm – though it is typical of Australian rural life that ways have been found of coordinating the activities of these pocket-handkerchief units of ownership through fifty-seven varieties of boards, pools, cooperatives and authorities. The private ownership of manufacturing, mining, and retailing has achieved scale in a different way, through the formation of companies. This is now the most important form of private ownership. The company is a device for fusing small units of ownership into the capital of a larger enterprise – in some cases, enormously larger – than any of the units would finance by itself. BHP, Australia's largest, had over 180,000 shareholders in 1974. At a rough estimate there are about a million people in Australia who are owners of shares, and about 200,000 companies.[1]

Two complexities appear immediately. One is that, in a mature corporate economy, the owners of capital do not usually confine their investment to a single company. The total of share-*holdings* is very much greater than the number of share-*holders*. Ownership itself becomes a kind of commodity, and markets (notably the ordinary share market) are organized to allow trading in it. The relationship of the owner to the company becomes attenuated, abstract: there is a circulation of owner-ship within the class of owners. The second complexity is that this circulation proceeds via companies as well as via persons. Almost exactly 50% of BHP shares in 1974 were held by other companies (who made up only 7% of share-holders). There is a very complex system of inter-company investment, which again attenuates the relationship between the owning person and the thing owned (and the person employed). For both reasons, one must look at the structure of the system of ownership, rather than the mere fact of private ownership itself, to understand what happens.

Plainly, a thorough analysis of ruling class structure, even in a small capitalist power like Australia, is a large undertaking. This chapter can offer only an outline. It first examines the structural ideas to be found in recent writings on Australian élites, and develops a criticism particularly of their treatment of unity; it then explores the extension of the ruling class and emergence of leadership groups within it, and the role of the state and the state élite.

Structural concepts in the literature on the Australian ruling class

Though the question has not been posed as a theoretical prob-lem and hence analysed systematically, there are structural ideas to be found in discussions of various élite groups in Australia. They relate mainly to three issues: the internal relationships of the business élite; the relationship between business and the state; and the sources of capital and personnel. I will take as the main texts for this discussion the works of Wheelwright, Encel, and Playford, the most important recent studies in the field.

The leading idea in discussions of the first of these issues is that of concentration. All three authors stress, to use Playford's words, 'the domination of key sectors of industrial, commercial and financial life by a handful of large firms',[2] and the centralization of the ownership of companies in the hands of a small number of shareholders.

A number of studies of market concentration and monopoly have been done, which stress the level of concentration in Australia relative to other capitalist countries, and its maintenance through much of the twentieth century. As the most extensive of these studies concludes: 'A high level of industrial concentration appears to have remained stable throughout Australia's industrial development.'[3]

On share ownership there is now systematic evidence over a span of twenty years. Wheelwright's study of 102 large companies in 1953 estimated that the top 5% of shareholders held about 53% of the shares. The study of 299 large manufacturing companies in 1962–4 by Wheelwright and Miskelly showed that the top twenty shareholdings in each company accounted for 58% of the shares. A journalist's study of 251 companies in 1972–3 (after the stock exchange obliged listed companies to publish their top 20 shareholders) estimated that the top twenty, making about 4% of shareholders, held about 55% of the shares.[4] The comparisons are not exact, but the orders of magnitude are similar: it is reasonable to conclude that the concentration of ownership has remained much the same over the last two decades.

This evidence refers to concentration of ownership within the group of owners (implying that most owners have only small lots of shares), and concentration of market shares among all companies (implying that most companies are small and weak). The degree of concentration with respect to the population as a whole is obviously much greater.

Almost as important as the concept of concentration is the idea that the leading figures in the ruling class are linked to each other individually. Tracing out the links produces a kind of sociometric map of the ruling class, with the most powerful men appearing in it as sociometric 'stars'.

Research on this has followed two lines. The directors of companies can be mapped in this way, using membership of the same board as the definition of relationship. The most

important study of this is by Rolfe, who examined the fifty
largest Australian companies in 1963 and found interlocking
directorates of a number of kinds. There were board connections between companies that were rivals or customers of each
other, and between manufacturers and their financiers, as well
as interlocks that reflected investment interests.[5]

The last of these leads to the other group of 'network'
studies, those which trace out the investments, board member-
ships, and intermarriages of the leading business families.
Earlier left-wing descriptions of the ruling class along the lines
of Campbell's *Sixty Families* (1963) were mostly based on this
kind of study. Of recent authors, Encel in particular has
explored this.[6] His work illustrates the role both as entrepreneurs and rentiers of the Robinsons, Fairfaxes, Knoxes,
etc., and above all the Baillieus – whose Collins House investment complex also appears as a major element in Rolfe's
boardroom sociometry. Both Wheelwright and Miskelly, and
Playford, caution against overestimating such evidence.[7] The
rich families only account for a fraction of total capital, and
over-concentration on them may seriously distort the picture
of the ruling class. They are the greatest beneficiaries, but are
far from being equivalent to the beneficiaries as a whole.

Classical economic theory stressed competition between
businessmen; the recent literature on the ruling class in contrast stresses its fundamental unity. Wheelwright argues that
the emergence of giant companies that are mostly self-financing
has largely freed big business from the constraints of competition. Playford stresses, in an argument over a number of
points, that men of wealth and property, however divided on
particular issues, are 'fundamentally united'; and Encel speaks
of a loose collection of élite groups linked by a 'governing
consensus'.[8]

Playford's formulation, the most precise, stresses that the
upper class consensus is about 'defending the social order
which affords them privileges': that is, it is a unity with respect
to the working class and its interest in change, a unity imposed
by the opposition of classes. Wheelwright, by contrast,
stresses that the consequence of centralized corporate power
is freedom:

Thus, within quite wide limits, the market will permit managements
to choose their own ends: these may be profit-maximising, empire-

building or merely satisfaction and the quiet life. The essential point is that – irrespective of how they use their power – a small number of men possess it, and they are not publicly accountable for it.[9]

These formulations could lead to different views of the ruling class: in the one case to the idea of a class with systematic divisions on various points that are overridden by unity on the issue of its relations with another class; in the other to the idea of chunks of a class that have largely broken loose from each other and which operate under very little constraint at all. Clearly the role of competition and internal conflict needs close examination.

The idea of 'neo-capitalism', expounded by Playford in particular, is based on the view that there has been an increasing integration of business and the state. The most important feature of this is taken to be support of business and its interests by the state élites, both bureaucrats and politicians. There is 'support' in the sense of attitudes: bureaucrats and politicians are favourable to business and unwilling to act against its interests. This is the main thrust of Playford's account of influential people in the state, such as party leaders and arbitration judges. The massive evidence he and Encel have collected about the movement of officials into well-paid jobs in business provides support for this judgement, and points to one of the ways the link is maintained.[10] On the other hand there is support of business by the actual policies of governments: tariff policies that benefit manufacturers, subsidies, provision of infrastructure, etc. This has been documented in particular detail by McFarlane for the period of Liberal rule, and by Catley and McFarlane for the period of the Whitlam government.[11]

A good deal of attention is given by Playford and Encel to organizations that link government and business. These are the boards of public corporations like TAA and AIDC on which leading businessmen sit; the liaison and advisory committees that are set up by government for this particular purpose; the peak organizations of industries that function as lobbies in Canberra; and the finance committees of the Liberal Party (we may now add the Labor Party). These provide a series of links which, be it noted, go below the level of directorships and involve executives of the large companies.

The basic concept here is of a negotiating or bargaining

relationship. The businessmen, and the politicians and bureaucrats, are thought of as having independent power bases, and finding mutual benefits to exchange. In the process a new decision-making structure is constructed, independent of elections, parliaments, and public scrutiny, which takes over much economic policy making.

According to the theory of neo-capitalism, 'the scale and pervasiveness of state intervention has been increasing in recent decades'; but this is to the benefit of business. The minor constraints on property imposed by governments are in its own interests in the long run. Reciprocally, the commitment of government to capitalism 'curtails its freedom of action on a vast number of issues and problems'. The state is 'subject to the structural constraints of the capitalist system'.[12]

To some extent this is a tautology: if the state organization exists in a capitalist society, then obviously officials, if they are to act at all, have to deal with a capitalist system, its constraints included. The argument becomes a significant structural principle if it is claimed there has been a historical change in this reciprocity, as Playford argues, or if the forms it takes become central to the strategies of either party, as Encel argues:

Leaving the rural sector aside, the Australian economy might be accurately described as a system of monopoly capitalism, operating through a highly regulated structure of output, prices and wages, which is interlocked with and maintained by an extensive system of government activity.[13]

The third line of argument about structure relates to the sources of capital and élite personnel. On the face of it, an analysis of sources would not appear to say anything about structure; but this has in fact provided one of the main structural concepts in Australian discussions, the distinction between locally-owned and foreign-owned business. Wheelwright raised this issue in his first monograph, and explored it in detail, with Fitzpatrick, in *The Highest Bidder*.[14] He has consistently stressed the growing weight of overseas ownership and overseas (potential) control. Official surveys confirm the results of academic research: a Treasury white paper of 1972 estimated overseas ownership at between one quarter and one third of the Australian corporate economy.[15] As is shown in more detail in Chapter 5, this became a first-class political issue in the early

1970s, with both major parties developing policies to 'protect Australian ownership'.

The evidence of overseas ownership has led to contradictory inferences. Encel argues that 'the local agents and beneficiaries' of the capital inflow 'continue to be the established economic elite'; while Playford suggests that it has led to 'the relative weakening of the "native industrial bourgeoisie"'.[16] How far the fact of foreign ownership is reflected in a division among managers, or in differences in company policies, has yet to be established. There is evidence of a greater profitability of foreign, especially American, owned companies in the 1950s and 1960s.[17] But there are as yet no detailed studies of the movement of managers in and out of foreign-owned companies, or comparisons of their marketing and labour policies.

On another front, personnel studies have been done, by Encel in particular, stressing the common social origins of the native business, political and administrative élites. Though personnel recruitment is not in itself a structural matter, it is relevant to such points as the ideological unity of élite groups. And organisations that handle training and recruitment, such as the élite private schools, may in the process of reproduction of a class become important elements of its structure.

Concentration, competition and unity in business

The discussion of concentration immediately raises the question, concentration of what? Wheelwright, Encel and Playford all speak of domination, control, or power. The evidence, however, is not about this. The evidence is mainly about ownership of shares; and in his original study, Wheelwright was careful to distinguish that from power in the sense of initiative in decision-making. At most, the study of ownership can yield information about 'ultimate control', meaning 'the power to select or change the management of a company'.[18] To be blunt, what we have here are conclusions based on inferences about what might happen if the shareholders attempted to mobilize. This, clearly, is only one element in an analysis of power, and not necessarily a very important one (given the usual passivity of shareholders). The studies of market concentration also yield, at best, inferences about a potential for control of an industry (or an economy). It is altogether another matter to show that control is in fact exercised, or with what results.

The same kind of thing can be said about the studies of networks of directors and family ownership. These provide evidence not of organization itself, but of a potential for organization. From inferring that they could function as systems of power within business, it is a long step to showing that they do. This requires a case-by-case study: and the politics of business is an extremely ill-researched field. There are however some useful instances. Perhaps the best-known is the case of the newspaper companies and their attendant radio, television, and magazine enterprises – now mainly concentrated in three national media empires.[19] The personal power and political adventures of media entrepreneurs, such as Keith Murdoch (who built the Herald and Weekly Times chain), Frank Packer (controller of the *Women's Weekly* and the Sydney *Telegraph*), and more recently Rupert Murdoch (Keith's son, but the creator of a new corporate structure), are well known. But the most detailed study of family ownership, Poynter's account of the Grimwade family in the glass and chemical industries, paints a different picture. Here the interlocking investments appear as the residue of an earlier period of business history, when the enterprises were being launched in the late nineteenth and early twentieth centuries. The personal power of the Grimwades declined as their family companies were merged into national monopolies and bureaucratic techniques of management developed; the family itself changed from being entrepreneurs to being rentiers.[20] The case of the Myer family, founders of Australia's largest retail empire, seems to be intermediate between these two. Here some members of the family have remained active in company management, but have not used it as a base for the kind of buccaneering that the media have seen.[21] These, however, remain instances. There is simply not the systematic evidence that would allow us to say, for instance, that a shift from family-entrepreneurial to management-bureaucratic control is the general pattern. We can say that the investment and boardroom networks provide a potential that may or may not be used; that evidently is in some cases and is not in others.

More profoundly, we can ask whether the actual performance of businesses would be very different, if these networks and potentials did not exist. If the controllers of companies are constrained to act in certain ways by pressures inherent in a system of private property, then it does not matter very much who they are. The nature of the constraints on businessmen, and the extent of their freedom from constraints, must be analysed to determine the significance of the evidence on concentration and networks.

Wheelwright argues that the size of companies, their 'domination' of markets, and the managers' independence of sanctions from shareholders, has conferred a great deal of freedom on the managements. He has also suggested that Rolfe's study of directors yields data more commensurate with the view that management acts in the interests of the propertied class than with the view that they have become separated.[22] The latter point is not proven because the data do not in fact bear on executives (apart from managing directors). But note that if the first point is true, the second can be true only by the *choice* of the managers: they are not *constrained* to maximize profit, exploit the workforce, etc. In Wheelwright's formulation there is no structural imperative acting on company managements that determines the use of their power, the direction in which they will act.

It is at precisely this point that the issue of competition becomes important. For there is competition between businessmen, of a much greater variety than simply competitive selling of products in the marketplace. The system of share ownership of public companies makes management in principle vulnerable to rival groups buying up shares and attempting a takeover. (As the takeover battle between the transport firms TNT and Ansett showed, even corporate heavyweights are vulnerable to this.) Managements which do not maintain a high rate of profit on their assets are vulnerable to 'asset stripping' raiders (who buy up a company's shares cheap, take over, and sell off the undervalued assets, like Gordon Barton with the publishing firm Angus & Robertson).[23] A declining market share and profit performance may provoke a coup within the company (e.g. British Leyland, which axed its Australian management very suddenly in 1974).

These observations become more significant in the light of foreign investment in Australian business. To say that there has been increasing foreign investment is, conversely, to say that Australian business has become increasingly integrated into the world capital market. And big capital is highly mobile, both between countries and between industries – as the multinational conglomerates like ITT very clearly show. These competitive forces, we may infer, have increased in the Australian economy, however internal market competition may have declined. One of the consequences is that managers of the Australian branches of multinationals must try to squeeze growth and profits out of the local firm in order to get on in their international careers.

We may argue, then, that conflict in business has a continuing and systematic importance. It is a constant force on the actions of businessmen, pushing towards profit making, corporate growth, and resistance to working-class politics. Note that this applies as forcibly to managers as to directors. We do not have to assume anything about the attitudes of managers, nor even postulate with Playford 'a basic community of interests' between managers and owners, to explain this tendency.

The concepts of concentration and network are useful, but it is necessary to distinguish between them and the full concept of a structure of power, which by almost any definition includes the effective exercise of command or constraint. Parker may be wrong in claiming that in Australia power 'plays an unusually restrained role',[24] but at least he is talking about power and not simply a possible base for it. To move from the one to the other it is necessary to work with a concept of mobilization, one of the keys to a historical understanding of the ruling class. One does not have to suppose a continuing structure of rigid control: one can observe the ruling class mobilising in periods of crisis such as the bank nationalisation campaign of 1947–9.[25] And it is noteworthy, in view of the research attention given to directors and owners, that it was managers such as McConnan of the National Bank who were politically decisive in this process.

The concept of competition must be brought in as a fundamental structural category for the analysis of the ruling class, but in a wider sense than simply competition in the product market. Competition in the capital market is of major importance – a worldwide capital market – and also competition in what we can describe as the 'person' market, i.e. competition between businessmen for the control of companies and their assets, which is also now conducted on a worldwide basis. Such a concept is necessary to account for the systematic character of the ruling class's activity in a stronger way than simply postulating attitudinal consensus. The concept of 'fundamental unity' thus can be dropped, in favour of an analysis of the institutional basis of the power of the ruling class; a concept that relates to the structure of the whole society rather than the ruling class alone.

The class and its leadership

The argument just offered implies that the ruling class is not simply to be equated with businessmen. Their power, as entrepreneurs and bureaucrats, rests on something wider and deeper.

The class, by the basic hypothesis of class analysis, is initially constituted by the system of private ownership and what I have called elsewhere its 'generative capacity', its capacity to enter into and structure a wide range of social transactions, as property is used as capital in production and for other collective purposes.[26] Some, but only some, of the owners of property actually use it in these ways. They are however able to mobilize the property of others who are not personally involved. The most important channel for this is the system of company share capital sketched at the beginning of this chapter; other channels are the financial institutions such as banks and insurance companies which mobilise capital through deposits, fixed-interest loans, and insurance premiums. The men (there are hardly any women at the top of major companies) who mobilize and direct the use of property-as-capital through these means are not a class, but rather the most active section, the business leadership of the class of owners.

The organizational structure of mature capitalism is thus predicated on the passivity, or at least very marginal involvement, of most of the owners. One consequence of this is that the boundary of the class becomes difficult to fix. On the one hand, people who are dependent for survival on the wage from a job can be owners of small packages of shares, savings accounts, etc. On the other hand, the top employees of a firm like BHP, who may not be owners of any shares at all, can be pulling down salaries of $50,000 or more that make them very much richer than most of their nominal employers.

This paradox can be resolved, though it requires an extension of the initial definition of ownership and the concept of profit. We have to take into account the changes that occur when many small properties are combined in a mature corporate structure. Profit may be taken, by those who control these agglomerations of property, in other forms than the payment of dividends, forms that on the surface resemble the payment of wages. A simple example is the payment of directors' fees, a form of payment that, as a fixed annual amount, resembles a salary, but is plainly not given as a labour-market exchange. It is a cut from entrepreneurial profits, dependent on the directors' relationship with shareholders (in practice the directors' ability to mobilize proxy votes to keep themselves in office). The inflated salaries of top management (and fringe benefits and bonuses on top of them)[27] are basically to be understood in the same way, as entrepreneurial profits, claimed by virtue of the organizational power of the executives concerned. The form in which income is received masks its nature.

As we come down the scale of salaries, an increasing percentage can be attributed to the sale of labour-power and the market conditions affecting it, notably the market for different kinds of skill. Here analytic difficulties arise, particularly in the case of professional and technical workers where the labour market is partly controlled by professional associations which claim a kind of property in certified skills, and enforce income differentials reflecting professional status. A full theory of income is obviously a complex matter, but it is not needed for the main argument here: that the income of upper salaried groups is still dependent on the structure of ownership, though the dependency has become more complex with the growth in the scale of enterprises. It should not be assumed that because the *form* of income is a continuous gradation of wages and salaries, the *differential* between property-based and wage-based incomes is any the less. Indeed, it may be easier for an entrepreneur to extract a high personal income from a large corporate structure as salary-plus-benefits, than to extract it as dividend from a less bureaucratised enterprise.

It is important, then, to acknowledge the difference made in property relations by the corporate structure. And this gives a grip on the other horn of the dilemma, the small-property-owning wage earners with packets of shares, life insurance policies, etc. These are of course a minority of wage earners, and a small minority of manual workers, and there is evidence that they account only for a small fraction of the ownership of major companies;[28] but they do exist, and hence blur class categories. On the face of it they would seem to be, through the corporate structure, their own employers; and this point is naturally taken up by business propaganda about shareholders coming from 'all walks of life'. The typical shareholder of course drives rather than walks, but some fringe of ownership does extend into the ranks of pedestrians and public transport users. No organisational power, however, comes with it. Here the relations of ownership are so attenuated that they have the practical status of small interest-bearing loans.

It makes little sense to think of people whose main 'property' consists of consumer goods, cars, and equity in a house, and who are dependent on wages for all but a small fraction of their income, as members of a class of property owners. It does make sense to think of them as being integrated – in what may be a fragile and temporary way – into the extended fund-raising networks of corporate capitalism. Here the function of supplying capital extends beyond what would normally be thought of as the class of capitalists. As in the case of the salaried hierarchy, the boundaries of the class appear to be in principle indeterminate.

This is a difficulty, if one expects a preliminary economic definition to yield an unambiguous and final system of social categories. It is not a theoretical difficulty, but an interesting empirical fact, if one thinks of classes as emergent groupings within an overall structure which itself is the main object of theory. The chief purpose of class analysis, after all, is to get a grip on the way the whole society works, not to arrive at a neat system of social pigeon-holes. From the point of view of its actual working, the ruling class in this society can still be understood as the group which lives off profits generated by property, provided it is recognized that this can take several forms – profits of personal entrepreneurship; dividends, rents and interest; and corporate profit appropriated as salaries. As a matter of fact there is considerable overlap in the groups who drink from these various streams of profit (the percentages of share owners, for instance, are markedly higher among professionals and managers than among other occupational groups), but this is a contingent, not a necessary, feature of the system.

51

The business leadership is related to the rest of the class basically by the mobilization of capital. The main features of this relationship were laid down with the introduction of limited-liability companies and the organization of local capital markets, which occurred in Australia around 1860–80, during the first long boom.[29] There have of course been changes since, such as the declining importance of the banks, and the recent rise of insurance firms, as channels of business finance. The relationship is guaranteed by the state through the law of property and the fraud provisions in the Companies Acts. But it has on the whole been remarkably unregulated, as is shown by the absence of a national company-regulation body, and the absence of control of the share market demonstrated by the Rae Committee's enquiry in the aftermath of the 1969–70 mining boom.[30]

The business leadership of the ruling class is self-appointed, consisting of those people who succeed in mobilizing capital or in winning or inheriting control of established accumulations of capital. It acts not so much by consent of the bulk of owners, as in default of their opposition: i.e. it acts by its own lights unless in a particular case they mobilize against it. This practically always occurs as mobilisation under the leadership of some rival entrepreneur. Organization of shareholders simply as shareholders is extremely weak. There is an Australian Shareholders' Association, but it has no more than nuisance value; and attempts to organize policyholders to win seats on the boards of such institutions as the National Mutual have, practically without exception, failed.

The conduct of business, however, is not the only purpose for which the ruling class needs leadership. The expansion of the union movement in the later nineteenth century, its rise to electoral success in the Labor Parties of the early twentieth century, and the deepening militancy of industrial workers around the time of the first world war, posed a threat to the entire position of the ruling class. (However mild the Labor Parties may appear in historical retrospect, they were certainly seen as a wild and dangerous force by property owners at the time.) One response, as is well known in the history books, was a closing of the ranks, a 'fusion' of free-traders and protectionists against Labor in parliament. Another response, less well recognized because it developed over a longer time, was the emergence of a new leadership in the ruling class. A specialized political cadre emerged, a group of men who took on the political leadership of the ruling class as distinct from its business leadership. In the nineteenth century, business leadership and political leadership had been so closely intertwined they were often impossible to separate. Now they were prised apart: in the case of men like Bruce and Massy-Greene in the inter-war years, by a temporal division of a business segment from a political segment in the one career; in the case of men like Playford in South Australia, and Menzies nationally, by a full-time specialization in politics with only the faintest traces of a personal involvement in business.[31]

In the leadership of the Liberal and Country parties, then, we have a group not separate from the ruling class, but separate from its business leadership: the two are now parallel specializations within the one class. Like businessmen, the political leadership is made up of entrepreneurs; but these are entrepreneurs whose field of action is the state organizations, and whose success depends on mobilizing and using political support rather than capital. In this process, of course, money is necessary; so the collective operations of this leadership draw funds from the business leadership, and individual members of it may have close relationships with individual business entrepreneurs. But there is no need to assume that conservative politicians are typically the agents of particular groups of businessmen: indeed the general situation is that they are not.

This argument leads to a rather different view of the bodies linking business and government that Playford has carefully mapped. These now appear, not as signs of an increasing integration of business and politics, but as consequences of their historical *separation*. The specialization in the leadership of the ruling class and the growing independence of the political wing has created a need to re-establish coordination in political tactics, social and economic planning. There have been hitches and conflicts in doing this, as when Menzies threw out the scheme for national economic planning devised by the Vernon committee (headed by the general manager of CSR), as too great a threat to the parliamentary leadership. But the need has remained, and an untidy system of consultation has grown up to meet it.

The state and the state élite

The theory of neo-capitalism argued by Playford raises very broad questions about the role of the state in class society. So far as the structure of the ruling class is concerned, two are most obvious: what is the relationship between the leadership groups just outlined, and the state structure; and what in particular is the place of the upper-level civil servants, the élite of state employees?

So far as the political leadership of the ruling class is concerned, the basic point is simple: its aim is to gain and hold state power; or at the minimum, to prevent state power from being used against the interests of capital. The details of course are infinitely complex, both in terms of the political tactics involved (some of which are explored in Chapter 6), and the uses – coercive, cultural, etc. – to which state power is put (some of which are explored in Chapter 10).

The business leadership poses more difficult problems. Broadly, the point made by Playford, Encel and McFarlane about a considerable integration of the business leadership with the state is correct. The slightest observation of the actual behaviour of companies like BHP and CRA is enough to dispel the view of businessmen argued by Parker, that 'what they want is to be left alone'. Their operations impinge on, and are affected by, the state at every level from the granting of mining leases to the negotiation of sales; and the sophisticated executives of the big companies have little time for the backwoods anti-state rhetoric of conservative ideologues.

But when we come to look at the details of business-state integration, particularly at the nature of state support of business, difficulties arise. Tariff protection, for instance, is often cited as a prime example of this support. But tariff protection to manufacturers disadvantages other businessmen, notably in the pastoral and mining industries. Integration of the state with one group implies dis-integration with others.

Similarly one might observe of much of the lobbying activity noted by Playford and Encel, and of the bodies which permit and conduct it, that most of this is directed against other businessmen, not against labour. There is integration of the state with one lobbying group only to the extent that its rivals have failed; or, to see it from the other side, to the extent that it is in the interests of political and bureaucratic entrepreneurs such as McEwen, when he was leader of the federal Country Party, to form stable links with a particular business group. The point is that there is really no lobby that reflects the interests of businessmen in general. To get to the level of the collective interests of businessmen, one has to penetrate to a very basic institutional level: to the institution of private property itself. *At no other level is there unanimity in business*; not even on an issue such as conceding wage demands to the unions, as the repeated conflicts between the metal trades employers and other employer organizations attest.

At that level, there is nothing new about an integration of business and the state. In white Australian history, business has always depended on the state for a guarantee, by force and suasion, of private property rights; and has never depended in vain. The very foundation of Australia as a penal colony was part of the enforcement of this system – the great majority of the convicts were sent out from Britain for offences against property. We are still serving out their sentence.

It is useful to distinguish between the *state*, in the more general sense of the sphere of direct enforcible social relations, and the *state organizations*, the departments, courts, schools, etc., which form the machinery of government.[32] The connection of the ruling class with the state in the broader sense is profound, as the enforcible relations of property are constitutive of the system within which the class, as a concrete group, arises. Yet this is not a matter of a pattern of causation that would make the state the *fons et origo* of the class structure. The nascent ruling class of capitalism had to struggle to win control of state organizations already existing, and as they gained strength were able to modify fundamental rules to make their economic position secure (such as the laws against usury), and to allow the fuller development of their economic organizations (such as the law of liability – the modern corporate structure depends on the principles of limited liability introduced little more than a century ago). The state is one section of the total organisation of power that defines a capitalist society: a crucially important section, in terms of the maintenance of the structural pattern; but not the section from which the principal dynamic of the system arises.

The state organizations play more limited and specific roles.

Their connections with business are similarly limited and specific. Broadly, these connections are to be understood within the
analysis of faction formation and factional conflict within the
ruling class, rather than as a characteristic of the ruling class
as a whole. Members of the conservative political leadership,
and members of the state élite (of civil servants), are perfectly
capable of taking their own line in these factional conflicts. Of
course they will define their policies as representing the interests of the people, or the system, as a whole; but there is no
need to believe that this is so, nor that they normally stand for
the common interests of the ruling class in anything but the most
abstract sense. The 'abstract sense' becomes concrete when
there is, or is believed to be, a threat to the stability of the
system; and at such moments the political leadership can
become the focus of a broad class mobilization.

What of the state élite itself – the holders of the top positions
in the state organisations? Encel has argued that the growth of
the public service since before World War II amounts to a
'bureaucratic revolution'[33]: first greatly increasing the size and
scope of the central administration, then leading to a marked
status differentiation within it, with the emergence of the
Second Division of the Commonwealth public service as an élite
corps by the 1960s. 'Revolution' is hyperbole; but there is
no denying the power that members of this group hold. In
an executive sense, the top civil servants in Canberra, along
with a few of the more influential ministers, are certainly
the most powerful men in the country. Their government is
the biggest employer, with the widest range of functions.
Though they may only occasionally (e.g. in the 1972–3 shakeup)
have the possibility of making big 'investment decisions'
about the application of resources in the public service, their
routine decisions affect the mass of the population in a range
of ways unmatched by executives even of companies like BHP
and CSR.

Again, it is worth stressing, this is not new. The top bureaucrats and ministers have always been the most powerful executives in the country, from the convict period when officials
like Lt-Governor Arthur exercised almost totalitarian control
in Van Diemen's Land, through the colonial period when public
investment decisions on matters like railway building were
among the most important social commitments being made.[34]

The emergence of a recognized élite corps does not necessarily signify a change in power relations extending outside the bureaucracy.

To a certain extent, the top civil servants can be seen as bureaucratic entrepreneurs parallel to the business and political entrepreneurs already discussed. But though they come from mostly similar social backgrounds, as Encel's research has shown, the analogy breaks down in that their power is not based on a mobilization of the resources of the class from which they arise. It is directly based on the system of command relationships, of coercion and consent, on which the labour market itself is based through the institution of property. Within the state organizations the bureaucratic entrepreneurs, when mobilizing resources, mobilize influence within a fairly narrow group, rather than mobilizing capital or support on a mass scale. There are, then, irreducible differences in the bases of power that make it impossible to equate them to the political and business leaderships of the ruling class, and thus arrive at an analysis along the lines of Mills' power-élite theory.

On the other hand, it is inadequate to analyse their relationship to the ruling class as Playford does, in an argument that makes the central fact their *attitudes*, their general social conservatism and support for the capitalist order.[35] Playford's facts are correct, and are not seriously affected by the recent appearance of rather more progressive people in the upper echelons of the civil service under Labor (the 'political appointments' about which the Liberals made such an outcry); nor even by the point that the Liberals used a good many civil servants who had entered the federal bureaucracy in the 1940s and who personally held fabian or reformist beliefs. The point is rather that the attitudes of senior officials are not normally a principal determinant of the way the bureaucracy functions, of its *major* effects. Their attitudes will influence which of a limited range of options may be taken (which, e.g. in decisions about tariffs or rural subsidies, may seriously affect particular groups of businessmen), and will influence who gets promotion within the civil service, etc. But their attitudes will not, except in a crisis of unusual urgency and uncertainty (e.g. where military officers decide for or against a coup), affect major choices about the application of state power.

It is necessary to distinguish arguments about the similarity of the state élite and the business élite from arguments about their respective role. The similarities are evident. They arise from common social backgrounds, have common levels of comfort and income, and common patterns of work. The problems of managing a large organization are reasonably similar whether it is a state department, a public corporation, or a big company; the routines of work – the offices, conferences, air travel, and so forth – are much the same; and the outlook fostered by it, the tendency to see the world as something to be administered from above, is naturally shared. Some bureaucrats (Coombs is the most striking example) resist the social complacency that all this fosters, but the smooth integration of government officials into corporate employment that Playford has traced argues a general compatibility of outlook.

Senior officials, then, are readily able to become members of the business leadership, and there are some cases (e.g. Ellicott, who recently went from being federal solicitor-general to being a Liberal front-bencher) to show that they can move into the political leadership. But this does not imply that, as officials, they *are* part of the leadership of the ruling class. Their power, as already suggested, rests on a quite different basis.

It may seem odd to argue that the society has a ruling class, and then to suggest that the most powerful officials in it are not members of that class, or at least not members of its leadership (since civil servants may well be small property owners). Yet this is what the argument implies. The difficulty is partly an ambiguity of language: the phrase 'ruling class' does not imply 'rule' in the sense of executive control (no one, and no group, rules a capitalist society in that sense). What is implied is a collective domination, the maintenance of an institutional structure within which the class appropriates benefits, the choking off of alternatives – the only sense in which a *class* can intelligibly be said to rule.

On the other side, this argument points to limitations of the power of the state élite that are not immediately obvious when one looks at the scale of their executive activity. Paradoxically, their power as individual office-holders is more marked than their collective power as a unit within the social order. The rhetoric of conservatism, which attacks the expansion of 'unproductive' government as a 'burden' on the productive sections of the community, here reflects in a distorted way, an important truth about a capitalist social order: that the central dynamic lies in private profit and capital accumulation, and the social conflict to which that gives rise. The state élite manages important regulatory and service functions – arguably essential functions, given entrepreneurial capitalism's inability to regulate itself – but activities that are superimposed on a social dynamic whose roots are elsewhere.

The major companies

The main form of ruling-class organization in Australia is the company; a fact so familiar, so mundane, that it is often overlooked. News about companies is generally tucked away in the 'business section' of the press, where it is fated to be read only by capitalists and left-wing academics. We have studies of company ownership and financial performance from Wheelwright and Sheridan[1]; but there are not half a dozen decent histories of Australian businesses, and not one good up-to-date analysis of the internal structure and politics of any major firm. The contrast to the attention historians and political scientists have given to parties, parliaments and unions is remarkable. Yet it is in companies that the daily life of capitalism occurs – power exercised, profit extracted, accumulation made possible. A serious analysis of a capitalist social order must be grounded in a knowledge of its chief organizations.

As already mentioned, there are about 200,000 companies in Australia. Most of course are small, being modest-size businesses, or paper entities created for the purposes of share dealings and tax evasion. Though this chapter will be focussing on the few largest, it is worth reflecting a moment on the importance of small companies to the system. They carry out, in aggregate, a large slice of actual production; even in manufacturing, it has been estimated, plants employing less than 100 people account for about 40% of total output.[2] They represent a means of entry to the class of property owners, and a route into the business leadership for energetic and lucky entrepreneurs. They provide real models for the rhetoric of 'free enterprise', and otherwise hamper working-class mobilization, since small plants are usually hard for unions to organize. As family firms they are an important point of articulation between the economy and the structure of kinship.

Nonetheless it is the big companies that are economically and politically crucial, that are fully characteristic of developed capitalism. They control key technologies – mechanized mining, oil refinings, steel making, motor manufacturing, air transport, and so on – and often have flocks of smaller companies closely tied to their operations. The oil and motor industries, for instance, both have a few very large producers and then a wide spread of agents, distributors, parts suppliers, etc., in various relations of dependence.

To study the major companies it is necessary to identify them; so the first step is to draw up a list. I stress that this is the first step, not the last. A list of 'top companies' is in danger of being taken as a definition of the power centre of Australian capitalism. This would be a mistake. It would reify a criterion of size alone, and ignore the processes by which power is gathered and exercised. A vigorous entrepreneur in a smaller company may have more widespread influence than the somnolent management of an established giant. And the existence of a list, of course, directs attention away from companies that don't get in it – and which add up to the greater part of total capital. The top companies are not the capitalist economy, nor their owners the ruling class, *per se*. With these cautions in mind, a list can be taken as a useful, indeed a necessary, tool, defining a field within which one can search systematically for power structures and study the accumulation of wealth.

A top 50

To produce a list of the biggest companies, however, is not as simple as it sounds. For one thing, there is a problem in defining 'biggest'. Size could be judged by number of employees, annual turnover, profit, or several possible ways of measuring capital; and each would produce a different final list. Processes of production vary in their capital-intensiveness, and companies are financed through different balances of share capital, retained profits, and loans. Compare for instance these two firms with almost equal share capital (1972 figures):

	Woolworths	Alcoa
Issued capital	$53 m	$50 m
Funds employed	$222 m	$404 m
Employees	34 000	3 500

Alcoa, like most of the giant mining and refining operations that developed in the 1950s and 1960s, is highly mechanized, and raises much of its capital in the form of long-term loans; thus it has nearly double the operating capital of Woolworths, but a workforce only one tenth the size. Plainly a composite criterion of size is desirable if a general-purpose list of companies is to be produced.

Another problem is determining scope. Geographical boundaries cut across the operations of large companies, even when they have not reached full-blown multinational status. The ANZ Bank is commonly regarded (and is listed here) as an Australian company, but is incorporated in London and has a substantial trade in New Zealand. The big shipping firms which trade to Australia are equally important in the country's economic life but are usually not regarded as 'Australian' companies. In compiling her list of 50 largest for *The Controllers*, Rolfe omitted all overseas-owned companies – not a promising start for an analysis of the local business élite, as it excluded the controllers of General Motors-Holden, ICI, and most of the oil majors.[3] Lists based on the stock exchange, such as the 'top 1000' or 'top 200' published by newspapers and business magazines, or the list studied by Sheridan in *The Firm in Australia*, necessarily miss important types of company: wholly-owned subsidiaries of overseas firms, and insurance funds such as the AMP.

These problems can be met, but at some cost in elegance; there is simply no definitive 'top 50', and to be comprehensive one must be a bit messy. I have taken two criteria of company size: shareholders' funds, and number of employees. The first is one of several possible measures of capital; it seems more practically relevant, than share capital alone as a measure of the direct owners' stake in the business, but excludes loan funds which involve a different structure of ownership. The second reflects the scale of the company's operations in the labour market, and is one possible index of its importance to the working class. The list then includes all companies that have (a) more than 6000 employees; or (b) shareholders' funds of $100 m or more. The capital criterion has been stretched to include a couple of firms with shareholders' funds just under $100 m but $50 m of it as subscribed share capital; and mutual insurance funds, which do not have shareholders in the ordinary sense, are included if their assets exceed $900 m. All these

62

figures are arbitrary, as any cut-off point in a nearly continuous distribution of company size must be. They are chosen simply to produce a list of about fifty companies, with about equal numbers getting in on the workforce and capital criteria. About a third get in on both.

The scope of the list is companies whose principal operations are within Australia, regardless of where they are owned and whether or not they are listed on stock exchanges. The only important group of companies excluded is the semi-government corporations such as Trans-Australia Airways and the Commonwealth Bank. These are plainly important, but have to be analysed separately by a study of the state as an agency of capital formation.

Some 45 companies or groups of companies, plus a few of their large subsidiaries, meet these criteria. They are listed in Table 1, which shows their names, major activities, head offices, workforces, and shareholder's funds. (For insurance firms, policyholders' funds are shown in brackets). Details are given for 1972 as far as possible: the calendar year if that is the company's basis of reporting, or whatever is the closest approximation to it. (Where the accounts are drawn up from 1 July to 30 June, the report issued in 1972 is used.) Where the reports distinguish a major company's own accounts from 'group' or 'consolidated' accounts including subsidiaries, the group figures are taken. Subsidiaries are not listed separately, even where they would meet the criteria on their own; thus Australian Guarantee Corporation is not listed, as the Bank of New South Wales took 51% ownership of it in 1972. Companies substantially but not majority owned by others are included, e.g. Comalco (45% owned by Conzinc Riotinto of Australia) and John Lysaght (50% owned by BHP).

The list was compiled initially from business directories, starting with a search of *Kompass* (the most extensive listing), supplemented by *Jobson's* and various other directories and lists.[4] No single directory is complete enough to yield a full list, and there are many minor errors and inconsistencies in them. The details for all companies that seemed likely to meet the criteria were therefore checked in their annual reports and various other publications and information supplied by the companies. Company reports vary a great deal in the amount of useful information they let out – the Collins House com-

Table 1. Major companies, 1972

Company	Major business	Head office	Employees (to nearest 500)	Share-holders' funds ($m.)
Alcoa of Australia	Aluminium mining, refining	Melbourne	3500	94
AMATIL (British Tobacco)	Tobacco, food, packaging	Sydney	10000	145
Ampol Petroleum	Petrol	Sydney	2500	113
Ansett Transport Industries	Air transport	Melbourne	12500	43
ANZ Banking Group	Banking, finance	London	19000	143
Australian Consolidated Industries	Glass, plastics	Melbourne	22500	162
Australian Mutual Provident Society	Insurance	Sydney	5000	(2959)
Australian Paper Manufacturers	Paper, board	Melbourne	6000	136
Bank of New South Wales	Banking, finance	Sydney	18000	217
BP Australia	Petrol	Melbourne	4000	146
Broken Hill Proprietary	Steel, oil, mining	Melbourne	55000	1104
Burns, Philp and Company	Merchant, shipping	Sydney	4000	98
Carlton and United Breweries	Brewing, hotels	Melbourne		127
Chrysler Australia	Car manufacturing	Adelaide	6500	69
G. J. Coles and Co.	Retailing	Melbourne	28000	112
Colonial Mutual Life	Insurance	Melbourne	4500	(1041)
Comalco	Aluminium mining, refining	Melbourne	5500	136
Commercial Bank of Australia	Banking, finance	Melbourne	6500	56
Conzinc Riotinto of Aust.	Mining investment	Melbourne	12000	362
CSR	Sugar, building materials, mining	Sydney	16000	258
Dunlop Australia	Rubber, footwear, textiles	Melbourne	23500	120
Elder Smith Goldsbrough Mort	Wool broker, merchant	Adelaide	5000	94
Ford Motor Company of Australia	Car manufacturing	Melborne	13000	124
General Motors-Holdens	Car manufacturing	Melbourne	24000	236
ICI Australia	Chemicals	Melbourne	12500	187
David Jones	Retailing	Sydney	12000	97
John Lysaght	Sheet steel	Sydney	7000	122

Table 1. (cont.)

Company	Major business	Head office	Employees (to nearest 500)	Share-holders' funds ($m.)
Mayne Nickless	Transport	Melbourne	9000	28
Metal Manufactures	Copper manu-facturing	Sydney	7000	78
MIM Holdings	Mining, refining	Brisbane	7000	166
MLC	Insurance	Sydney	4500	(1113)
Mobil Oil Australia	Petrol	Melbourne	2500	
Myer Emporium	Retailing	Melbourne	29000	170
National Bank	Banking, finance	Melbourne	9500	94
National Mutual Life	Insurance	Melbourne	3000	(1182)
North Broken Hill	Mining, investment	Melbourne	1000	127
Olympic Consol. Industries	Rubber goods	Melbourne	6500	50
Philips Industries Holdings	Electrical goods	Sydney	10000	51
Repco	Automotive parts	Melbourne	12000	75
Shell Australian Securities	Petrol	Melbourne	5500	242
Tooth and Co.	Brewer	Sydney	2000	126
Tubemakers of Australia	Tube, pipe manufacturing	Sydney	8000	89
Waltons	Retail, finance	Sydney	8000	54
Western Mining Corporation	Mining	Melbourne	3500	194
Woolworths	Retailing	Sydney	34000	100

panies, discussed below, are among the worst; BHP among the best. Various uncertainties therefore remain in the list. In particular, information about the workforce is hard to come by, and has had to be gathered from any source available. There are no doubt inaccuracies and inconsistencies in these figures. They should be taken generally as estimates – the orders of magnitude should be right. Where companies operate overseas, the Australian workforce (if available) is shown.

Here then, within the obvious limits of this technique, is a guide to Australia's corporate heavyweights of the early 1970s. One is struck immediately by the absence of pastoral capital – only one pastoral firm (Elders GM) creeps in, and that only by bending the criteria. Apart from mining, which is well represented, it is urban activities – retailing, manufacturing, and finance – that dominate. The largest industry group here is the motor and oil complex, which accounts for nearly a quarter of the companies on the list and some big ones that did not quite make it. But the largest urban industry, building, is not directly represented at all; though a very large employer, it has a more decentralized structure of companies.

Even within this list of heavyweights, size varies a good deal; BHP, which is well in front on both criteria of size, is more than ten times as big as the smallest firms listed. After BHP the biggest employers of labour are the chain retailers, Coles, Myer and Woolworths, followed by the biggest manufacturers and banks. On the criterion of capital, BHP is followed by a mixed group of miners and manufacturers, CRA, CSR, Shell, GMH; and though one cannot directly equate the measures, the massive investment funds of the AMP Society, nearly three times the size of the next insurance firms', put it in this league.

Patterns of growth

The obvious question to ask about such a set of companies is how they got there; and a study of their origins and growth should give useful insights into the processes at work in Australian capitalism. What I can offer here, given the lack of monographic studies, is only an outline, compiled from the company histories that are available and abstracts in sources such as *Jobson's*; but it still has some interest.

A general idea of what has happened can be gained very easily by charting the dates of formation of the companies in the list. This is done in Table 2, which classifies them by type of industry and four periods in the development of the Australian class structure.

A date of formation is not always easy to fix. In some cases like the Bank of New South Wales and BHP it is perfectly clear as the beginning of the business, the incorporation of the company, and the achievement of large size, all more or less coincide. But in other histories these events may be separated, sometimes widely. In cases like Australian Paper Manufacturers and Australian Consolidated Industries, each of which began as a number of separate partnerships or family businesses and then grew by a complex chain of incorporations and mergers into a large monopoly company, it is very difficult indeed

Table 2. Dates of formation of the major companies

	1788–1840	1840–90	1890–1930	1930–70
Finance	1817 B of NSW 1835 ANZ Bank	1848 AMP 1858 Nat Bank 1866 Commerc. Bank 1869 Nat. Mut. Life 1873 Col. Mut. Life 1886 MLC		
Merchants		1883 Burns Philp 1888 Elders GM	1906 David Jones 1917 Myer 1921 Coles 1924 Woolworths 1926 Waltons	
Manufacturing (other than transport)		1855 CSR 1885 BHP 1888 Tooth 1895 APM	1904 AMATIL 1907 C & UB 1916 Metal Manufac. 1916 ACI 1921 John Lysaght 1926 Philips 1928 ICI 1929 Tubemakers	
Transport			1900 Shell 1904 Mobil 1920 BP 1922 Repco 1925 Ford 1926 Mayne Nickless 1926 GMH 1929 Dunlop	1933 Olympic 1936 Ampol 1936 Ansett 1951 Chrysler
Mining			1912 North BH 1924 MIM	1933 WMC 1960 Comalco 1961 Alcoa 1962 CRA

to nominate a date at which the present company was 'formed'.
Table 2 can therefore only be an approximate guide, but it is
accurate enough to indicate the general trends. The date given
is normally that of the original incorporation. Some companies
such as David Jones and Tooths have a considerable pre-history
as unincorporated businesses before these dates. In some cases
a date after the initial incorporation is given. Where a big merger
created an entity that was obviously a new force in business,
such as the brewery merger that produced Carlton and United,

the glass merger that produced Australian Glass Manufacturers (now ACI), and the mergers of the Australian holdings of British firms following mergers in Britain that gave us British Tobacco (now AMATIL), ICI, and CRA, the date of this amalgamation is given. In the case of the ANZ Bank, however, the date of incorporation (1835) of the first of the two banks merged in 1951 is given, as both had been major companies throughout the intervening period. The recent trend towards reorganization in a holding-company structure has been ignored; it would for instance be absurd to regard the MLC as dating from 1962, though that is when the present holding company was formed.

The pattern that emerges in Table 2 is clear. The top companies of the present date from all stages in the evolution of Australian capitalism from the convict period to the present, and reflect the changing character of its economy. The columns should not of course be read as a list of the major companies in each period – merely of those that have survived as majors to the present. Of the pastoral investment and agency companies that loomed large in the nineteenth century, only one reminder (Elders GM) is on the list, and that only by dint of multiple amalgamations. None of the gold-mining companies of the period is represented – the richest, Mt Morgan, is long defunct. But the predominance of mercantile and financial capital in the colonial economy has left its mark on Table 2. All of the major financiers, both banks and insurance companies, of the early 1970s were established in the nineteenth century. The industrialization and urban expansion of the twentieth century are still clearly reflected. A majority of the manufacturers, and all the big retail chains, date from the first third of the century. The 1920s especially was a vintage decade for big mergers and promising foundations. Companies established then grew hugely in the industrial boom that followed the depression; and at that time the motor and oil complex became a leading force. The youngest group of companies, curiously, is mining – given the hoary age of the mining industry by Australian standards. But the largest miners on the scene at present reflect the inflow of British and American capital into mechanized mining, mostly in the north and west of the country, under very different conditions from the original rushes.

The current set of leading companies, then, was created by

the growth of an industrial economy over a mercantile and pastoral base within an imperialist context. Apart from the absence of building firms, they nicely sum up the grand trends of the last hundred years of economic history. But what of their individual formation?

To get a grip on this it is useful to examine the sources of capital involved in a company's origins – at least the immediate sources, leaving aside the more general questions of the generation of profit. With some of these firms the source is conspicuous, as there was a direct import of a large bloc of capital from overseas. The Union Bank and the Australasia (now merged in the ANZ Bank) were created in this way in the 1830s; as were Mt Isa Mines, Chrysler, Comalco, and others of the last generation. With others the source is a consortium of local businessmen or companies who each put in fairly large shares. Some of the earliest companies in the list, including the Bank of NSW, CSR, and AMP, were formed in this way, reflecting the character of early nineteenth-century companies as committees of merchants and propertied gentlemen. In a number of twentieth-century cases there is a consortium of local and overseas capital. Metal Manufactures and Tubemakers are examples, in both of which cases the overseas partners brought the technology that was wanted.

Plainly, companies formed in these ways reproduce the power of established businessmen. Often key shareholdings can be traced through a series of amalgamations and new companies, such as the Grimwade family interests in ACI and related firms, and the Baillieu family interests in North Broken Hill, Metal Manufactures, etc. As the Grimwade case shows, however, the new corporate structures can get away from their creators with the growth of scale and technique; new men can rise within them as bureaucrats and technologists.

New men can enter the corporate élite more dramatically, by rising with companies that did not depend on established capitals at the start. Companies of this kind, one might almost say, are of two separate species, the spectacular and the dull. The spectacular are those which struck a profit bonanza, such as the Broken Hill line of lode that launched (separately) the two major industrial complexes of the inter-war period, BHP and the Collins House group; or a rapidly growing new line of business, as did Coles and Woolworths with chain retailing,

Repco and Olympic supplying the motor trade. The dull are those which began as a small business, prospered respectably, and in the fulness of time resorted to the stock market for share capital: examples are David Jones and Tooths, a retailer and a brewer. In reality there is no clearcut division between these types; some combination of retained earnings and stock market raisings as sources of capital is typical.[5] Along these lines, some of the most important businessmen of the last generation have risen into the corporate élite: the Coles brothers with their retail firm, Frank Beaurepaire with Olympic, Reg Ansett with his transport firm, Charlie McGrath with Repco.

Perhaps the most notable feature of it all is this. One thinks of the accumulation of capital as a continuous and gradual process, and in the aggregate that is no doubt true. But in perhaps half the cases here, the capital that launched these firms into major status was assembled fairly suddenly – by a bloc investment, a consortium, a rich mineral strike, the extraction of monopoly profits, or some combination of these. In these cases the creation of a major company is a discontinuity in the process of capital accumulation rather than a routine extension of it.

The organizational growth of the companies is obviously affected by the pattern of capitalization, but can be distinguished from it. Two patterns of rapid growth can be seen. One is where a company is established at the start as a large operation, which obviously requires the participation of established businessmen, companies, or the state. This is seen in some of the earliest companies in the list (the Bank of New South Wales and ANZ Bank) as well as some of the most recent (Comalco, Alcoa). The other is the explosive growth of an initially small company as a result of a rich mine (the classic case is BHP) or the exploitation of a new market (Holdens, Coles). Such companies are often unstable; in a number of cases the initial growth has been followed by a major reconstruction or change of direction. Mt Morgan Mining, for instance, went out of business; BHP shifted into steelmaking, and initially was in serious difficulties with it; Holdens was taken over by General Motors. A variant of explosive growth is where an initially small or medium-sized company with an aggressive management is in a short period made into a giant by a string of takeovers. Waltons, Dunlop, Ansett, and TNT are the chief examples.

Other majors have been built up over a much longer period. Again one can distinguish two rather different patterns. In the one, a number of businesses grow up in a given industry as competitors, who at a certain point see the virtues of fellowship and merge their organizations in a monopoly. This may involve local groups (Carlton and United Breweries, ACI in glass, APM in paper), or the local subsidiaries of overseas firms (British Tobacco, ICI in chemicals). The event may be followed by diversification, but the merger itself significantly changes the scale of operation. In the other pattern there is a single company at the core, which gradually grows by successful trading in its original industry; this is often followed by diversification or takeovers to build a larger corporate structure. This is a common pattern in finance and retailing (e.g. National Bank, David Jones, Myer), and to an extent in light manufacturing.

These patterns are of course types, and one would have to sort fairly ruthlessly to fit all the companies on the list into them. The differences between them are matters of degree. Dunlop for instance diversified further and faster than Olympic, its fellow rubber manufacturer, and can now be regarded as a conglomerate. CSR, established en bloc (though with some travail) as a big company in the mid nineteenth century, grew steadily by consolidating a sugar monopoly but has now diversified into building materials and mining, and has begun to tread the takeover trail again. All major companies have a bureaucratic structure of course; but whether these differences in organisational histories are reflected in the way their bureaucracies operate remains to be discovered.

The four major groupings

So far I have treated companies as units, neglecting the connections among them. As was shown in Chapter 2, there are a good many pitfalls in analysing business linkages and alliances; but it is necessary in order to understand the politics of business, the allocation of resources within the ruling class.

The biggest company is of course BHP. Its history is well known. It began with the discovery of phenomenally rich silver ores at Broken Hill in western New South Wales in 1883, and rapidly earned very large profits – twice, in the depressed 1890s, declaring a million-pound dividend. As its silver mine became exhausted the company turned to steel manufacturing, setting up blast furnaces at Newcastle. Under the control of Essington Lewis it survived a financial crisis in the 1920s, stimulated the development of companies that used its steel, and in 1935 achieved a monopoly by taking over Australian Iron and Steel. Under Lewis' successors in the last twenty years it has diversified into mining on a large scale, and has become, in a joint venture with Esso, the country's main oil producer. Its growth has been largely internally financed out of profits (though its move into steel initially depended on a large loan from the young Commonwealth Bank). The present company is itself a steel manufacturer, but is also the holding company for 60 subsidiaries (at the time of the 1974 report) of which the most important are:

Australian Iron and Steel (steel manufacturing)
Dampier Mining (iron ore)
Groote Eylandt Mining (manganese ore)
Hematite Petroleum (gas/oil production).

It also has a large interest in some other companies in related fields:

Tubemakers of Australia (44%)
John Lysaght (Australia) (50%)
Blue Circle Southern Cement (43%).

It is, basically, a very large vertically-integrated monopoly whose immense resources have allowed it to diversify more or less at will. In practice its management has been fairly cautious, staying mostly within the steel-and-mining field.[6]

The second largest company in terms of capitalization (omitting the insurance funds) is Conzinc Riotinto of Australia. The Australian origins of this firm go back to 1905, to the formation of the Zinc Corporation, which was in 1907 sold to British interests, and in 1949 merged with a British smelting company to form Consolidated Zinc. It kept up its Australian mining operations, and made a major aluminium discovery in the 1950s at Weipa. CRA however had its main source in the British Rio Tinto Company, which dates from the 1870s when British capital moved into the Spanish Rio Tinto mines. In the early 1950s most of this interest was sold off, and the proceeds were used to finance a new multinational mining investment operation, masterminded by the late Val Duncan. Rio Tinto began operations in Australia in 1954, buying into uranium and exploring in the Pilbara. In 1962 it merged with Consolidated Zinc in Britain to form Rio Tinto Zinc; and the Australian holdings of the two companies were united under a new holding company, CRA. This company immediately became the base for a spectacular expansion of large-scale and highly mechanized mining and refining ventures in aluminium, iron ore, and copper, financed in part through long-term loans based on long-term export contracts. The group is now by far the largest mining empire in Australia, comprising about 40 companies held together by common ownership through CRA (itself 81% owned by RTZ) and interlocking directorships. Duncan himself before his recent death was active in major negotiations involving the subsidiaries. The main subsidiaries are (1972):

Hamersley Holdings (54%: iron ore mining)
Bougainville Copper (53%)
Mary Kathleen Uranium (51%)
Australian Mining and Smelting (72%: silver–lead–zinc).

It has also a 45% interest in Comalco. The pattern here is very different from BHP: the group was created by financiers and is integrated only by finance and common ownership. Its rapid growth is a dramatic demonstration of the impact of international capital in a small economy; and also of its political caution, as RTZ has been careful to provide for minority local ownership in all its Australasian operations.[7]

The local group which is most analogous to this, and indeed was involved in the history of the Zinc Corporation, is the so-called 'Collins House' group (named for the building in Collins Street which used to house many of their head offices). This began with a group of Melbourne businessmen who bought into the Broken Hill mines in the 1900s and struck it rich in the areas outside BHP's control. Led by the redoubtable W. L. Baillieu, they reinvested the profits in a series of metal processing and manufacturing companies, maintaining close links with British interests; indeed several of the leading figures emigrated to England. In this group there is no one parent company; rather, a series of companies which have been used to invest in each other under *ad hoc* arrangements for each new enterprise. The first two, North Broken Hill and BH South, now function substantially as investment companies; but the others cannot be regarded as their subsidiaries. The major companies involved are (showing NBH ownership as an example of the interlocks):

North Broken Hill (mining and investment)
BH South (mining and investment; 2% NBH)
Metal Manufactures (copper products: 16% NBH)
EZ Industries (zinc refining: 7% NBH)
Broken Hill Associated Smelters (30% NBH)
Associated Pulp and Paper Mills (19% NBH)
Alcoa (12% NBH).

This is a looser investment structure than CRA's. It is indeed a little difficult to say where the 'group' begins and ends: there are for instance significant investment links with Western Mining Corporation (originally promoted by one of the Collins House entrepreneurs and now a partner in Alcoa). On the other hand there is a greater vertical integration of the enterprises, from extraction to final processing, than in the case of CRA.[8]

These are the three largest groups that can be readily identified by the traditional method of analysing chains of ownership and the history of the formation of companies. There are of course other kinds of links, such as the joint ventures and temporary alliances that have recently grown up around CSR, but have not reached any formalization in terms of ownership (and may never do so). On the other side, the insurance companies are major owners of shares in practically all the companies on the list, but they have invested for income and the relationship rarely has any implications for the operations of the other companies.

There is one other complex of companies on the scale of the three just discussed, though it is not a 'group' in the same sense: the companies involved in motor and oil manufacturing and supply. The motor transport complex grew up outside the previous corporate structure, being partly created by technically-minded entrepreneurs in Australia, and partly by the entry of overseas firms, mostly American. They now form a a fairly tightly-knit oligopoly, protected from competition by the immense costs of entry to the industry under modern conditions and the limited size of the Australian market. There is no pattern of interlocking ownership or directorates in Australia. There is however an interesting indirect connection. A number of the oil firms involved can be traced back to American companies which are linked in the USA by the Rockefellers and are derived from the original Rockefeller monopoly company, Standard Oil. Mobil, Caltex, Esso and Amoco are all subsidiaries of Rockefeller companies; H. C. Sleigh is partly owned by American Caltex; Ampol has been partly financed by a Rockefeller bank, for a long period distributed Caltex's oil, and is now partly owned by American Caltex. The Australian motor fuel industry is thus to a significant extent a product of the overseas expansion of America's most powerful financial and industrial empire. Rockefeller interests, particularly the First National City Bank of New York, have also recently moved in strength into Australian finance, taking a 40% share in IAC and setting up FNCB–Walton's as a 50%-owned joint venture with the Sydney firm. The relationships among all these companies are indirect. It is possible, but most unlikely for political reasons (trust-busting in the USA as well as nationalism in Australia) that the Rockefeller interests in Australia could at some time be rationalized and integrated in the manner of the RTZ interests.[9]

It would be unwise to suggest that the era of large-scale foreign investment in Australia is over. But it does seem unlikely that future empire-building will take the forms that it has with BHP or CRA and Collins House. New major groupings in business are more likely to emerge by a process of cartelization, which can create operating units out of firms whose capital structures remain distinct, or very remotely related. Something of the sort has already emerged in petrol and in construction materials; a kind of state-controlled cartel already exists in banking; the process was actively encouraged in the mining industry by Connor, and is unlikely to be reversed by the Liberal government. In the last two decades there have been significant trends towards holding-company structures for big firms, and diversification of their enterprises. If these trends continue – and the recent BHP–CSR struggle for the cement industry suggests that the latter does – the future structure of big business in Australia may well be a series of conglomerates based on holding companies, whose major subsidiaries are cross-linked in industry-by-industry cartels.

Conflict in the ruling class, 1970–72

Discord and disunity are problems that beset the ruling class and its leadership as much as they do the labour movement, though of course in different ways and at different times. The struggles of the last decade in both the political and business wings have been unusually bitter, and are worth studying closely. Not only does the barrage of publicity surrounding them provide a unique chance to examine the *modus operandi* of the top leadership. A close analysis of the patterns of conflict can help rectify some of the characteristic weaknesses of class analysis as it has been practised in Australia.

In the first place, it is an empirical truth that conflict within the ruling class is chronic. It is the stuff of politics in Canberra, it is the stuff of business life. It is so widespread, so frequent, so ordinary, that it leads very many observers, including many journalists, economists, and political scientists, to regard it as the basic structure of politics; to adopt, that is to say, a pluralist interpretation of the structure of power. One of the reasons why pluralism, a profoundly unsatisfying intellectual position, keeps bobbing back (in tacit forms even if not as a theory), is that it points to truths that other interpretations persistently ignore or deny. It is really true that different businesses have different interests, which really are opposed. That the conflicts arising from them are genuine is demonstrated quite simply by their savagery, by the fact that some businessmen are actually destroyed in them, occasionally whole companies, and sometimes even whole industries. The same goes for politicians and their parties.

To insist on these facts is not by any means to require a pluralist interpretation of them. Rather, it is to require that any interpretation of the structure of power that claims in principle to be complete, must deal with them. And in dealing with them, class analysis will recover some of its own strength. For in denying the reality or the importance of conflicts in the ruling class, the theories advanced by Australian radicals in the past have repeatedly tipped towards a conspiracy theory of social power. They have developed into a thesis of 'the monopolists against the people', and have thus wound up in a populist rather than a socialist position.[1] This tendency is again apparent in much of the current left-wing criticism of foreign capital. Now conspiracies do occur, and at times the ruling class does close ranks in the face of an actual or perceived threat – as in the bank nationalization campaign in the late 1940s, and more briefly but equally successfully in 1975. But conspiracy, or solidarity at the top, is not the *basis* of the power structure; it is, rather, one of its emergency defences. A recognition and exploration of the patterns of conflict that are normal in the ruling class is important in driving the analysis back to the concern with the institutional bases of the structure of power that is necessary for a socialist theory. Indeed, as suggested in Chapter 3, internal conflict is one of the forces that produces consistent action from the ruling class as a whole.

In the second place, an attention to episodes of conflict forcibly raises the question of process. Class analysis often suffers from a kind of constipation, produced by the 'categorical' approach outlined in Chapter 1. The analyst with great care sets up a system of sociological categories, investigates the background of people and families, and fits them into the scheme. Once they have been got in their boxes, the analysis jams. There is nothing much more to do with them after they have been classified, except to state the obvious general consequences of their class membership.

Such analysis can wind up in the awkward situation of being quite unrecognized by its own objects. Show a businessman a piece of analysis which makes him out to be a member of a neo-capitalistic ruling class, and he (it is practically always he) is likely to protest that it does not correspond at all to his own experience of competition, obstacle, difficulty and frustration. While coloured perhaps by false consciousness, such a protest contains an important truth. A static analysis of a system of classes is liable to pass over the activity of its members, the very activity by which the system, as a structure of social relationships, is constituted. And in passing over the activity, the experience of the people concerned must be ignored; or at best fragmented and stylized, as usually happens in polls of 'class consciousness'.

The general answer to this difficulty in class analysis is to approach classes from a historical point of view. But that is a rather grandiose style to adopt when one is interested in particular people or companies. An attractive model for events at this level was suggested some time ago by the American sociologist Long (ironically, in a polemic against power élite analysis) when he described the politics of a city as 'an ecology of games'.[2] Within a given area, power-holders will be playing a variety of different games, each with reasonably definite goals and a distinct audience: a banking game, a newspaper game, a political game (narrowly defined), an ecclesiastical game, and so forth. They will make use of each other, and of current events, to further their strategies in their particular games. Thus a cleric may make use of a businessman, a businessman of a politician, and so on. Out of the interplay of their private strategies and diverse games come social consequences that no one of them may have intended.

The 'game' analogy is useful at precisely the point where static class analysis breaks down. It draws attention to the continuing activity of power holders; to the fluctuations of their fortunes; to the rationality, within limits, of their behaviour; to the constraints upon them and the opposition they meet. Above all it stresses their continuing need to decide strategies, to choose tactics, and to enact them. But it is only a preliminary guide. A game played with fifty million dollars is a rather different matter from a game played with fifty dollars a week, and to call them both 'games' says nothing about why both are being played together. An analogy is not a theory; though it is useful, this one becomes effective only within the context of a structural analysis. It is vital to consider the nature of the resources available to players at the start, and those they try to assemble in the course of playing.

The players in the ruling-class power games of 1970–2, from the peak of the mining boom to the defeat of the McMahon government, were drawn mainly from four groups: (a) owners, directors and managers of established Australian businesses, such as the banks, the insurance companies, and big manufacturers like BHP and CSR, who mostly figure in the top 50 of the previous chapter; (b) managers of multinational corporations with investments in Australia or capital to be invested here, such as Rio Tinto Zinc (RTZ, British) and International Telephone and Telegraph (ITT, American); (c) new entrepreneurs, the managers of local companies which moved up to wealth and influence in the 1950s and 1960s, such as the leadership of the Minsec and Patrick groups to be discussed shortly, who mostly have not quite made it into the list of top companies; and (d) the political entrepreneurs, the top parliamentary and executive leadership of the Liberal–Country Party coalition. The two other leadership groups which are most important in the power relationships of the period, the Labour Party and trade union leadership and the federal bureaucracy, will be left aside in this discussion except for those occasions where their games impinge as major constraints on those being played by the businessmen and conservative politicians. The chapter focusses on the national conservative leadership, and mostly leaves out state politicians. Figures such as Askin, Bolte and Court obviously have had power and importance beyond their local houses of parliament; in WA and SA especially, state politicians have been vital in bringing in the multinational corporations. Conflicts of interest between state and federal conservatives are only briefly considered in the section on the Liberal leadership below. But though the analysis is thus incomplete, the very considerable centralization of state power in Canberra in the last generation, parallel to the centralization of economic power through the major companies, which practically all now operate on a national scale (and a few on an international scale), makes it proper to focus on the national leadership.

The basic division of the leadership of the ruling class into specialist politicians and specialist businessmen, as suggested in Chapter 3, happened long before this period. Having fought off the first and most serious challenge from labour in the years around 1920, this leadership, partly deliberately and partly by default, launched Australia after the depression on a course of industrialization. Intensified by the second world war, the process of import replacement and industrial development continued after it and developed into what the economists talk of as the second 'long boom' in Australia's history, three decades of largely unchecked population growth and economic expansion. A heavy inflow of migrants, a less conspicuous but also heavy inflow of capital, and rising standards of living and levels of demand from the local workforce, sustained the expansion. The conservative politicians swept back into office after the war on a programme of freeing the economy from constraints, and rode the boom with such skill that in 1969 they had held office continuously for twenty years. A considerable degree of central management of the economy was by this time accepted as normal, in fact one of the major services that the political wing was expected to provide for the business wing. The central management for most of this period was expansionary; one of the few experiments with policies of restraint (by Holt as Treasurer in 1960–1) had led to a temporary split among businessmen and nearly to a Labor victory at the polls. The mistake was not repeated while Menzies and Holt held the reins.

But the policies through which the conservative politicians contributed the government's support to the business boom could not roll on to the crack of doom. Migration was contingent on conditions in the countries from which the migrants came, and on Australia's capacity to absorb them; either might change. Holding Australia open to overseas capital could lead to conflict with local businessmen whose interests were threatened by it. Under certain conditions the clash of interests could become very sharp. At the end of the 1960s, in a society made rich by the long boom, but unsettled by conflict over war and cultural change, these conditions arose. The precipitating event was the stock market boom of 1969 and collapse in late 1970, which was followed by a general, if not very drastic, economic contraction. The three years 1970–2, roughly the lifetime of the 27th parliament, were marked by a series of conflicts within the ruling class of a range and intensity not seen since the 1940s. They can best be approached by looking at particular episodes and analysing the games being played by those involved and the resources they deployed. I have chosen three episodes, arranged by the widening range of involvement, from the clash of two investment companies to the political split with which the whole electorate was finally concerned.

Giants of the mining boom: Minsec and Patricks

The curious and dramatic events surrounding the collapse of Mineral Securities Australia Ltd in February 1971 have been well ventilated in the press at the time, the enquiries of the Senate Select Committee on Securities and Exchange, and the debate over the long-drawn-out process of liquidation. They have also become the subject matter of criminal charges. No doubt further details of the story will emerge, but the main outlines are already reasonably clear. It is necessary to set out a narrative of events to make clear the strategies and resources involved.[3]

Minsec was formed in 1965 by two mining consultants, K. H. McMahon and T. A. Nestel: one became its chairman and the other its managing director. Its purpose was to trade in shares, particularly mining shares, and with the profits of buying and selling on the stock market, to finance prospecting and new mines. In practice the mining mostly occurred on the stock exchange. Some early successes in share trading in the rising market of the late 1960s placed the company in a healthy position as part owner of a number of oil and mining companies, and sharpened the management's share-trading skills. When the mining market took off for the sky on the announcement of Poseidon's nickel strike (see Figure 1), Minsec went with it. It became, for a time, the largest share-trading operation in Australia, relying on quick turnover and inside information, not to mention more organized manipulation of the market such as the 'privileged trading in the shares of subsidiaries' documented by the Senate enquiry. In a stock market awash with rumours, where organized runs on particular stocks were (on Nestel's evidence) commonplace and more exotic techniques of turning a dollar were also familiar, Minsec, with an efficient information system of its own, gambled intelligently and won repeatedly. Its net profits soared from $21,000 in its first year to nearly $2 million in 1968–9 and a phenomenal $15 million in 1969–70.[4] It spun off two investment funds, and with the mining companies it had bought into, was well on the way to forming an interlocking finance and mining group.

If that result was remarkable for a company only six years old, something even more spectacular was on the horizon. In 1958 a company called Kathleen Investments had been floated

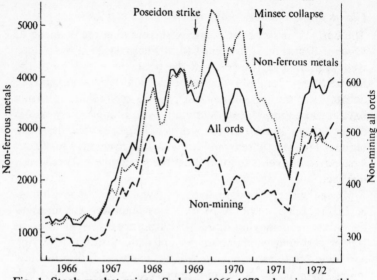

Fig. 1. Stock-market prices, Sydney, 1966–1972, showing monthly averages of ordinary share prices. Source: ordinary share price index, *Sydney Stock Exchange Gazette* and *Australian Stock Exchange Journal.*

to take over a 35% Australian interest in Rio Tinto's subsidiary in Queensland, Mary Kathleen Uranium. A subsidiary of Kathleen Investments, Queensland Mines, was exploring for uranium. In 1969 it announced a substantial strike in Queensland. In April–June 1970 it did better, striking paydirt at a place now called Nabarlek in an Aboriginal reserve to the east of Darwin. A preliminary announcement was made on 3 July, and on 1 September the managing director, E. R. Hudson, publicly announced details of the find: 'indicated reserves' of 55000 short tons of uranium oxide at an average grade of 540 pounds to the ton of ore – the richest uranium deposit in the world. The Geiger counters went off their scales at Nabarlek. Whoever controlled this deposit, given the high concentration of the ore and the slack state of demand, would be in a position to dominate the world uranium market. Minsec moved in and began buying shares in both Kathleen Investments and Queensland Mines. But the price had flown so high that a controlling interest was beyond even Minsec's capacity to buy. It needed an ally, and found one in another large investment company,

Castlereagh Securities, a new creation of the stockbroking firm Patrick Partners.

Patrick Partners (which changed its name from Patrick and Co. in 1970 and will be called Patrick Partners for simplicity, throughout) was formed in 1953 by the merger of two small sharebroking firms. It carried on an expanding broking and underwriting business into the 1960s, when a new strategy emerged under the influence of M. R. L. Dowling, who was senior partner during the boom. This was to use the stockbroking business as the base for the creation of a group of Australian finance companies capable of acting in the big league of world finance. To reach this position it needed to take a strong position in local industries capable of quick and sustained growth; and the firm recognized mining as a suitable candidate. Investment in Australian mining generally expanded at a brisk rate from 1963–4 on, rapidly becoming the main growth point of the economy. In 1967 Patrick Partners floated a company called Mining Traders, intended 'to trade in company shares but principally to purchase large interests in mining ventures'. Like Minsec, it was in a strategic position when the mining stock market took off. Vigorous operations again netted huge profits from a small base. Mining Traders' profits over the years 1967 to 1970 totalled $7 million; and its associated unlisted investment companies also reaped rich rewards.

Part of this was from ordinary share trading, as in the case of Minsec; but a large part of the Patrick companies' profits arose from operations connected with the business of the parent firm. Patrick Partners had a huge turnover purely as stockbrokers, for thousands of investors, large and small, plunged into the speculative market. The firm had about 25,000 clients at the peak, and is said to have handled at times as much as 40% of the entire Sydney mining share market. (There were 62 firms on the Sydney Stock Exchange in January 1970.) This business created a glorious range of new opportunities as the boom developed and the appetite of investors for new mining stocks became apparent. The Patrick group became extremely active in launching new companies and raising new capital for old ones: from 1969 to 1971 they raised over $60 million from such issues. A particularly lucrative side of the business was underwriting and sub-underwriting new issues, with the opportunities this gave for 'stagging' (being allocated new issues at or near

83

face value, and selling out when the stock came onto the open market and its price leapt). The Senate enquiry uncovered an example of such transactions in the shares of one company, Australian Consolidated Minerals, which alone netted $1.5 million nominal profit in about six months for the Patrick companies, about half of this being realized profit. The broking house, its partners, and its associated public and private companies were in every aspect of the boom: prospecting, selling leases, floating companies, underwriting and sub-underwriting floats, arranging loans, advising on investment, broking shares, buying and selling in their own right, and acting as directors of companies. They met themselves coming back in highly profitable ways.

The proceeds from these activities enabled the Patrick organization to expand very rapidly and turn towards other fields of finance. The details need not concern us; it is sufficient to say that in 1970–1 the parent firm and a series of closely associated companies came to cover most aspects of the finance business. They were in broking, share trading, underwriting, the short-term money market, other aspects of merchant banking, and industrial and housing finance. In July 1970, Patricks also launched a large new investment company, Castlereagh Securities, intended to complement Mining Traders (called Patrick Corporation from August 1970) by taking long-term investments and exercizing control of mining companies. The issue of shares raised $20 million. By great good fortune, as it seemed, this company was floated just at the time of the first Nabarlek announcement. It immediately bought into Queensland Mines; and after Hudson's announcement of the quantity of ore, took quick profits by selling its Queensland Mines shares but began to buy heavily in Kathleen Investments.

Minsec's plans for Nabarlek thus came up against an equal and opposite force; possibly a stronger one, as the Patrick group, though it had only small shareholdings initially, already had directors on the boards of the two uranium companies. (Patrick Partners had underwritten the original float of Kathleen Investments and had kept close links with the company since. Dowling personally was on its board at this time.) Realizing that they were bidding against each other, the boards of Minsec and Castlereagh began to consider ways of cooperating. They were not strangers: McMahon, as a mining consultant, had worked for Patrick Partners in the 1960s and was on the original board of Mining Traders in 1967. The details of their negotiations are still disputed, but it appears that at least three schemes were considered. The final one agreed to, late in 1970, was for Castlereagh and Minsec to continue to buy Kathleen Investments shares, up to 20% of the total – a figure that should have given decisive influence in that company. These they would shortly sell to a new company (to be called Power and Resources of Australia, PRA) that was to have other energy investments, and was to be floated when stock market conditions were right. (In case the reader is now a little lost, Figure 2 sets out the relationships among the principal firms.) The buying continued, on a large scale; but the market at the end of 1970 was in a general decline, and the conditions for the PRA float never did appear.

As the delay grew longer, Minsec's position grew more and more awkward. Their success had been phenomenal; but they had failed to reckon with the market's downturn, and began to lose heavily in share trading across the board. They financed their purchasing in late 1970 with short-term loans from other companies, a technique they had used a little before for rapid share trading, and now extended on a much greater scale. But Nabarlek was a long-term investment – at least in the absence of PRA – and the company became increasingly vulnerable as its borrowings mounted and the value of its shareholdings fell. Minsec had also been buying heavily in the more expensive Queensland Mines shares; and its big slice of Nabarlek was causing doubts as rumours circulated in December and January that the ore deposit was not nearly as rich as claimed. The Minsec directors have claimed that as part of the PRA deal there was a verbal agreement with Patrick Partners to provide bridging finance of c. $30 million, which was not fulfilled; Dowling has denied this, reasonably arguing that finance on that scale would never have been so informally arranged.

The crisis came over transactions in another company. After the peak of the Poseidon boom, Minsec had become involved in the flotation of the Robe River iron-ore project, which happily gave them tax concessions to set off against their startling share trading profits. Late in 1970 two of the Minsec companies sold about six million shares in Robe River Ltd to a broker, register-

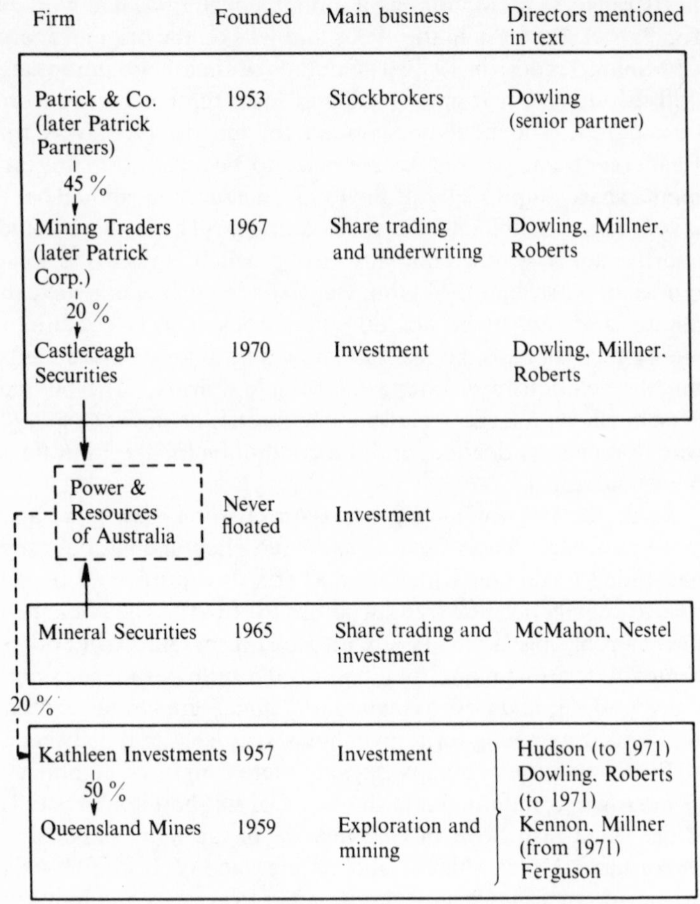

Firm	Founded	Main business	Directors mentioned in text
Patrick & Co. (later Patrick Partners)	1953	Stockbrokers	Dowling (senior partner)
↓ 45%			
Mining Traders (later Patrick Corp.)	1967	Share trading and underwriting	Dowling, Millner, Roberts
↓ 20%			
Castlereagh Securities	1970	Investment	Dowling, Millner, Roberts
Power & Resources of Australia	Never floated	Investment	
Mineral Securities	1965	Share trading and investment	McMahon, Nestel
20%			
Kathleen Investments	1957	Investment	Hudson (to 1971) Dowling, Roberts (to 1971)
↓ 50%			
Queensland Mines	1959	Exploration and mining	Kennon, Millner (from 1971) Ferguson

Fig. 2. Main companies involved in the Nabarlek conflict, 1970–1971.

ing a healthy profit on their books and allowing Minsec to claim $3½ million net profit for July–December 1970. But other companies in the group had bought them back from the same broker, in order that control of Robe River, and access to the 'greatly enhanced profits' expected from it, should remain in the house. When both transactions were consolidated in the group's accounts, the Minsec board were forced to acknowledge that their claimed profit was actually a loss of $3 million. The crisis came at the beginning of February 1971: some creditors moved in to safeguard their money, and the company could not pay. Its shares were suspended on the stock exchanges on 4 February, and the company shortly went into liquidation. The Australian business world shook as the Minsec empire crashed. In a hectic round of negotiations between local firms, multinationals (including the Rio Tinto subsidiary CRA), the federal government, and the liquidator, several schemes were proposed for selling Minsec's assets and preventing the rot from spreading. Some were quickly sold off, with results that shall be seen; it took three years, however, to dispose of the Robe River shares.

That was the end of the road for Minsec; but it was far from the end of the story for Patricks. For as the Minsec details came to light, the agreement with Castlereagh Securities to buy a large holding in Kathleen Investments, formerly a complete secret, was made public. The role of Dowling and Roberts of Castlereagh Securities, who were also directors of Kathleen Investments and Queensland Mines, came under sudden scrutiny. The opinion of Kathleen's chairman and many shareholders, who believed that Dowling and Roberts had tried to win control of Nabarlek in a clandestine operation, swung violently against them. At dramatic annual meetings of the two Nabarlek companies in May–June 1971, they withdrew from the boards, leaving Hudson apparently in complete control.

But it was now Hudson's turn to taste the ironies. He had agreed earlier in the year to take onto the boards the nominees of the AMP Society and Noranda (a Canadian mining firm), which had bought Kathleen Investments and Queensland Mines shares from the Minsec liquidator. This deal, it appears, had been initiated by members of the Patrick group, as the shares involved had been held as security for a loan to Minsec by one of the Patrick finance companies. Hudson thought the new directors would not combine with the Patrick–Castlereagh interests (even suggesting in evidence to the Senate committee that there was an understanding that Noranda and AMP would 'hold the shares against them', though this seems anachronistic), and certainly expected them to support his own position. He was soon to be disillusioned, though as the result of a new factor. The rumours about the size of the uranium deposit, which had played their minor part in Minsec's collapse, were in fact correct.

Hudson's bonanza announcement in September 1970 had little more foundation than guesswork by Queensland Mines' chief geologist, who had been pressed to make an estimate before the first drilling assays were in; the basis of the calculation, as a technical consultant to the Senate committee later put it, 'can only be thought of as geological doodling'. Systematic drilling and assaying in the following months showed the uranium deposit to be smaller, and of much poorer average grade, than at first believed. But neither Hudson nor his board enquired very deeply into the matter, or retracted the original announcement, until T. A. Rodgers, the new director from Noranda and an experienced mining executive, gathered some of the technical results and began to press for their disclosure. A complex and bitter boardroom dispute blew up over the issues of public disclosure and Hudson's credibility – one debate was so heated that he physically collapsed – in which a majority of the directors coalesced against him. Rodgers resigned from the boards in August, but he was immediately replaced by J. S. Millner, the chairman of Castlereagh Securities, and Queensland Mines made an announcement downgrading the deposit to about one-sixth of the size originally claimed. Shortly afterwards Millner replaced Hudson as chairman of directors of both companies.

Hudson then resigned as managing director, calling for a general meeting of Kathleen Investments to get the new controllers voted out, and put up a team to replace the existing board. The sliding scale of voting in the company weighed against big blocks of shares such as Castlereagh's, but they could be split up into small shareholdings to maximize effective votes, and were. On 15 December 1971, about 500 share and proxy holders turned up to an acrimonious general meeting. The small shareholders at the meeting mostly supported Hudson, but the company holdings mobilized against him were overwhelming. Millner was voted back by a ratio of 4 to 1. A year and a half from the first discovery, members of the Patrick alliance were back in control; and it was they who held it through the subsequent disputes with the Whitlam government over Aboriginal rights in the mining leases at Nabarlek.

The most striking thing about the companies involved in this tangled story was their small size. At the height of the Poseidon boom Patrick Partners employed about 550 people. This is very large for a stockbroker, but tiny in comparison to the amount of money being handled. Mining Traders in the boom was even less. It consisted of a board of directors, a secretary, and an assistant secretary! All the work was done by Patrick Partners. In four years as Indyk observes, Patrick Partners earned seven million dollars for a company that was not much more than a name in the companies register.[5] Minsec was a similar operation. There was actually no 'company' in the ordinary sense of the word: just directors, owners (8000 of them), and money. 'Mineral Securities had no staff whatsoever', its chairman explained after the crash, 'not even typists'. The management was done under a management contract by Kenneth McMahon and Partners, mining investment advisers, and its employees. They also managed Minsec's associated companies and funds.

The implication of this is of course that there was no mining being done by these companies (nor by Kathleen Investments). They were legal entities formed to own other companies; their operations were on ownership rather than on minerals. The 'mining boom' of 1969–70 is misnamed. It was, strictly, an ownership boom.[6] In the cases of Queensland Mines and Poseidon, there was not yet a mine – merely a deposit of ore and the expectation of a mine. In other cases, such as Tasminex, there was not even that. The battles for control were fought out at several removes of people and time from actual mining. So if one asks who the Minsec and Mining Traders profits were made from, the answer is evident: other capitalists.

It is difficult to form an accurate picture of the numbers of investors involved in the mining boom. The figure of 25000 for Patrick Partners' customers would be very large for one stock-broker, both because of Patricks' large share of the market and their reputation for taking on any customer. One would think ten times that figure would be an outside estimate of the numbers involved. But there is some Gallup Poll evidence which suggests as many as half a million Australians may have been in the stock market in the smaller boom of 1968.[7] The number will hardly have been less in 1969–70. An estimate somewhere in the range of a quarter to half a million will have to do. However, we can say with complete confidence that the types of people involved were mainly the already affluent – managers, professionals such as doctors, and administrators

– and of course other companies. Such events as the temporary rises of Patrick Partners and Minsec thus represented a shift of power within the propertied class, rather than a shift of power between classes. As financial journalists at the time noted, financial power was moving in the boom from Melbourne to Sydney. We may add, within the one class. Those against whom the balance of power moved naturally reacted, as was shown by the hostility of Melbourne financial interests to Patricks in 1971.

Mining Traders and Minsec were similar kinds of company, conducted with equal flair; but the bases on which they had been erected were different. Minsec was more a bootlaces operation, Mining Traders an outgrowth of a well-established broking business, which could use the resources of the Patrick group at need. The difference in the positions becomes evident when the role of credit in this kind of enterprise is considered. Minsec's collapse is commonly attributed to mistakes in management, which over-extended itself on a falling market. True; but other companies also made mistakes without collapsing. Minsec was vulnerable because its later operations depended heavily on short-term borrowing from other companies, and any shock to its credit would interrupt this essential support. That shock was delivered by the Robe River blunder. There was no actual monetary loss, but the damage to its credit network, which depended on decisions by managers of other companies pursuing their own strategies, could not be absorbed.

Castlereagh Securities also lost heavily on Nabarlek; and in the long run this contributed to the whole group's collapse. But the Patrick-Castlereagh alliance survived the immediate aftermath of the Minsec crash when the whole inter-company loan market dried up, and was able to come back to control of Kathleen Investments, because of another resource – a purely political resource created by the 'game' of company finance. This was the cooperation of a group of businessmen outside the broking partnership proper. Over a period of years, Patrick Partners had become associated, as financiers and brokers, and through interlocking directorships, with a number of expanding Sydney firms: notably Washington H. Soul Pattinson, Thomas Nationwide Transport, Pioneer Concrete, and of course various mineral companies such as Longreach Oil. Like other large brokers in Sydney and Melbourne, the firm and its group of finance companies thus became the centre of a looser alliance of businessmen, who brought business to the finance house and could be relied upon to act in cooperation when the need arose.

A wide range of support was in fact mobilized in the struggle for Kathleen Investments in late 1971. The critical step in the comeback was getting Millner, chairman of Castlereagh Securities and Soul Pattinson, onto the board of Queensland Mines. This was done by the votes of H. B. Ferguson (a director of Longreach and Pioneer Concrete) and E. C. Kennon, the AMP nominee. At the voting in December, Millner's supporters appear to have controlled the Castlereagh, Pioneer Concrete, Soul Pattinson, AMP, and Noranda blocks of shares; though they no doubt had support from other shareholders also.

While there undoubtedly were very bitter feelings involved in the clashes of the second half of 1971, it would be wrong to see the anti-Hudson forces as inspired by personal animosity or lust for power. They or their companies owned large blocks of shares in the Nabarlek companies, and after the market downturn, and particularly the downgrading of the reserves, could not dispose of these shares without taking a very heavy loss. Hudson was regarded, rightly or wrongly, as the man who had landed them all in the bog by a wildly misleading announcement and refusal to correct the error. His opponents argued that Queensland Mines would be unable to establish trading links as foreign companies' confidence in its management had been destroyed. One of the first acts of Millner's board was to bring the representative of a large American miner onto the boards and arrange with him for technical assistance at the site.

We thus come back to the basic feature of the mineral exploration of the period, that very little of the production was finally intended for consumption in Australia. It was to be fed as raw material into the world economy – or at least, the world capitalist economy – and the involvement of leading organizations of this economy, in the long run, was essential. Both for trading reasons, and because of the fact that Australia was a promising investment anyway, a great deal of interest was shown by foreign capital in the developments of the period, and large slices of Australian companies were bought. As the liquidator of the Minsec empire struggled through 1971 and 1972 to sell its holdings without too great a loss on the depressed market, it was foreign companies which bid highest. Uranium shares went to one Canadian company, tin shares to another; beach-mining shares went to a South African, some of the iron shares to an American bidder. And that perhaps was only just – as it turns out that many of the owners of Minsec itself had been overseas investors.

The controversy over foreign control

The gradual liquidation of Minsec with these results gave further impetus to an argument over foreign control that had been simmering for some time, and that boiled up into a public controversy in late 1971 and 1972. The argument was heated, but also vague, and became increasingly confused; at one stage it found the chairman of BHP, the federal Labor Party, Sir Henry Bolte, and militant trade-unionists, apparently all on the same side. The diffuse character of the dispute, itself a fact worth explaining, permits no simple narrative. It is necessary to sketch in a little background before looking at the main events of the controversy.

Australia, as a country settled by emigrants from industrializing Britain, had in a sense been created by foreign investment – though it was a long time before many Australians were to think of Britain as 'foreign'. The capital with which most early Australian entrepreneurs operated was brought from Britain or sent out to them. But it was not until later that absentee investment on a large scale developed: in the pastoral industry in the second quarter of the nineteenth century, then in banking and government loans, and towards the end of the century on a large scale in mining. The extent of British investment, in government loans especially, was one of the leg-ropes that hobbled Australian governments in the Depression and led to the collapse of Scullin's administration. In the second long boom that followed the Depression, and especially after World War II, American investment was heavier and grew to rival the British stake. Japanese investment in the 1960s was growing too. By 1970–1 the total foreign investment in Australian business was of the order of $10 000 million. This involved almost complete ownership or control of some important high-technology industries such as motor manufacturing and oil, substantial interests in many other industries, and a general position in Australian corporate business which was officially estimated as control of one-quarter to one-third of the whole.[8]

The policy of the Liberal government under Menzies and Holt had generally been to encourage the inflow. On occasion Menzies blocked a foreign takeover attempt (e.g. for Broken Hill South in 1961), and McEwen went on record, on a celebrated occasion, against the policy of 'selling a bit of the farm each year'. So it is not correct to describe the government as having a completely open-door approach. But there is no doubt that it saw a continued capital inflow as a necessary part of the continued expansion on which its political fortunes depended, and did a lot to encourage it.

When Gorton came to power in 1968 this was one of the established policies he began to question. He developed a reputation for economic nationalism later that year by blocking an attempt by a British insurance group to buy into the MLC. A couple of steps were taken to make it easier for Australian firms to resist takeovers (though this machinery remained unused); and after nearly a year's vacillation the government in September 1969 announced a policy which attempted to use the old guidelines on local borrowing by overseas firms as a lever to get Australian shares in the companies. McEwen seized the chance after the 1969 elections to revive his scheme for an industrial development corporation to tap loan funds from abroad for Australian manufacturers and miners; this was established during 1970, with stress on protecting development from overseas control. Gorton became involved in the Nabarlek story in September 1970, a fortnight after the first announcement of the strike, when (evidently on Hudson's initiative) he announced an intention to limit foreign ownership of the supposed bonanza. An ordinance putting a 15% ceiling on total foreign holdings was made in December. In February 1971 Gorton was involved in the negotiations to organize an Australian consortium to take up Minsec's assets. His efforts, however, were cut short by the Liberal Party crisis of March in which he lost the leadership, and with it control of economic policy. McMahon as Prime Minister withdrew active federal government participation in the negotiations, and the Minsec liquidator was left with the consequences we have seen.

But though no continuing policy had been established, the issue had been publicly broached at the very highest levels.

Criticism of foreign investment was no longer the preserve of pamphleteers and left-wing academics. Gorton's actual stand had been thoroughly ambiguous. He made some sharp criticisms of the 'tickle my tummy on any conditions' approach to foreign investors; yet opened his major policy statement by saying 'the importance to Australia of a strong and continuing inflow of overseas capital has never been questioned by my Government'.[9] (Why not? one might ask.) Similar bromides softened other actions, and Gorton never stated a general policy on acceptable maxima of foreign control. It was McEwen, in pursuit of his old scheme of a Country Party–manufacturer (and now miner) alliance, who created the more substantial prop for local business. Yet in the aftermath of the boom Gorton's style rather than his content was remembered, and the aftermath gave plenty of scope for economic nationalism.

The collapse of the boom in mining shares in 1970–1 was accompanied by a general depression of prices on the stock market. Turnover in Sydney fell to a quarter of the volume of mid-1970 as overseas and small investors withdrew from the market. In several ways a situation was created that was ripe for takeover merchants. The slump in prices uncovered many firms whose assets were greater than the current value of their shares on the stock market. PA Management, a consultant firm, estimated that no less than 64% of listed companies were in this position in May 1971. The host of small mining companies spawned by the boom were ripe for rationalization. It was hard for local companies to raise loans on the inter-company market in the aftermath of Minsec, or capital by new share issues. In these conditions, big overseas firms could offer capital and skills hard to come by, and could buy in at attractive rates. A wave of takeovers and mergers followed in 1971–2, in which foreign companies were prominent as bidders.[10]

Some of the most spectacular of the takeover struggles were between local firms, for the same logic appealed to local corporate raiders. There was a protracted battle through 1972 for control of R. W. Miller Holdings' shipping interests, between Ampol and Bulkships on the one side, and the shipping and investment company Howard Smith plus the old Miller's management on the other – eventually won, after a very costly legal fight, by Ampol and Bulkships. Sir Peter Abeles, a director of Bulkships and of Millers, was involved in another spectacular struggle in March–April 1972 as director of TNT when he tried to engineer, with financial support from Patricks, a takeover of Ansett Transport Industries. The story of the bid's eventual frustration by Sir Henry Bolte's appeal to Victorian state chauvinism is well known. It shows that local groups too were on the takeover trail – and shows also the sensitivity of the foreign ownership issue, as one of Ansett's defences was the claim that TNT, though an Australian firm, had too high a percentage of foreign shareholders. A Senate investigation duly showed some 34% of TNT shares were owned overseas, as were about 10% of Ansett's.[11]

The procession of undoubted foreign takeover attempts continued through late 1971 and 1972, with sufficient resistance to make headline news. English-owned Rowntree battled Life Savers to take over James Stedman (makers of Minties and Jaffas, representing a high point in Australian technology); simultaneously Burmah Oil absorbed the explorer Woodside over the bitter protests of one director. Two English subsidiaries competed for the Melbourne retailer Patersons; ITT bid for Frozen Foods (makers of Chiko Rolls) in April 1972 and a few months later Chlorox of California bid for Kiwi. These were only a few of the bids actually being made, the ones that attracted publicity because of resistance or the reputation of the firms involved. Some idea of the others can be gathered from the fact that the very cautious McMahon government froze five current takeover offers for study on 20 November 1972 (including one for the soft-drink maker Tarax – there seem to have been some undernourished capitalists abroad). The Senate Committee investigating the issue had a list of 37 takeovers announced from July to September 1972. And in the first three and a half months of the Labor government it had no less than 63 bids to consider. (39 were reported at that time as approved, 1 prohibited, the rest pending.)

The wave of takeover attempts ran into considerable, though inconsistent, resistance from local businessmen. The basic technique of a takeover is an offer to the shareholders of the company to buy their shares, either for cash or by exchange for other shares, at a higher price than they could currently get. It is normally in the short-term financial interest of the shareholders to accept the offer – if it is not, there is little point in the takeover attempt. The offer can be made with or without the approval of the company's directors. If it succeeds, they may find themselves out of a job (unless the offering company has agreed to keep them on); but in order to prevent it, they have to convince the shareholders apparently against their interests. There are various ways of doing this, and various other ploys that can be used in defence, as demonstrated by Ansett. The study of takeover and anti-takeover tactics makes a fascinating branch of the theory of games. Particularly where there is more than one bidder and where the directors of the company are divided, as in the R. W. Miller affair, the possible permutations and combinations appal the mind. But we need be concerned here only with two.

The first, which was given a vigorous test in October–November 1971 in the Woodside and Stedman struggles, is a direct appeal to the nationalism of the Australian shareholders. R. N. Hughes-Jones, a director of Woodside, opposed his fellow directors' plan to merge with Burmah (having run out of funds and being unable to raise loans), declaring the scheme a 'sell-out to overseas interests of the last vestige of Australian control of the immensely potential (*sic*) oil and gas leases on the North-West Shelf'. Life Savers, bidding for Stedman, described the issue as 'a very real test of Australian investors' attitudes as to whether Australian companies will remain Australian owned or be absorbed by foreign capital...they have to make a decision to either back two Australian companies to form a substantial local group or to completely sell out to foreign interests'. 'Do not be misled by arguments irrelevant to the real issues', replied Rowntree's advertisements, and it appears that the real issue of $2.85 per share proved more interesting to the Stedman board and shareholders, for they accepted Rowntree.

That was the catch in the tactic of nationalist appeal: shareholders normally held their shares for profit, not sentiment, and the foreign bidders could offer more. A big overseas firm, as economists at the time pointed out, could afford to pay more for reasons that might have nothing to do with the immediate local situation: it might pay simply to a get a foothold in the local market, or to assure a raw materials supply, or to gain some other benefit of internal reorganization. As in the case of Kiwi, it might even be interested in the Australian firm's overseas operations. A more solid line of defence was needed than vague appeals to shareholders, and one could be found. As MLC demonstrated with Gorton, and Ansett with Bolte, governments could be approached for support; and they had the power to block takeovers. These were specific cases; could the principle be erected into a more definite policy than Gorton's stated intention to keep an eye open? It appeared, in 1971–2, that a substantial sector of Australian business wanted the federal government to do just that. No less a personage than the chairman of BHP made a speech in March 1972 warning against the rising foreign domination of Australian resources.[12]

The McMahon government had pulled back from Gorton's initiative in the Minsec liquidation and had allowed substantial mining assets to pass into foreign hands. Its ministers on various occasions had made the traditional noises about capital inflow and economic growth. McMahon himself was closely identified with the economic policy of the Treasury, a department regarded as the bastion of laissez-faire thought within the federal government. But under persistent sniping from the Labor Party – some of whose members led by Al Grassby had made a grand public relations exercise of opposing the sale of land in the Simpson Desert to some hapless Americans – and now under pressure from members of its own class, the Government began to give ground. Toward the end of 1971 a Treasury inquiry into the problem was launched, and about the same time, at DLP instigation, the Senate set up a select committee to investigate foreign ownership. In March, the Deputy Prime Minister Anthony issued a government directory of foreign-owned firms and made a speech to a meeting of American businessmen saying that there were limits to foreign investment. In April the giant ITT (about the eighth largest corporation in the USA) was revealed as the bidder for Frozen Foods, and there followed a brisk salvo in the Senate from the Labor Party and the DLP on the takeover and the political tactics of that particular company, criticizing its intervention in Chilean politics. The Government gave way: after a series of Cabinet discussions on the takeover, McMahon announced on 4 May that a general review of policy in the area would be launched; ITT suspended its bid.

In June the Senate Committee began its public hearings; but already, it appears, some businessmen knew the general outline of the Government's future policy. (It was finally announced before the Senate Committee made its report.) In July the foreign control issue again heated up in a strike of oil company workers: the Government supported the companies' attempts to hold down wage claims, and was denounced by unionists for supporting the interests of foreign monopolists against Australian workers. The issue was ticklish in the run-up to the election, now only four months away, though the Government no doubt hoped to get some mileage out of an anti-inflation stand. In August Whitlam weighed in with a proposal for government encouragement of Australian investment, and the Attorney-General for the third time pegged foreign holdings in Nabarlek. On 26 September McMahon announced his policy, and in October the necessary legislation was passed, and the Senate Committee trailed in with a hastily-compiled report. In November several takeovers were frozen. That was as far as it went: the Government was defeated at the polls in early December.

The policy actually announced in September, given the electoral situation and the heat of the debate, was remarkably mild. It consisted of four points. Short-term loans from abroad were reduced; foreign-owned firms were allowed to borrow locally; Australians were given limited permission to buy shares abroad; and the Government was given power to block foreign takeovers judged by an independent authority to be against the national interest. Even this was hedged around with references to the possible benefits of takeovers and the rights of shareholders, and the traditional salute to the role of capital inflow in economic growth. There were no general guidelines on acceptable limits of foreign shareholding, nor statements as to which industries were to be protected; everything was left to be decided *ad hoc*. The Government in fact had the power to block or hinder any takeovers, but was signalling its intention to do this as little as possible.

The policy on which the Government finally settled bears all the earmarks of conflict and indecision: conflict as a result of its own earlier indecision, and further indecision flowing from the unresolved conflict. For while some sections of business had been pressing for controls, others had resisted them, and others again had evaded the controls announced. Noranda, for instance, was not entitled to its Kathleen Investments and Queensland Mines shares under the original Nabarlek ordinance; but Gorton approved this purchase and others of the kind, and in March 1972 the McMahon government stretched the ordinance to accommodate them. Some really ingenious techniques of avoidance were invented by others, such as the device of leasing a local company's business, leaving the company, as a legal entity, *virgo intacta*. Naturally enough, foreign groups publicly opposed controls. The American Chamber of Commerce in Australia, for instance, spoke out in defence of foreign investment and the benefits it had brought to Australia in the way of technology and export income. Those in the mining industry stressed the importance of 'risk capital' for prospecting, which was hard to raise in Australia, except in the boom. Those who realised that some form of control was politically inevitable, called rather for a definite long-term policy on acceptable levels of investment so that foreigners would know just what they had to contend with.

While foreign companies were a large section of Australian business, their political influence would have been slight if they were isolated, if they were pitted in a straight fight against Australians. But they were not, and never had been. This is the most critical point in the story: the mutual interests of foreign and local businessmen. Three very substantial interests in Australian business stood to benefit from relatively uncontrolled foreign investment. The first we have already discussed: the present owners, i.e. the shareholders in Australian companies, who could get higher prices for their shares if foreign firms were in the market. The organized shareholders' pressure groups which stated this point of view have always been weak, but the underlying interest is a major one, and McMahon himself raised it as the principal defence of takeovers in his September policy statement.

The second interest, closely connected with the first, is the Australian business houses who handle the inflow of foreign capital – the 'financial intermediaries' as the Senate Committee called them – banks, stock exchanges, investment companies and a range of more specialized finance companies. Bankers and brokers had defended the unrestricted inflow of foreign capital in Gorton's time. Now the president of the Associated Stock Exchanges again spoke out in defence of foreign takeovers, calling opposition 'the offspring of muddy thinking. . . sheer ignorance and incredibly ill-conceived'. He happened to be an Englishman. The point is not purely symbolic: some of the most important banks in Australia (now merged in the ANZ group) had been set up by English capital; and though the trading banks were by now tightly under federal government control, other financial enterprises were not. Foreign capital was very prominent in the mushroom growth of merchant banking around 1970. Even Patricks, that bastion of nationalism, had gone shares with an American, a Japanese, and a French bank in setting up its company in this field (Patrick Intermarine) in 1971. The reason is obvious: since much of the business involved is handling international transactions, it is advantageous for both the local and the foreign firms to have a permanent link. In broad terms, we can say that the capital inflow had created, in the very groups which handled it, a local interest in its continuation; and we can also see that this interest was taking a permanent organizational form in these years in joint ventures in the money market.

While merchant banks were involved as advisers and financiers in takeovers, they also did a large business in arranging international loans. We have already seen how important loan finance was to a company such as Minsec. One of the moves by which its management attempted to stave off trouble had been an attempt to arrange European loans through the big merchant bank Ord-BT. While the political debate focussed on the dramatic issue of takeovers of established companies, a great deal of capital was coming into the country in other forms, notably joint ventures with Australian companies and loans at fixed rates of interest. Official estimates suggest overseas loans totalled about $2800 million by September 1971. The biggest firms could raise very large sums overseas at relatively low rates: for instance, in late 1971 the sheet-steel firm John Lysaght (part-owned by BHP) raised $60 million in a deal of this kind to finance a new mill at Westernport, through one of the merchant banks. Joint ventures, sharing the cost of development, were a common arrangement in the mining field, the ill-omened Robe River project being a case in point. It was also common for a small local company to prospect for minerals, and if successful, look for a heavyweight to buy them out. Thus a 'takeover' would actually be the purpose of the local firm. Woodside Oil was one which requested a merger as it needed the finance. The defenders of foreign investment stressed that an open field for investment was important in keeping overseas businesses involved with Australian operations, i.e. that it was important for psychological reasons. (Whether this is essential may be doubted – given the rude shocks Australian companies have delivered to overseas investors from the first gold rushes, through the 1893 collapse, all the way to Minsec.) In short, the business conducted by foreign firms and foreign-owned firms in Australia created an interest in the defence of such capital, in the local firms which did business with it: and given the scale of foreign penetration already, this third interest was even wider than the second.

Thus while some businessmen were hostile to foreign capital because of competition, others because of direct threats to their control of their own companies, and others were agitated about the question for electoral reasons, there were large sections of Australian business which had a definite interest in the maintenance of the flow of investment. There was a structural tension within the class of owners and its most active section, the managers and directors of companies. The tension came out in amusing ways in the Senate enquiry into the issue. By the end of September the Committee had sent out about nine hundred requests to authorities, associations, and firms to make submissions – and had got about ninety in return. As they drily reported, 'There has been a reluctance by many large associations to place submissions before the Committee because of the wide range of differing viewpoints held by their members...The news media have been singularly reluctant to put in submissions, many pleading that they have no information or knowledge of this subject, a point of view which is hard to reconcile with the articles and editorials so continually published.'[13] This is a particularly telling instance of the indirect influence of the presence of foreign capital, as overseas ownership of the news media, at least those involved in broadcasting, is restricted by law and very slight in fact.

Given this structural tension, the Liberal Party, whose historic *raison d'être* is the defence of property and private enterprise against labour, was unable to crack down without offending a large part of its supporting class. McMahon's policy of September was the minimal concession he had to make to the critics of foreign capital to relieve himself of political pressure (from the DLP as well as the Labour Party) in the election year. It was an exercise in symbolic politics rather than an actual shift in commitment.

The Liberal leadership

The rising level of conflict in the federal Liberal Party after the departure of Menzies in 1966, and the decline in its electoral fortunes to the defeat of 1972, have commonly been blamed on the inadequacies and personal rivalries of its successive leaders. This was the burden of press comment on successive explosions of the 'leadership crisis', and is the preoccupation of Reid's book *The Gorton Experiment*. Even Oakes and Solomon in their much more perceptive *Making of an Australian Prime Minister*, declare that 'the Liberals' problems...were of their own making', and locate the flaw in the factionalism of the party leadership group.[14]

Gorton very fairly remarked, in his famous reply, that Reid's reporting had rarely been concerned with ideals and issues, concentrating rather on deals and organizational manipulation.[15] We may take the hint a bit further. The conservative political leadership in 1970–2 was divided by a number of issues, and troubled by its inability to resolve others. If we trace back the major issues as they presented themselves at the level of federal politics, we find that all the others stemmed, like the foreign-ownership issue, from a conflict of interest within the propertied class. The political leadership, in fact, was paralysed by a rising level of conflict within the class from which it arose and on which it depended.

We may make a *prima facie* case that the prolonged Liberal leadership crisis was not simply an internal problem of the federal parliamentary leadership, by observing other instances. These were not the only clashes within the Liberal's ranks. The most striking case outside Canberra was in South Australia. The Liberal and Country League, after Playford's defeat in 1965 and Hall's accession to the Premiership in 1968, entered a period of sharp internal conflict that led to a leadership crisis of its own in 1972, the formation of the Liberal Movement, and a breakaway from the old party in 1973.[16] Within the Liberal party machine, the federal president in 1971 publicly criticised the parliamentary leaders for ignoring the party membership, and foreshadowed moves to establish tighter machine control. (They did not eventuate – but there is evidence of poor relations between leadership and machine in the election preparations).

Such events could still be regarded as cases of factional politics within the party; more conclusive is evidence of conflict in the relationship between the party and business. Both the Gorton and McMahon administrations conducted affairs against a background of public and private criticism from business. That this went far beyond the normal pushing and pulling for sectional advantage derived from the economic role of the state is shown by its publicity, scope, and sharpness. 'Government economic policy strategy in 1971 could only be described as ineffective – even disastrous', wrote the economic correspondent in the first issue of the national *Australian Stock Exchange Journal*, for February–March 1972. The comment is typical of that time. The extent of conflict is shown, closer to the hip-pocket nerve, by election finances. The Liberal Party found itself acutely short of funds for most of the election year; there was an obvious reluctance of businessmen to kick in, comically so at a special fundraising dinner for McMahon held by Abeles where no one was willing to ask the guests for their money. Only late in the day were large sums raised by the party, enabling it to outspend the opposition. By contrast, the Labor campaign was from the start rolling in unfamiliar wealth, estimated at over $700 000 in retrospect – a great deal of it from business. And businessmen were prominent in the campaign itself, from Rupert Murdoch, the newspaper owner, and Patrick Sayers, sponsor of the dramatic 'Business Executives for a Change of Government' advertisements, to Kenneth Baillieu Myer, as establishment a figure as you can get, who signed a public appeal to elect a new government.[17] Clearly there was a political split in business itself; and such things do not happen at random.

Underneath the surface fluctuations of the parliamentary game, four issues can be seen as standing points of conflict. The first is the one just discussed, how to deal with the inflow of foreign capital. Gorton's handling of the MLC case in 1968, in such a way as to circumvent Treasury opposition to his policy, was one of the first episodes to draw criticism of his 'shoot from the hip' style of government, and there was obviously protracted conflict in the government over the investment and borrowing 'guidelines' in 1969. We have seen how the issue burned on from start to finish in McMahon's administration. The conflict of interest outside the party did not lead directly to a factional division within it, rather it created problems which were insoluble for it, in practical terms. Were the government to do what it was repeatedly called on to do, lay down general rules specifying maximum percentages for foreign ownership and which industries protection would apply to, it could not help but offend powerful interests. The troubles it had with the Nabarlek ordinance are proof enough of this. The *ad hoc* policy-making for which both administrations were criticized was, from the point of view of their political survival, the only rational response.

The second continuing issue presented itself at the parliamentary level as the problem of maintaining the coalition, the alliance of the Liberals and the Country Party. This is a tangled skein that goes right back to the formation of the country parties around 1920 as breakaways from the conservative parties of their day. Their commitment to the special interests of country capital, i.e. farm owners and graziers, had hardly wavered through the vicissitudes of coalition and opposition, until McEwen's chequered attempt to form a producers' coalition of Country Party and city manufacturers in the 1960s; and it was still the *raison d'être* of the party in the 1970s. This involved direct conflict over government economic policy where the interests of some or all of the Country Party's clientele clashed with those of urban business.

The issue that is usually taken to illustrate this conflict is tariff policy. In this period exchange policy was equally prominent, especially with the increasing integration of Australia into the financial system of world capitalism and the accelerating disintegration of the capitalist countries' monetary order in the late 1960s. Not that the issue was a novelty: one of the more striking public events of the Depression has been the devaluation of the Australian pound against sterling engineered by the Bank of New South Wales, in the interests of its grazing clientele, over the protests of the Melbourne banks. In 1967 when sterling was devalued by the Wilson government, the Country Party tried to get a corresponding devaluation in Australia in the interests of primary producers. Holt, and McMahon as Treasurer, had successfully resisted. McMahon's reputation on this and other grounds as an opponent of the

Country Party had led to their veto on his rise to the leadership in 1968. At the end of 1971, after he had become Prime Minister, there was yet another currency crisis when the American dollar was devalued. Snedden as Treasurer battled to maintain parity with sterling; but the Country Party leaders threatened to wreck the coalition if no concession was made to the farmers' and miners' interest. McMahon finally came down on the side of concession. The conflict of interests in this field, and at other points where concessions to country capital were made, had multiple repercussions in politics. It set up a direct clash of factions within the coalition. It created a series of problems whose inconsistent handling damaged the reputation of the leadership; while the handling had to be inconsistent, for a complete commitment to either side here would certainly have wrecked the coalition. And it led to tensions within the Liberal Party machine, as urban sections harried the leadership for its apparent disregard of 'national' interests and those of its own rank and file.

If Gorton acquired a rather undeserved reputation as an economic nationalist, and McMahon as an opponent of country interests, there was no doubt where each of them stood on the issue of centralism and federal government power. Gorton wanted it extended, McMahon committed himself to the status quo. Gorton brought down on himself a heap of conservative criticism, on this as on the related claim that he governed in despite of his Cabinet. McMahon avoided criticism on the first issue, but attracted some on the second, and blew it wide open again in the biggest gaffe of the election campaign when in a television interview in Brisbane he appeared to criticize the competence of his own ministers.

At first sight the locus of decision-making within the federal constitutional framework, or within the federal cabinet, seems a completely formal issue, of concern only to the professional politicians, and perhaps the bureaucrats, directly involved. In fact it is an issue of much wider significance than that. The reason is that the Liberal Party has never become a centralized national organization. It and its predecessors were formed by an alliance of conservative groups from the different colonies that made up the Commonwealth. An alliance, rather than a fusion, it has remained ever since. The principle was entrenched in the conservative custom of always having at least one representative in the cabinet from each state.

The specialization of political leadership within the ruling class mentioned at the beginning of this paper is most marked in federal politics. The composition of the state parties corresponds more closely to the social groups on which the parties' power is based. This is true of Labor as well as Liberal. There are more unionists, and more businessmen, in the state parliaments. Descendants of the colonial ruling classes and members of currently upper-crust families retain much greater power in Legislative Councils and state party organisations than they have in federal politics, given their regional roots and family influence. In pushing for an extension of federal power Gorton was striking in an unmistakable way at the power of the social groups that stood behind the conservative state premiers. McMahon did not reverse this trend from pure spite: he was a member of the Sydney social élite himself.

The state 'establishments' were not the only people with an interest in a division of government power. With state governments competing for industrial development, businesses considering new investment have a distinct chance of winning concessions they would never get from a single central government. The party complexion of government matters little here, given that the Tonkin government in WA was as hot after development as Brand's had been, even more grandiose in its schemes for the Pilbara; and the Dunstan government has pursued investment just as Playford did, though it speaks a different language of environmental protection. The businesses which suffer are those which operate on such a large scale across the continent that dealing with a multiplicity of governments is a serious nuisance; and those which are involved in extensive transactions between states that are hindered by state taxes, particularly banking and finance. These groups never became articulate in support of Gorton's centralism; but one notes that, for all his *gaucherie*, Gorton got on well in negotiations with very big businesses such as BHP, and McMahon did not.

Where business did become articulate, on the margin of the issue of federalism, was in calls for economic planning. Business criticisms of McMahon's administration regularly included a demand for some firmer direction in policy, some set of goals. This, as we have seen, was the line that foreign businessmen moved towards on the issue of foreign ownership. Local businessmen too complained of incoherence in the government's economic policy, to the point where Snedden as Treasurer was complaining that the chairman of the Sydney Stock Exchange seemed to have joined forces with the Labor Party in the demand for central planning.

The desire for central planning, at least indicative planning, on the part of governments, is characteristic of the very large firms which are in no serious danger from competition and which want predictability in their environment for their own planning purposes.[18] Some Australian companies have already reached this Galbraithian state, and a number of the multinational corporations operating here are accustomed to such relationships with governments elsewhere. Yet central planning runs against deeply ingrained traditions in Australian business, and the name, if not the fact, strikes a chord of fear in those who remember Labor's rapid move from attempts at central control to attempts to nationalize the banks immediately after World War II. A party which had come to power on a wave of reaction against nationalization and controls could not take easily to a public commitment in the other direction.

Yet the Liberals under Menzies had implemented central banking controls, and had accepted the task of central management of the economy, in fact if not in rhetoric. They had fairly successfully acted to keep up a growth rate and keep down unemployment. Businesses of all kinds had come to assume conditions of continual expansion. The calls for planning that came out in 1971–2 were in large part a response to an apparent failure here. The mining boom was followed not only by a slump in share prices, but by a contraction or at least a slowing of growth, elsewhere in the economy. McMahon ran into heavy criticism of the cautious, anti-inflation budget of 1971 as unemployment rates rose and other economic indicators did not. Whether the government had anything to do with it is a moot point, but it was certainly blamed for it. Within a few months in 1971, a sequence of business pressure groups, important ones at that, lambasted the government for lack of a policy in the first place and too restrictive a policy in the second: the Australian Industries Development Association (June), the

Associated Chambers of Manufactures, Federal Chamber of Automative Industries, and Master Builders' Federation (July), the Associated Chambers of Commerce, and the Manufacturers again (September) – though a new president of the latter group consoled the government in December by agreeing with their long-term policy (whatever that was). The government was gradually levered away from the stand it had taken and pushed towards more expansionary policies. The budget strategy was practically abandoned in early 1972. Again a conflict of interest, here a many-sided one, had led to inconsistency in the political leadership's behaviour and a loss of credibility in the run-up to the election.

The developments of 1970–2 argue that under contemporary conditions a conflict of interest within the propertied class does not lead automatically to a factional division in its political leadership, as it may have done in colonial politics. It may 'use' an established factional division (counting the Country Party as a faction within the conservative framework), but it may not find factional expression at all. One important reason for this is that the pressure-group activities of businesses are now concentrated at the level of the bureaucracy, from which most policy initiatives come, and not the parliamentary parties. (One may infer a factional structure at policy-making levels in the executive, though it is difficult to get solid proof of this.) Yet such conflicts still register on the parliamentary seismograph, very obviously at election times, but also in between, by creating problems which the ministry must handle but which they cannot in fact resolve. The strategies that leaders evolve to cope with such situations, and their behaviour under fire, are essential to their winning support or hostility among the back-benchers, and hence affect the occurrence and the outcome of leadership struggles in the parliamentary party.

Conclusion

The discussion has covered a number of different types of conflict, and it may be useful to attempt a rough classification of them. There seem to be three distinct patterns. Under conditions of mild expansion, or a steady state, there is an 'administrative' form of conflict, a jockeying for marginal advantages; normally, at the higher levels in Australia, in an oligopolistic context. Bargaining and persuasion are the tools.

In conditions where there is a sudden expansion of opportunity there is a scramble to seize the prizes. Innovation, risk-taking, and entrepreneurship come to the fore; and a wider range of players can enter the game. Under conditions of contraction or decline, the knives come out. Those in established positions are under threat of losing them, and collective decision-making becomes choked by the interaction of many defensive strategies.

What happened to the political and business directorate in Australia was that in a period of three or four years they went through all these conditions in quick succession. The long steady expansion of the politico-economic structure under Menzies was characterized by administrative conflict; he is rightly given personal credit for containing latent conflict in the Liberal Party, but it must be admitted that for the most part the conditions were not very difficult. At the end of the 1960s the pattern was broken by the mineral boom and the stock-market boom, in which many establishment figures got their toes trodden on by vigorous firms such as Minsec and Patricks; by international changes such as the breakdown of the monetary order; and by rural contraction. The stock-market collapse and the recession of 1971–2 generalized the conditions for defensive conflict.

At the same time a recession was occurring in the electoral fortunes of the Liberal Party, and a similar pattern of behaviour was evident there. 'Some of them were the greatest bunch of bitches you could ever have imagined', remarked the Minsec liquidator (in a newspaper interview) about the defensive strategies of that company's creditors; and that nicely sums up the atmosphere in the Liberal Party at the time. Given the close interaction of business and political decision-making, not to mention the structural connection of business and the conservative parties, this series of conflicts had to register in politics. Their succession was too rapid and their scope too wide for the party leaders to be able to evolve a formula for managing them.

Thus we do not need to postulate a shift in the balance of power between classes in order to explain Labor's accession to office for the first time in a quarter-century. Nor do we need to suppose that the Labor leadership had become a tool of business to see how it could come to office in a society where the social roots of business power were untouched. The co-incidence of a revival in party and trade-union leadership with a period of multiple conflict within the ruling class created the conditions for Labor's electoral victory. Whitlam himself stressed the restrictions on what his party in the 28th Parliament would be able to do. In this, at least, he was right.

Responses to Labor, 1973–1975

The pattern of national politics

The modern Australian party system was created by a working-class challenge to the bourgeoisie that dominated the colonial societies of the later nineteenth century. Towards the end of that century working-class organizations took two strategic decisions: first, to undertake political mobilization on a large scale; second, to challenge capital within the arena of the state organizations, by attempting to influence, and then control, councils and parliaments. In the generation from 1890 to 1920 the Labor parties that embodied these decisions developed enough strength to take office in several parliaments, and have remained as governments or pensioned oppositions ever since. They also developed enough strength to fight off the more radical strategy, represented within the labour movement by syndicalists and Communists, of mobilization to seize power by action against the state. Though this alternative achieved a certain following in the unions, especially in the 1940s, and has at times had some following within the Labor Party too, the mainstream of working-class politics has remained strongly reformist. A modernized version of this traditional reformism came to office in the 1972 federal election.

The early theorists of the Labor party had thought of themselves as completing the work of nineteenth-century democracy, and had anticipated (though the point was rarely made explicit) that the party would keep parliamentary power as the large majority of the people swung behind its programme. That this did not happen was partly due to internal contradictions in the labour movement, but much more to a successful counter-mobilization by the ruling class. Conservative nationalism, fear of anarchy, and established class interest combined in the formation of mass conservative parties. The apparently irresistible growth of 'socialism' was stopped in the decade 1910–20, and a long-term parliamentary deadlock was achieved. The dominance of urban capital was challenged in several states by the formation of country parties, but in all states except Victoria the logic of class conflict soon forced them into coalition or merger with urban conservatives. The new organizations were electorally successful but organizationally unstable, and a series of internal conflicts culminated in a dramatic fragmentation in the early 1940s. A united party was then formed under the leadership of Menzies, with a welfarist economic programme made possible by the increasing productivity of the industrialized economy. This became the dominant political force in the period of sustained industrial growth after the second world war. At the beginning of the 1970s Menzies' successors still clung to office in Canberra, but were having increasing trouble in handling the problems created by industrial and urban growth.

In Chapter 3 I indicated how these struggles had led to a change in the structure of the ruling class, with a separation of political and corporate leadership. Though both arose from the same class, and were united in their defence of its property system, they were largely independent of each other in day-to-day operations, and frequently came into conflict over details of policy. Yet the degree of separation should not be exaggerated; important connections have been maintained. The political leadership in the 1970s has continued to rely on the corporate leadership for its finance, especially at election times when party bagmen do the rounds of business. The conservative parties carefully preserve the secrecy of these arrangements – they used their Senate majority in March 1975 to throw out a bill providing for the disclosure of sources of campaign funds – though details sometimes trickle through in the press, such as the property developer Alan Bond's $20,000 donation to the West Australian Liberals in 1974.[1] Militant businessmen also provide organizational support in elections, and sometimes take a leading role in producing anti-Labor propaganda (some examples will be discussed later). Under Snedden's leadership of the Liberal party from 1973 to 1975 there was an interesting revival of direct involvement in the party machine, with men from some of the more sophisticated sections of business attempting to apply up-to-date management techniques. Even the most hidebound of the state branches, the Liberal and Country League in South Australia, appointed a young marketing manager as its first executive director in 1973.[2]

To some extent also, conservative politicians retain personal and family connections with business. Snedden had only a minor flirtation with commerce, and his successor Fraser, though personally wealthy, is outside the corporate leadership; but Lynch, deputy to both of them, was a management consultant and keeps close to Melbourne businessmen, while Anthony, the Country Party leader, is connected by marriage with a northern NSW farm supply and media combine.[3] Business continues to recruit from the ranks of civil servants and conservative politicians in the way that Playford showed for the 1960s – an ex-MP, R. J. Solomon, was appointed executive director of the Advertising Federation of Australia in 1975, while an ex-minister, Sir Allen Fairhall, became chairman of an insurance company in 1973, and in 1975 was one of the insurance companies' spokesmen in their short and bitter campaign against a federal insurance commission. (At the state level the ties are closer – the WA Liberal Premier Sir Charles Court is a well-known entrepreneur, and politicians' involvement in business has been a staple of debate in the Victorian parliament for years.) It is not the case that the conservative federal leadership is typically in business; but it arises from the same social groups, often comes into politics through business, and moves constantly in business circles. Their solidarity is periodically reinforced by a curious social custom in which groups of businessmen meet semi-publicly to exchange congratulations with Liberal Party leaders. Thus in March 1974 Snedden addressed 600 party cadres and businessmen across turtle soup, imported salmon and roast pheasant at the Melbourne Town Hall, and was rewarded with over $200,000 in campaign fund promises; in May he was treated as if already Prime Minister at an Institute of Directors luncheon. After his disappointment, the Victorian Premier Hamer addressed the Australian Society of Senior Executives, read them extracts from his party platform, and promised that the state of Victoria would remain a 'shield and haven for free enterprise' against the depredations of the federal government.[4]

The industrial boom that had underwritten Menzies' political hegemony had left a series of intransigent political problems.

Perhaps the most striking and novel were those related to the growth of cities. A massive shift to a car-based system of transport had occurred, with the motor manufacturing, servicing, and fuel industries becoming the country's major industrial complex. Governments had promoted this by tariff protection and other forms of aid to the companies concerned, and were now caught in the classic dilemma of high prices and protected jobs. The private car allowed, and in turn was stimulated by, a vast spread of suburban housing, which outpaced the provision of state-financed services like sewerage as well as the more intangible resources of education and collective leisure. A large migration programme, feeding the labour-demands of industrialization, increased pressure on housing. By the end of the 1960s steep price-rises were under way and sections of the working class were being priced out of the housing market.

The finance of economic growth also left problems. The federal and state governments, with the general support of local business, had allowed a heavy inflow of funds from the major capitalist powers. This, as shown in the previous chapter, produced a rising level of conflict within business, while the labour movement also became increasingly vocal about control by overseas interests, especially in the mining industry. Regulation of the economy by the state was made more difficult by international money flows, the increasing confusion of currencies, and the effects of international inflation.

The long boom had also seen changes in the pattern of private life which surfaced as political problems around 1970. Two are of particular importance. The rising standards of living which industrial growth had allowed workers within the framework of a generally stable distribution of income, threw into relief the problems of those groups who were outside the wage system or peculiarly ill-served by it: pensioners, single mothers, large working-class families, aborigines, and others. Intellectuals formulated the issue as the problem of 'poverty', and the reconstruction of the welfare system to deal with it became a leading political issue. Advanced industrialism also suddenly accelerated the long-term but previously slow movement of women into the paid workforce. The difficulties of combining marriage and employment gave a material edge to an increased awareness among women of sexual discrimination and the pervasiveness of controls. This awareness rapidly matured, in the cities, into a campaign of resistance to the whole structure of sexual subordination that produced the most radical and creative oppositional movement that Australia had seen in fifty years.

The conservative politicians who controlled the federal government and most of the states at the end of the 1960s had increasing difficulty in handling these problems. The essentials of their political programme – economic growth, anticommunism, moderate welfare provision – had been formulated early in the boom and gave little guidance in handling its later stages. The parliamentary leaders who made the first attempts to modernize the programme, notably Gorton in Canberra and Hall in Adelaide, struck stiff opposition within their own parties. The problems were made insoluble for the conservative leadership, at least in the short term, by the fact that some of them arose from substantial conflicts of interest within their own class (the foreign capital issue, for instance), and others could only be tackled by pitting the state against entrenched and previously unchallenged groups (such as the attack on doctors' economic independence required to provide effective medical services to the poor). The result was the period of factionalism traced in the previous chapter, that was felt in several of the states but was most severe at the level of national government. It was not ended when the McMahon government fell.

The Whitlam leadership of the Labor Party gained a strong propaganda position by developing, with a good deal of care and sophistication, policies that addressed themselves precisely to problems that the Liberal government had to fumble. We can distinguish three main strands in the Labor programme of the early 1970s. The first, and initially most visible, grew out of the progressive liberalism characteristic of the professionals newly prominent in the party leadership: a pluralist and antiracist foreign policy, action to improve the position of aborigines and of women, attempts to involve local 'communities' in the process of planning. The second reflected the interests of the working-class mass base of the party: protection of unions from penal clauses, support of wage claims in arbitration and some equalization of the wage structure; increases in general welfare provisions and a state-run medical insurance system; a shift to a 'needs' basis for the funding of schools.

The third strand, which was central to the Whitlam government's strategy, is not so easily related to the internal composition of the Labor Party. It reflected, rather, a new approach to the situation of being a party of government, holding itself responsible (and being held responsible electorally) for the general management of economy and society. It involved policies – and sometimes not even 'policies' in the accepted sense, but rather a network of authorities and activities – attempting a rationalization of the process of growth. The centrepiece of this, in the run-up to the 1972 election, was the attempt to develop an urban programme: to control the growth of the major cities and promote new ones, to fill in the gaps in the provision of suburban services, and to control the housing market. What attracted most attention after the election was the attempt to control and rationalize the mining industry and develop a resources policy. The government also moved, in a rather more halting way, towards a prices and incomes policy as an answer to inflation; and quietly proceeded with a large increase and administrative rationalization of central government funding of education.[5]

In its main thrust, plainly, this was not a class programme. It implied large increases in central government activity, but these were to be financed out of the proceeds of growth rather than by a direct attack on the class distribution of income. (In practice, they were partly financed by the proceeds of inflation, and involved some indirect redistribution.) It was a programme that, in principle, the ruling class could wear; and progressive sections of the ruling class did support Labor in 1972. The advent of the Whitlam government did not represent a shift in the balance of class forces, even at the electoral level. Only a marginal gain in the vote was needed (2.5% from 1969 to 1972), and the Victorian election won by Hamer soon showed that the federal Labor vote did not necessarily carry over into state politics.[6]

Nevertheless a distinctly new situation, with a new range of problems, was created for the ruling class by a working-class-based government, however moderate, in office. At the very least, the business leadership would have to adapt to men like Cameron and Connor who were far from being socially familiar. The political leadership responded with systematic intransigence, blocking a series of government measures by use of its Senate strength; in April 1974 forcing a new general election, which it lost; and in November–December 1975 forcing a second, which it won. The corporate leadership was more cautious. Groups of businessmen had held talks with Whitlam and with Crean, who was to be the new treasurer, before the 1972 election. We may now turn to examine their responses to Labor in office.

The operating relationship of business and government

The obvious place to start is the advisory committees and semi-government bodies which, as McFarlane and Playford noted, provided channels of consultation under the Liberals.[7] These, it seems, mostly continued to function in much the same way as before. The Labor government continued the appointment of established businessmen to existing bodies such as the investment corporation AIDC. It also sought businessmen to serve on new bodies such as its land-tenure enquiry (appointing Dusseldorp of Lend Lease Corporation) and its enquiry into manufacturing (Jackson, general manager of CSR). Perhaps the finest hour came in May 1973 when the socialist tiger in person, J. F. Cairns, travelled as Minister for Overseas Trade to red China – taking along directors of Myer and BHP. The essential point is that the business leadership, by and large, accepted the government's overtures and continued to man such bodies. There was however a clash over extension of AIDC powers, which will be discussed below.

Of course public consultation and cooperation of this kind represents only a fraction of the normal contact between business and the federal government. Most occurs in a much less visible way, in negotiations over specific issues. There is plenty of evidence that this too continued in much the same way as before, though details often become public only when negotiations are finished, or when a dispute arises. Thus we have public evidence of negotiations with the motor industry over the long-vexed question of the entry of Japanese manufacturers into Australia, recently bearing fruit in a plan for a jointly-owned motor foundry; over sales tax on cars, etc.[8] A constant process of enquiry and negotiation occurred over foreign takeovers, which the Liberal government had begun in 1972, usually with favourable results – such as when the government allowed an American majority interest in the large finance company IAC in early 1975. There were negotiations for a new sugar agreement in 1974 – an upsurge in the buying of big models from the computer companies in 1973 – negotiations on the provision of infrastructure for mining in the Northern Territory in 1973 – and so on and so forth. On occasions the new government proved reluctant to get involved in companies' affairs. It kept aloof, for instance, when the Mainline Corporation, a large building firm, collapsed in September 1974, though asked to rescue it. But some of its plans effectively implied an extension of involvement with business, and an extension of services to it. This was plainly true of urban policy, where the Liberal government had left little administrative machinery. The Labor government set up authorities which contracted out a good deal of planning and research to private companies; while its plans for new cities required a series of incentives to business to locate in them.[9] The range of persisting business contacts is nicely indicated by the fact that in 1973 a Sydney firm launched a management newsletter entirely devoted to 'Government and Consumer Interaction with Business', at a modest subscription of $65 per year.[10]

Despite this, it is clear that by the end of 1973 there was some discontent among businessmen about their ease of access to the federal government. The financial press began to speak of a 'business–government gap', and some public noises were made. The president of the Associated Stock Exchanges, for instance, complained in October 1973 that he had not seen a minister for three weeks![11] On the same occasion the managing director of Leyland Australia blasted the government as 'uninitiated, inexperienced twits'; and the emergence of this kind of criticism after an initial period of cautious silence by most companies was no doubt behind the Bank of NSW's ill-judged attack on AIDC a few months later. Certainly the government took the problem seriously, as in August–October 1973, Whitlam went on a speaking campaign to businessmen's dinners to reassure them that his government's intentions were honourable. It is possible, of course, that much of this criticism was simply the traditional rhetoric of complaint and buckpassing in situations where interest groups are in trouble.

In one area contact undoubtedly was strained, and at times abrasive. The mining industry occupied a peculiar position in Australian business: the area of most rapid growth in the 1960s, but also the scene of the most spectacular collapses in the 1970s, from the Tasminex and Minsec fiascos to the failure of the Patrick group in 1975. It was also a sector in which there was a very high concentration of foreign capital, which had already attracted much nationalist criticism. The policies developed by the new minister, Rex Connor, were decidedly nationalist though hardly socialist. The government imposed a require-ment of majority Australian ownership on new mineral de-velopments, which in practice meant an increased role for Australian companies – this was imposed for instance on the abortive Redcliffs petrochemical project, over the opposition of the South Australian Labor government. Connor bullied the mining companies to form cartels for export negotiations, and rapidly got higher iron ore prices for them from the Japanese. He pushed for the development of uranium exports, and the government undertook to develop the necessary infrastructure in the Northern Territory. This was all in the interests of the companies, though the minister was rhetorically rather abusive of them, on one famous occasion calling mining executives 'hillbillies and mugs' for their errors in export negotiations. As his plans unfolded, it seemed that he intended to reorganize the industry by constituting the federal government as a kind of super-company, buying and distributing fuels, undertaking ex-ploration and presumably production in its own right.[12] The response to moves in this direction was public and hostile. There were complaints over the fuel proposals in 1973, and mining companies as well as the opposition parties came out against the Petroleum and Minerals Authority Bill in 1974. (It was passed after the 1974 double dissolution, but has since been declared unconstitutional.) Mining executives traded insults with the government, and continued to abuse it through 1975.[13] This sentiment no doubt was part of the reason behind the huge outcry over the government's overseas loan fiasco in 1975, involving money that seems to have been intended to finance Connor's projects. Despite all this, the companies knuckled under on the distribution issue, and accepted the Australian equity requirements in new projects.

The principal dangers a reformist party in office faces are not those involved in direct negotiations with business or disputes arising out of them. Barring a coup [this was written in August 1975, and seems amusing enough to leave unchanged] which has been the fate of many reformist governments, and has been known in Australia (a military coup was contemplated against Lang in the depression, and a constitutional coup in fact succeeded) – the most effective sanctions at the disposal of the ruling class are through the collective mechanisms of the property system itself. A flight of private capital is a serious danger to a government that bases its economic strategy on general growth in a mixed economy. Though government loans, with a few hitches as a result of rising interest rates, went ahead under Labor, there were rumblings of a withdrawal of capital from private development projects, especially by multinational companies. This was threatened in response to Connor's minerals policies, and at least two foreign-owned mining groups (Anglo–American and CRA) directed their exploration activity overseas. A survey of US firms by the American Chamber of Commerce in 1974 announced that most had become reluctant to invest in Australia. So far, however, the effects of this have been marginal. Development of the iron-mining projects, for instance, one of the most politically sensitive areas, has continued, with multinational participation.

The area where a market-type response has emerged, and appears to have been effective, is in the labour market itself; specifically, in its connection with commodity markets. The government came into office as the representative of a union-based party, and proceeded to support the unions' wage claims, or at least stop opposing them, in the arbitration system. Money wage rises do not necessarily mean a shift of real income to the working class, if their effects can be passed back to the working class as rises in the price of goods. (This process may nevertheless produce a redistribution of income within the working class, e.g. towards the employed or towards strongly-unionized industries.) The business leadership here had a handy strategy for resisting pressure for redistribution, which hardly required conscious political thought. The attempt to protect profits by such means is part of the ordinary rationality of the firm. Generalized to the whole economy, however, it represented a defence of class income and, equally important, a defence of the corporate organization of class power.

The government's attitude to this was ambivalent. In the short run it stood to gain from inflation, which increased its tax share and eased the finance of its programmes. This came under

120

increasing criticism from business, and by the end of 1974 the government was willing to call a halt by announcing cuts in personal and company tax. Earlier it had made several moves to hamper the business leadership's use of the inflationary strategy, by direct attempts to control prices under the limited legal powers it had, and by a general tariff cut in July 1973 which made manufacturers more vulnerable to price competition from imports. An attempt to get power for the federal parliament to legislate prices failed at the constitutional referendum of December 1973.[14]

The government was then left with the attempt at moral suasion through the Prices Justification Tribunal it had set up earlier. This was a quasi-judicial body, with no power of enforcement but with a power of public enquiry, intended to look at price rises by all large companies. The threat of a public examination of their accounts was enough to scare some businessmen into withdrawing proposed rises. But others responded by attacking the whole concept of price control, such as the Adelaide establishment figure Sir Norman Young who roundly declared:

The clear intention of the Government is to use its prices justification law to intimidate persons who are responsible for safeguarding the huge amount of capital tied up in major private business operations.[15]

Others declared they would ignore it: GMH when making its submission in November 1973 stated it was 'impossible' to take anything less than what it sought; while a Macquarie University survey in mid 1973 found only 28% of companies intending to abide by the findings of the PJT.[16] But the most effective tactic was that of BHP, the first customer of the PJT, in fact the subject of a judicial price enquiry before the PJT was properly constituted. It brought a claim for steel price rises forward, and accepted the compromise figures proposed; but then came back again and again for more, meanwhile making dignified remonstrances in its own reports:

. . . if because of low prices now we are unable to generate a reasonable cash flow for future investment . . . then the established Australian steel industry must languish . . .[17]

The company eventually seems to have got the PJT to accept its logic; and indeed, in the final analysis, the government had to accept it. Short of actually adopting a socialist strategy for accumulation, it had to buy a measure of acceptance from business by agreeing to maintain 'fair profits' – a position Whitlam was already spelling out in the middle of 1973, though without making the mistake of actually saying what profits he thought were fair.

There are of course other market mechanisms through which businesses can put direct pressure on the government. GMH in December 1974 threatened to sack 5000 workers unless the government cut car imports and reintroduced export incentives – and sent the government, highly sensitive over rising unemployment figures, into a tailspin. The price gambit, however, seems to have been the most widespread, threatened in response to environmental pollution controls as well as wage demands. It is, perhaps, the least politically dangerous for the business leadership, being the one which is most readily compatible with the prevailing ideology within which government–business interaction takes place.

The ideological field of business–government interaction

So far I have stressed the economic logic and political pragmatics of the interactions. Australian politics is, as often remarked, highly practical. But the negotiations do not take place in a cultural vacuum, and what is practical is judged only within a framework of shared beliefs. The 'economic facts of life' that business propaganda groups like the IPA are fond of apostrophizing are 'facts' constituted by a given social structure; and following out their logic constitutes an affirmation of that social structure. In this sense, Australian politics is highly ideological, and ideology is a constraining force of the first importance in the everyday functioning of the social order.

A significant commitment is made in the basic reformist strategy itself, in which the labour movement agrees to act within the law and carry on its struggle with the tools provided by the organizations of the capitalist state – parliaments, arbitration courts, etc. There are however many varieties of reformism, and many things which one can use those tools for: some of them very radical, some of them not. The particular reformism of the Whitlam government, with its basic strategy of rationalizing the process of growth and paying for welfare reforms out of its proceeds, involves a much more extensive commitment to the dominant ideology. If we scan the economic pronouncements of the ministers and officials of this government, we find them (with a couple of significant exceptions) to be entirely within the framework of the legitimacy of property rights and the legitimacy of the business leadership; to accept, even defend, the profit mechanism; and so on.

An illuminating example of the consequences of these commitments is the rhetoric of 'business confidence'. To get growth requires investment in productive resources. Within the dominant ideology, investment decisions are largely made by company executives, on criteria of future profitability. The consequence is the truly comic sight of government going on bended knee to capitalists and begging them to make healthy ('fair', 'equitable') profits; even the sight of a Labor Treasurer making reassuring noises to try to bolster prices in the share market. This point was not academic: as early as April 1973 claims were being made that the government's activities depressed share prices; and the rise in share prices that accompanied the loans scandal and hostile rumours about Connor in July 1975 argues for a widespread distrust of Labor among share buyers.[18] The government had to give at least the appearance of being favourable to business; one observes Whitlam naming the reborn Tariff Board the Industries *Assistance* Commission, though the civil servant who drew up the plan had proposed to call it merely the 'Industries Commission'.

Conversely, businessmen can use the 'confidence' argument as a tactical weapon to fight off the more trenchant parts of a reformist programme. This was repeatedly done in arguments against Connor's minerals policy and Cameron's wages policy. It is of course only one of the ways the government can be blamed. Where it is involved in a regulatory or protective capacity – as it is now in every major industry in the country – it becomes a convenient scapegoat for sackings, profit failures, price rises, mismanagement, indeed all the ills that business flesh is heir to. Not that this is peculiar to the Labor government:

AMPOL LASHES GOVERNMENT AFTER
FALL IN EARNINGS

was a headline of 1971, not 1974.[19] Such complaints are of course discounted by the press, and no doubt by many of its readers, but they still become a staple of political discussion and regularly put the government on the defensive. There is practically a convention of public rhetoric that businessmen may attack the government but the government may not attack business. Connor and Cameron attracted so much business hostility partly because they broke it.

The rhetorical balance-sheet showed by no means all loss to Labor. If Whitlam's reformism acknowledged the legitimacy of business, it was partly because it shared some common ground and could occupy it to the government's advantage. An admiration for rationality and efficiency had been obvious in Whitlam's outlook long before he came to office, and he made good use of the theme in defending the 1973 tariff cuts. In his speeches to businessmen that year he claimed, with tongue not wholly in cheek, that his was the first real free enterprise government in Australia in 23 years. The tough trade-practices legislation that Murphy brought in as Attorney-General was in the strictest tradition of economic liberalism; though it was stalled by the opposition parties, it got support from Snedden personally. Connor's cartelization policies were not so classically liberal but these at least were nationalist and developmentalist. The belief that social welfare was essentially linked to economic growth, another constant in business ideology, was also able to be used offensively. In the 1974 campaign Whitlam, in tones of ringing indignation, claimed that it was the Liberals who were trying to hold the country back from development and progress.

Reformism, acting within the national state, inherits the justifying ideology of that state; and the self-proclaimed nationalism of the new government gave it another political weapon. This too was shared ground with business, who had been using the 'national interest' argument against unions beyond living memory. In the dispute over foreign investment in the early 1970s the concept was vigorously revived, and there followed a wave of synthetic nationalism that infected manufacturers, miners, the media and the government itself, reaching a peak of silliness in a competition for a new national anthem. British Tobacco, one of the largest manufacturing companies, complained bitterly of being classified as a foreign company under the Liberals' rules in 1972, and shortly changed its name to the innocuous acronym AMATIL. Multinational miners, as well as BHP, vanished behind a cloud of advertisements stressing their essential Australian-ness. More seriously, the national interest argument provided a rationale for Connor's mineral policy and for the most cutting critique of the mining industry, the Fitzgerald report released in April 1974, which argued that government had in fact shown a net loss in its dealings with the industry. This provoked angry refutations from businessmen and conservative journalists, but they focussed on the arithmetic of the report, not its ideological presuppositions.[20]

However nationalist, the Labor government necessarily offended class-conscious sections of business, to whom it was simply an interloper – boorish, undisciplined, and dangerous:

The danger lies from inflation with its continued cost rises and eroding of confidence, and from socialistic Governments who distribute the taxpayers' money so recklessly, encourage indolence and make it plainly evident that their object is to reduce the thrifty, hard working citizen to the level of the spendthrift. It is clear their allegiance will be to the Unions and the urban dweller and that the man on the land will receive less and less consideration.[21]

That was from the president of the SA Stockowners' Association (who no doubt had Dunstan in mind as well as Whitlam), at a time of boom in the wool industry. Class consciousness here is tempered with fear of the city in a way typical of rural conservatism, which traditionally sees the government as a marketing organization, finance institution, and cost controller necessary to preserve the morally superior rural way of life – a framework of argument that even Labor country members had to accept.[22] The Whitlam leadership's stress on urban issues was bound to create antagonism, and its economic measures that trimmed concessions to rural entrepreneurs gave a handle for criticism. It was not long before conservative politicians were stumping the countryside about the government's war on farmers, to some effect: they took three country seats from Labor in the 1974 election, tipping Grassby, one of the government's most popular figures, out of his Riverina seat.

To some sections of urban business, too, nothing the government could do would be right. Despite the overlay of welfarism from the 1940s, there is in business a continuing tradition of hostility to state controls and welfare measures as tools of 'socialism'. For a couple of decades this rhetoric had been pushed out to the fringe of politics, cultivated by doctrinaire free-enterprisers and extreme-right splinter groups. In 1973 it enjoyed a sudden revival. By the middle of that year one could hear the Labor government being blasted as 'an inexperienced, power hungry, undisciplined parliamentary party' (to return to our friend Sir Norman Young), using its temporary authority to carry out 'frightening social and economic experiments based on emotional party political doctrine'[23] [i.e. price control]. 'Creeping socialism', 'centralism' (a term carried over from the days of Gorton, now much favoured by conservative state premiers) and government 'interference' with business were now often heard of. They were even seen, as cartoon images of the government as a snooping bureaucrat began to pepper the propaganda of business and professional groups. The Australian Medical Association and the General Practitioners' Society in their struggle with Hayden over medical insurance gave good play to these ideas, as did the Bank of NSW in its attack on the AIDC proposals in early 1974, and the insurance companies in 1975.[24] Most important, they were picked up by Snedden, who very probably interpreted this rhetoric as a sign of a new business mobilization, and certainly took a more doctrinaire position than the Liberal leadership had done since the early 1950s.

But this was not a position on which all, or nearly all, of business agreed. Since the 1940s and early 1950s there had been an enormous growth in the scale and sophistication of the major companies, and with it a growth of the ideology of corporate liberalism (in the American sense), both in major companies and in sectors of business such as advertising and public relations. To many people in such circles, the class-conscious rhetoric of these attacks must have seemed simply atavistic. The attack on the AIDC could hardly have been worse judged: its board members included prominent directors of Ampol, Repco, BHP, and the Bank of NSW itself – Sir John Dunlop, who resigned from the bank board, rather than the AIDC board, over the issue. The Melbourne Chamber of Commerce was criticized from within its own ranks for misleading rhetoric about 'centralism', and the hardline advertisements produced by Singleton in the 1974 elections were criticized from within advertizing as well as by the Victorian Liberal Party.[25]

From circles such as these there were certainly criticisms of the government; but also a stress, as in Whitlam's speeches, on the interdependence of business and government. At Annual Report time in 1973 BHP gently chid the government for the obscurity of its long-term plans, but made plain its ability to accommodate to the new regime. The chairman of Hamersley Holdings, one of the CRA companies, changed his earlier tune and argued that business had to learn to live with the government – it was reported, at the prompting of his boss in London.[26] A number of prominent businessmen supported the appeal to build John Curtin House, a national headquarters for the Labor Party, though sharply criticized by the Queensland premier. The concept of profit itself was played down. There was embarrassment at the huge mining profits of 1973, and by 1975 the chairman of CRA (one of those involved in the reconstruction of the Liberal machine mentioned earlier) had come to the pleasing conclusion that 'business was not in business to make a profit. It exists to serve the market and produce goods and services for which people are prepared to pay. Profits are only a means to an end.' Meanwhile the general manager of CSR was arguing that the issue was not capitalism or socialism, but 'how to get people to work together'.[27] Along these lines a public *persona* was constructed for big business that stressed compromise, social responsibility, efficient management and social collaboration. The intention was to be, in BHP's words, 'a good corporate citizen'.

This cannot have sounded plausible to many of their workers who heard it. At the same time as it was announcing its sweet reasonableness in public, BHP attempted to deregister 11 unions over a pay dispute in NSW; and 1973 was the year of one of the most bitter industrial struggles in recent years, the Broadmeadows dispute. Nor would it have sounded too plausible to smaller businessmen – BHP and CSR were both engaged in strengthening their monopoly positions at the expense of smaller companies in these years, BHP taking quite a battering when it ran up against CSR's opposition in the cement industry. Nor would it have appealed to consumers, if the reality behind 'social responsibility' projects like steel can recycling were examined.[28] It must be stressed that the arguments being discussed here are ideological, and what they represent is the rationalization at a public level of the inesca-

127

pable operating links of the big companies and the state organisations. It is a very effective defence of business, in the long run; enmeshing the labour movement leadership in a system of interaction, compromise and joint planning that in itself preserves the existing business structure, and shifts behind decent veils the facts of private property and profit uncomfortably exposed by the fundamentalists of 'free enterprise'.

And at some joints of the political mattress, this uncomfortable reality did still poke through. At the cabinet level it was mainly Cameron who registered the fact. He, for instance, took up the cause of the strikers at Broadmeadows, arguing that control by the multinationals' executives was responsible; and pushed through an attack on multinationals at the party conference in 1973. As Minister for Labor he endorsed wage rises and argued for an equalization of wage rates – his criticism of the 'fat cats' in the Canberra bureaucracy in 1973 is the most celebrated example of this.[29] One notes that he was shifted from the job when Whitlam felt sure of his position in the loans reshuffle of mid-1975. The former shearer was out to grass as Minister for Science at the time of the November catastrophe, when working-class support might really have been useful.

The conservative political response

The 1972 election gave Labor control of the House of Representatives, but not of the Senate; the opposition parties, when united, thus had a short-term veto over legislation. They used it to block or delay a number of initiatives, which Whitlam was to list in his call for a double dissolution: universal health insurance, industrial legislation, restrictive trade practices legislation, extension of AIDC powers, Petroleum and Minerals Authority bill, and the creation of a federal superior court.[30] All but the last, minor, item involved the defence of some group of entrepreneurs, or at least could be made to look like that, and some of these actions were taken in concert with the business groups concerned: the AMA on medical insurance, and the mining companies on the PMA.[31] Yet it is plain from the AIDC case that there was not universal backing for these stands; it is one of the ironies of the dual-leadership situation that the political leadership can be more militant in defence of business rights than parts of business itself. And the conservative parties still had not resolved the internal conflicts that had become evident in 1970–2. The Country Party was hostile to the Industries Assistance Commission, but the Liberals in favour; Snedden, with some support at the branch level, tried to swing the party round on restrictive trade practices; Lynch favoured controls on the multinationals, and even the Queensland government in 1974 came around to the principle of majority Australian ownership.

For these reasons among others, the most effective political responses to the Whitlam government in its first two years came not from the federal opposition but from conservative governments in the states. These had already proved a thorn in the side of Gorton; now freed from the inhibition of damaging a government of their own party, they harrassed Canberra with gay abandon. The NSW government became notorious for its non-cooperation with federal planning activities, for instance in its cities policy. State attorneys-general attacked the proposed uniform companies act (originally a Liberal government scheme) as an attempt to get 'complete control of all companies, including management', and the eastern states started negotiations to set up an interstate companies commission to preempt the field.[32] The tactic was particularly effective where it could be grafted onto a regional sentiment, an old Country Party technique; and it was the only Country Party premier, Bjelke-Petersen in Queensland, who used it most abrasively and effectively. It was he who devised the tactic that forced Whitlam into a corner in April 1974, and his campaign against Canberra produced a devastating if slightly irrelevant victory in the next Queensland state elections.

At the same time an ideological offensive was launched by some sections of business. The content of their attack on 'creeping socialism' has been described in the previous section. What is interesting organisationally is that most of it came, not from companies, but from groups of business ideologues organised in 'non-political' associations, like the Institute of Public Affairs in NSW (somewhat less militantly from the separate IPA in Victoria), and the NSW Constitutional League; and in peak associations such as the Melbourne Chamber of Commerce and the Associated Chambers of Commerce. There was also a vigorous fundamentalist response from businessmen like Singleton, whose advertising campaign has been mentioned, and the iron magnate Hancock. Hancock, who had been feuding with the WA Liberals, got diverted into a secessionist campaign in 1974; after its abject failure he joined hands with the splinter 'Worker's Party' (against 'human leeches, parasites, no-hopers and bludgers'; for 'less government, less tax, less inflation and more freedom') that emerged in 1975. In a similar way the most bitter criticisms of the government's health insurance policy came from the militants' General Practitioners' Society rather than the AMA.[33]

The language used in these campaigns was extravagant in relation to the actual proposals of the Whitlam government. One has a strong impression that they were intended as spoiling tactics, making it so hard for the government to achieve modest reforms that it would be intimidated before it moved to anything more substantial. This was hardly necessary, given the actual Labor leadership and its strategy; but it went with a traditional business belief that there were more sinister and radical groups 'behind' the moderate leadership. (One recalls the advertisements in 1972 that showed a Whitlam mask revealing the face of Hawke – not a bright idea, given that Hawke, the President of the Australian Council of Trade Unions, was at the time more popular than Whitlam.) There were grounds within this framework of belief to call for a general mobilization of business against Labor.

These calls duly came at intervals from mid-1973, particularly from the Bank of NSW.[34] There were a couple of attempts to organize such mobilizations from within business, in 1974 around the AIDC issue, and in 1975 around the insurance commission issue. The latter, with careful prompting by insurance company managements, achieved a public protest movement by insurance staffs, but did not go beyond that industry. The AIDC campaign did not even get as far as that, with the bank officers' union as well as businessmen like Dunlop supporting the government. One reason why there was so much rhetoric and so little action is suggested by a management consultants' survey in early 1974, which found businessmen mostly hostile to Labor but also optimistic about their companies' profits. The element of fear for class income and social position, so marked in the successful mobilization of the 1940s, was lacking. Profits however began to be squeezed in real terms in 1974 and 1975, and dividend incomes were reduced, so the material reasons for business discontent were building up.[35]

It was clear, as a CRA executive put it in 1974, that the public image of big business was low,[36] and a reorganization of a different kind occurred. The period saw the growth of a cadre of business 'spokesmen' and a wider use of public relations techniques both by individual companies and by industry groups: miners, advertising, and employer organizations as a whole. There was also an organizational closing of the ranks, with an attempt (still in train) to simplify the fragmented structure of business peak associations by amalgamations at the state level and the creation of a grand National Confederation of Industry on the British model.[37]

For all this, it was the conservative party leadership that produced the main political retort to Labor, and much can be learned from their two attempts. It is likely that Snedden, listening to the barrage of business criticism of the government through late 1973 and early 1974, and not realizing its relatively narrow base at that time, believed that an election would find a solid business mobilization behind him. He certainly thought that in the Gair affair he had found an occasion when the government was discredited by its attitude to Parliament. But he erred in choosing a *parliamentary* issue to bring on an election, for it was a matter of trivial concern to the electors (as subsequent polls showed), and was in no sense an issue between the government and the business leadership of the kind that might provoke a strong response from business. (In a similar way Whitlam erred in fighting the 1975 election on the parliamentary issue of how he was deposed.)

In the 1974 campaign the Liberals certainly enjoyed their usual superiority in finance. As already observed, there was business participation in the campaign machinery of a new level of sophistication, certainly far more effective than that available to McMahon. On the fringe of the party there was campaign support from business militants such as Singleton, who is said to have raised over $250,000 to finance his advertising. But there was no open alignment of the major companies, nor a grass-roots business-based campaign. The Labor Party too was getting money from business, its federal secretary saying he was 'pleasantly surprised' at the amounts.[38] It had its share of support from advertising and media people, getting much of its visual work done at cut rates. Most important, it had not damaged the existing interests of any group of major companies, and the periodic shows of industrial union militancy had not reached a point where they put the fear of God into executives and shareholders in general. The conditions of the conservative mobilization of the late 1940s were not reproduced, and could not be called into being by the will of the conservative politicians.

The 1974 campaign was compound of ironies. Whitlam, the constitutional innovator *par excellence*, discovered a great reverence for constitutional convention, especially that which forbade a Senate opposition to throw out a government. Snedden, who had made his first bid for the Liberal leadership as a man 'on the wavelength of his own era', found himself defending the eternal economic verities and aligned with the ideologues of the right. When the dust had settled, the Liberals replaced him with a wealthy squatter. The election in fact resulted in the passage of the laws that the conservative alliance had to that point successfully resisted. And within a year, the re-elected government had got itself into deep electoral trouble on its own chosen ground, the rationalization of the economy, and through inept attempts to tap the international capital market, reaching a point where it no longer required a widespread ruling-class mobilization to unseat it.

Fraser, on becoming Liberal leader in 1975, made a ritual call for a closing of business ranks against the government. But it is reasonably clear that when he struck by refusing supply it was a personal decision that the electoral fruit was ripe, rather than the outcome of a mounting mobilization. Indeed for some days it looked as though he had misjudged his tactics. The government did not immediately fall, morale in the Liberal's parliamentary ranks was wavering, and there were rumours that Fraser was looking for a face-saving way of climbing down, when the Governor-General came to the aid of the party. Yet that move itself was made possible by another instance of ruling-class opposition to the government. For it was the refusal of the private banks to accept a temporary finance arrangement that finally broke its delaying strategy and gave Kerr occasion to dismiss it.

In other matters of tactics the Liberal–business connection proved critical. The most important in all probability was the 'loans affair'. This was an absolute nonstarter as an economic or social policy issue – the debate never got on to the really interesting point about it, the proposed use of the funds. Rather, the Liberals saw in it a golden chance to discredit the government on the score of honesty and competence; the issue as it filtered down into the electorate became murkier and murkier, the government's backstairs dealing with a coloured (in some backblocks versions, Jewish) financier being the only point that registered. They worked through their local and international business contacts, particularly those of the Deputy Leader Lynch, to collect material on the matter and keep it alive through the boring months of nonevents. In seeking the money from the international capital market to finish his lifework, Connor can never have dreamed how he was handing himself over, bound hand and foot, to his political enemies. But that is precisely the kind of analysis that reformism lacks.

The end of the Labor government is still too recent to offer a full analysis; why it lost in a year electoral support that it had held for the previous six is not very easy to explain. I think the interesting problems here have to do with ideology more than with organization: the effects of the limitations within the Whitlamite programmes; the government's misunderstanding of the crisis when it came and its opposition to a working-class mobilization in response; and the social consciousness of the electors with inflation and unemployment under a reformist government. But each of these would require a lengthy analysis. The implications of the ruling-class experience in these years are easier to bring into focus.

In response to reformism there is, plainly, a range of options open to the ruling-class leadership, from class-conscious militancy to quite warm accommodation. The existence of a separate political leadership creates a definite push towards militancy, as the personal interests of those leaders are bound up with the earliest possible defeat of the reformist party. But reformism is not a pushover for the conservatives, and judgments about tactics and timing may vary independently of ideological position – it is noteworthy that Fraser, a strong conservative, was initially more reluctant to pull on an election than was Snedden, personally more liberal. For the business leadership, a great deal of time and energy can also be spent in fruitless rhetoric and abortive attempts at mobilization. The most fruitful strategy for them was probably that of CSR and

BHP – accommodation to the legal regime, reliance on ideological control and political opposition to keep it from doing anything dangerous, and patience, until a conservative government should return.

7. Class consciousness in childhood

Simply being a member of a class may have important consequences for action and experience; but it is only the shared consciousness of membership that can transform a class into a transforming political force. That idea has been the basis of socialist strategy ever since modern class structures began to emerge. The troubles of western socialism in the last generation have naturally led to a search for changes in the conditions of class consciousness.

The search has mainly concentrated on changes in industrial structure and family life, as in the 'embourgeoisement' debate, or on the psychological makeup of adults, as in Marcuse's theories of social integration under advanced capitalism. But the class consciousness of adults has a pre-history. As a number of social psychologists have shown, there is a knowledge of social hierarchy that exists long before a person enters a work situation or achieves adult genitality.[1] Taking class consciousness in its purely empirical sense,[2] to mean the understanding of the class structure and stances towards it held by members of a given social group, we may say that its roots go far back into childhood.

Davies, whose work has helped to make this point obvious, has sought the main clue inside the family, taking early relationships with parents, brothers and sisters as models to which later beliefs and feelings about class are assimilated. Before that kind of argument can be established, it is necessary to look at the evolution of ideas about class *per se*. Such ideas themselves go back to an early period of childhood, and might be found to have their own developmental logic.

The following discussion is based mainly on a survey of children in state schools in Sydney carried out in 1967 and 1968.[3] In the main part of this I interviewed 119 children aged 5 to

16 from three areas of the city, of high, middle, and low prestige by the usual criteria. The interviews, which were tape-recorded, covered mostly political topics; they included perceptions of wealth and poverty, ideas about jobs (introduced, for the younger ones, by showing drawings of people at work), and related topics as the children's individual answers suggested. The account that follows is based on a fairly close analysis of this material, and I am reasonably confident of the progression suggested, though it is not measured in a formal way. The extracts have been chosen to illustrate both the range of responses and some typical features. As in all such selections, the more articulate children are over-represented. The extracts have also been edited to cut out a number of repetitions and hesitations. Thus the fluency of answers is somewhat exaggerated; but the underlying ideas can be found very widely.

Understanding: three stages in the idea of class

Within the limits of a cross-sectional study, which cannot trace the development of one child's thought but can compare it with the ideas of older and younger children, the interviews show three main stages through which ideas about the class structure pass.

I: The stage of dramatic contrast (ages c. 5–8). Young children do not understand the word 'class' in its sociological sense, as I discovered in the pilot study for this project:

BOY, 6: (*Have you heard other people talking about an upper class, or a middle class or a lower class?*) Well...I've heard of a...only a middle class. And a middle class is . . . well they stay in the classroom for Scripture.

But children at these ages are not ignorant of economic differences.

GIRL, 5: (*Is Daddy rich or poor?*) Poor. (*He's poor?*) Yeah, cause he's got that much money [showing a height of about an inch with her fingers] and Mummy's not poor, she's got *that* much money [showing about four inches].

GIRL, 6: (*What's the difference between people who are rich and people who are poor?*) The people who are rich well they can buy everything but the people who are poor well they can't buy anything...It's not very good because the people who are rich well they're greedy.

136

GIRL, 7: If you don't pay your bill, you'll be an orphan and you won't have any home, you'll sleep out in the cold...(*What do you mean by an orphan?*) An orphan means that you'll be very poor. (*What does being very poor mean?*) It means that, sometimes, you mightn't have enough money to buy any food and you might run out...(*What would you say was the difference between people who are very poor and people who are rich?*) The people who are rich, they don't have to sleep out in the cold, like the orphans do. (*Why not?*) Cause they're very rich and they pay all their bills, cause they've got enough money.

BOY, 8: (*Why do we call someone rich?*) Cause they've got a lot of money. (...*And what about poor, when you call someone poor?*) They haven't got a lot of money, nearly dead broke...(*Do you know anyone who's rich?*) Yes, one of my uncles is a millionaire. (*Do you know anyone who's very poor?*) My mummy, she's real poor.

The interpretation of class differences at these ages is a curious mixture of vagueness and detail. The children have no idea of an overall class structure embracing the whole of society; they simply make the dramatic contrast between wealth and poverty. They have a firm idea that there are differences in amounts of money, though they have no realistic idea of the sums involved, and seize on such points as the height of a pile of change or the amount of pocket-money they have at the moment. Asked the difference between rich and poor, an overwhelming majority specify money; a few add things that can be bought, such as a house, or food. Asked how a person gets to be rich, they speak of immediate and tangible ways of getting one's hands on cash:

BOY, 5: (*How do some people get to be rich?*) They dig up gold from the gr, from the little water, from the water. (*Why is it that some people are rich and some people are poor?*) Because the poor people don't know that there's gold in the ground and the rich people do.

GIRL 5: (*What's the difference between rich and poor?*) The rich man has gold and poor man doesn't have gold. (*How is it that some people get to be rich?*) Because they steal gold. (*Do people get rich in any other way?*) Yes, and some people steal the money from the bank. I watch television and man stealed money from the bank and the lady screamed her head off...(*How is it that some people are rich and some people are poor?*) Cause some pe, umm, cause in the night time some people wake up and go and steal money, go and steal their gold and that's how people get poor.

BOY, 6: (*How does someone get to be rich?*) By getting money from the bank. (*How do you get money from the bank?*) Get a savings account.

These early conceptions of class reflect both the communications coming in to the children, and their limited cognitive capacity to deal with them. They learn about banks, etc., from their families (e.g. the 7 year old's discussion of bills), and sometimes from the mass media (e.g. the bank robbery). They are at this age being taught how to use money. This gives them details; but the most striking feature of their ideas at this age, the sharp contrast made between wealth and poverty, probably comes from another source. The chracter of the contrast, the frequent moralism of the children's references to wealth, the repeated references to gold, all suggest that this idea comes from the fairy tales, legends, Bible stories, songs and rhymes which depend upon the contrast. The rich–poor distinction is built into the traditional oral culture of childhood, which comes to the children both from adults and from older children.[4]

If these are the sources, it is clear that the ideas about class depend also on the children's level of intellectual capacity. Those familiar with Piaget's work on cognitive development will see in the passages quoted some of the symptoms of intuitive thought – the seizing on isolated details, the intuitive leaps from one point to another, the apparently inconsequential arguments, the tenuous grasp on objective reality.[5] The absence of an idea of an overall class structure at these ages must be attributed in part to the children's lack of the cognitive operations necessary for building up such a conception.

II: The stage of concrete realism (*c. 8–12*). In Stage I children do not have a class scheme, in the sense of an image of class differences embracing the whole of society. From about age 8 onwards there is evidence of an inclusive scheme:

GIRL, 8: (*What's the difference between rich people and poor people?*) Poor people, they don't have such nice clothes as rich people. (*Why not?*) Oh because they don't have very much money, poor people. (*Why do some people get to be rich?*) Because they save their money and um, they get a lot of money from their jobs...(*What about yourself, would you say you were rich or poor?*) In the middle. (*What about the people around here, around E. [an upper-status suburb]? Would they mostly be rich or mostly be poor?*) In the middle.

GIRL, 9: (*Why is it that some people are rich and some people are poor?*) Well, poor people they don't get a lot of money, they don't earn a lot of money, cause they don't go to work see, but the rich people go to work and they earn a lot of money. (*Well, then is everybody who goes to work rich?*) No. Some people sometimes they only get a bit, about seven dollars or something like that you know. My sister gets a hundred dollars each month, or week, I think. (*Why do some people only get a little bit every week?*) Because they don't do a lot of work. (*Do you think it's a good thing that there are some people who are rich, and some people who are poor, or is that a bad thing?*) Well, I think the rich people, it's a bit bad, cause they, see my father's medium, you know and I think they should be medium really.

BOY, 10: (*What would you say you were yourself, rich or poor or neither?*) Well not that rich I tell you that, ah well I'm, not that poor, oh just about half–half. (*What about most of the people round this district* [*a middle-status suburb*]?) Oh, I think they're rich I think I suppose. They might be half. I mean I don't know anybody poor around here.

As these extracts show, the children have constructed a rough but inclusive class scheme by inserting an intermediate group between rich and poor. The great variety of the names they give this *tertium quid* – 'in the middle', 'medium', 'half–half', 'not rich, not poor, enough', etc. – suggests that the children have constructed the category themselves, rather than receiving it from adult sources. And the stimulus to the construction is not far to seek. Children at these ages, who are moving far more freely outside the nuclear-family circle than Stage I childen, are learning a great deal about the concrete details of the class structure. They get realistic ideas about incomes, as the 9-year-old quoted shows. They are able to characterize the wealth of their own district, however mistakenly. To the questions about differences between rich and poor, and the reasons for wealth, the children give a much greater variety of answers than those at Stage I: they refer to luxuries, clothes, cars, etc., and they refer more often to work, ownership, and inheritance.

The most important change in this stage is that the children develop an idea of an occupational scale. Young children sometimes refer to jobs as a source of wealth, but usually with the idea that the rich have jobs and the poor have none. About the age of 9, the children begin to argue that a person becomes rich by getting a *good* job, and a little later, that the difference between rich and poor is the *type* of job they have:

BOY 9: (*How do some people get to be rich?*) Well they find a very good job which they can get a lot of money and they save. (*Why is it that some people are rich and some people are poor?*) Cause some people, well they, sometimes they have hard jobs and they can't do it, so they get a job like being a garbage man and you only get a little bit of money.

In one part of the interviews, the children were shown pictures or names of jobs, asked to pick the best, and then say why they thought it was the best. The younger children typically referred to the intrinsic satisfactions of the job; but from age 10 they commonly referred to the competitive advantages of the chosen job against others. Thus during Stage II the children develop a conception of an occupational hierarchy; though it is at this stage only loosely connected with the overall class structure.

As with Stage I, the characteristic ideas about class arise from an interaction of cognitive development with communications from the adult world. The children at this age have usually developed the ability to classify, and to order (logical) classes of entities; this enables them to conceive of an inclusive classification of all persons in society. The development of an occupational hierarchy presupposes the capacity to group objects both by similarity (aggregating jobs which are similar to each other) and by difference (distinguishing classes of jobs from each other). The subject-matter the children work on, as in Stage I, comes from the adult world, but it is now information about the present class structure rather than story and legend – particularly information about jobs from people in their immediate environment. It is quite probably this information that stimulates the transition from Stage I to Stage II, as the children realize the inapplicability of the extreme categories of 'rich' and 'poor' to the adults around them.

III: The stage of true class schemes (*c. 12–16*). The class schemes of Stage II embrace, potentially or actually, the whole of society; but their middle category has no properties other than that of being in the middle. True class schemes, where the classes described embrace the whole of society, and have distinctive attributes, appear about the age of transition to adolescence, and characterise the teenage years. They also diversify: one finds among teenagers the major types of class schemes that have been found among Australian adults.[6]

BOY, 15: (*If you were talking to someone who hadn't been in Australia before, a migrant for instance, and you wanted to explain to him what*

the main classes of people in Australia were, what would you say?)
Probably like middle class and upper class and that, lower class and
that stuff, probably be all middle class people, mostly. (*What everyone,
or mostly?*) Mostly everyone, oh, about sixty per cent'd be middle class
and twenty'd be upper and twenty'd be lower, but the most of them
would be in middle class. (*Well who would be middle class and who
would be the others?*) Oh, the people that, the people that got ordinary
jobs you know. (*Like what?*) Oh, I don't know, people who run shops,
just grocery shops and, taxi drivers and, you know, ordinary jobs and
that, but the people who run companies and businesses, they'd be the
upper class cause they'd get lot of money. And the people who haven't
got a good job, that just get a pension and that, they'd all be off and
that they'd probably be lower.

GIRL, 16: Well I'd say, well I think Australian people are, well firstly,
you know they go in for leisure and entertainment and that a lot.
And, first, I'd sort of say well there's a type of person, the middle
class person you know, and they're, the mothers who go to work, and
the fathers who go to work and, and the children at, public schools,
or Catholic schools. And then I'd say the next, the other class is the
socialists' class you know where they, people get into news and they,
they're the ones that shop at, LaSalle [an exclusive city shopping
centre], and they're the ones that always get their names in the paper
and um, send their children to private schools, and who drive a big,
you know who change their car every once a year to, the, car that's
in at the moment you know . . . They can be very nice people, but, they
tend to throw airs, I think . . . (*What class would you say you belong
to yourself?*) Well I think I belong to the middle class, but, the thing
is, it's not a strict, um, class to belong to because, you can come down
from the lower cl, you know you can go up and down all the time you
can, go places and things like that, I think that, and in between all the
time . . . there's no barrier.

GIRL, 13: Oh well, really pretty much the same, not many people are,
richer or, greater-minded or all this than you you're, all pretty well
the same, and there's not that many people that are real poor, they're,
like well no-one, no-one's poor, unless they, don't take care of things
. . . There's just those few people who, happen to get into a gooder job
get more money, bank more away, and they might go without some
things until they get, much higher than us. But otherwise I think we're
all pretty well in the same class of people.

These extracts show the ease with which teenagers use the
language of class (not true of all, but a definite change from
earlier ages), and the way in which ideas about job hierarchies,
wealth, education, etc., have been integrated into distinctive
images of a total class structure. It will not do to attribute

overmuch significance to the precise form in which a class scheme is expressed in response to a single question (one girl gave three different schemes to three different questions); but the total pictures presented are intelligible and can be sorted out into groups. The three cases quoted illustrate three of the types of class schemes identified by Ossowski, i.e. gradation, dichotomy, and classlessness.[7] Most of the teenagers' class schemes fell into these categories, and the distinction has more than a numerical basis. The gradation schemes were usually without affect, and seemed to be simply an elaboration of Stage II conceptions. The dichotomous schemes, the rarest and most emotional type, commonly involved some hostility to the upper class. The classless (or one-class) schemes usually went with an expression of satisfaction in the *status quo* and, like the dichotomous schemes, often seemed to be based on adult prototypes.

It appears, then, that the teenagers are constructing true class schemes and coming into contact with traditions of belief about the Australian class structure current in the adult world. The content of their descriptions of class incorporates that of Stage II, with two additions. At ages 11–12, in answer to questions about the difference between rich and poor, the children begin to mention a cluster of *differentiae* such as living area, snobbery, type of school, and privilege, that have in common a reference to segregation between the classes. The question of segregation comes through strongly in some class schemes – the 16-year-old just quoted discusses it at length – and some put their basic description of the class structure in terms of the different social areas of Sydney. This awareness can be attributed to teenagers' increased personal mobility away from home, and their much wider circles of acquaintances. The second development is that they add to the awareness of a job hierarchy the conception of a career. A projection of a complete life cycle is given by the 15-year-old quoted before:

BOY, 15: (*How. . . would you say people get to be rich, upper class?*) Ah, probably I mean like, if your parents don't have to be rich themselves, like if you were born and you, like you were pretty good at schoolwork, and, you liked schoolwork, and like say you went to a very good school well and there's nothing else to do except stay home and study on, well you just learn more and more, get a degree or some university and that, and you can actually have pick of any job you like, well that pays a lot of money and then you pick the job you want and you'd probably get about 150 dollars a week or something, and then when you retire, you, I don't know, you could be, before you retire you could invest and you could buy a company [word blurred] you know and just live rich like that.

The idea of a career is frequently connected, as here, to education as the first step in it; and this no doubt reflects the arguments that parents and teachers use to urge high school students on to their schoolwork, as well as the discussion of careers at school. It shows that the teenagers are developing, as well as an overall class scheme, an idea of the movement of people within it.

These are the major stages through which the understanding of class passes in the school years. We can see at each step how cognitive development, from intuitive thinking through to the synthesizing power of formal thought in adolescence, conditions the understanding of class; and we can see how at each stage communications from the adult world provide materials for the children's conceptions. By the end of this development, most teenagers have a moderately elaborate picture of a total class structure and the relationships of individual people to the whole. What of their stances towards it?

Stances: three traditions on equality

The children's feelings about social inequalities were probed by asking whether they thought the difference between wealthy and poor was fair (or right, or good). Their answers, stripped down to the barest essentials, are summarized in Table 3. There is a striking change with age.[8] The young children overwhelmingly say that the difference is not fair; less than a third of the teenagers agree with them. What is the reason for the change?

The answers given by the younger children provide a first clue:

GIRL, 5: It's not fair. (*Why not?*) Cause if the poor people haven't got the money well, the other people that have lend some from them, and, and that, if, if you got all the money and don't send them to the, that makes you, you greedy guts.

GIRL, 7: I think it's wrong. (*Why do you think it's wrong?*) If some people, are rich and the other people are poor, well the people that are rich, they think that, it's funny to laugh, at the people that are poor, but when they get poor, they don't feel so, happy.

Table 3. Children's views on whether the difference between rich and poor is fair, Sydney 1968

	5–6	7–8	9–10	11–12	13–14	15–16	Total
Yes	—	3	2	3	6	10	24
Sometimes yes, sometimes no	1	1	—	3	4	3	12
No	10	10	13	9	4	5	51
Don't know or unclassifiable	1	1	1	1	—	—	4
Total	12	15	16	16	14	18	91

BOY, 8: I think the poor people are quite, yeah that's a quite bad thing, sad thing. (*Why is that?*) Cause you, cause they wouldn't have much to eat and they wouldn't have much to drink.

BOY, 9: Sometimes it's a bad thing for poor people, bad thing for rich people cause sometimes when rich people are real rich, they don't give money to the poor people to live.

Such responses are obviously based on the dramatic contrast that is basic to the earliest understanding of class; the children's opinions are not so much a declaration for equality as a declaration of the need of the poor, conceived of as a deeply disadvantaged group, for succour. The pervasive moralism of these answers shows the influence of the tradition of Christian charity which is itself a source of the early class schemes.

A minority at Stage III agree that the differences are not fair. But their justification is very different:

BOY, 12: Well I don't, I think it's fairly wrong all, see some people, they get a job where they just practically do nothing and they're just sitting around and that, and they get an awful lot for sitting round . . . I don't think they should get as much as they really get because they're just sitting there some people they're just sitting there and they just sign a little thing and that's all they do, one day they might just sign a cheque or something and that's it, and he's just sitting in his office, and other people they work real hard, and they're not getting any, what, the amount of money they're worth. No I don't think so it all depends on the job I reckon.

BOY, 15: I don't think there should be any difference. (*Why do you think that?*) I don't know, everybody works, and a pilot, well, he does the same thing all the time so, it's not that any harder for him. (*Why do you reckon these differences exist?*) In pay? (*Yeah.*) Well they must think that a person that, sweeps the road well anybody can pick up papers and, sweep dirt off roads and everything but, I don't know I think, well after a while anybody could drive a plane after being taught. (*You said, 'they' think this, who do you mean by 'they' who decides?*) Well whoever, whoever made the, I don't know the government, they should give everybody equal pay.

These are quite typical of the older respondents who represent the famous tradition of Australian egalitarianism. Their argument is based on the conception of occupational hierarchy that emerges about age 9–10. It is not so much an abstract egalitarianism or levelling – there is only the faintest touch of this in the answers – as a deduction from the idea that reward should be proportionate to effort and the observation that effort and reward are not matched up in the present hierarchy.

The majority of teenagers take the view that inequalities are justified, or that they are justified in some circumstances.

BOY, 13: Well if they work for their money and they build up and build up until they've worked that hard they come to that good, I reckon it's pretty fair. (*And if they don't?*) Well if their, say their, great-grandfather [laughs] was pretty rich and he passed on the money to them, but say if he worked I don't think that's really fair cause they just sit at home.

BOY, 15: Oh they [communists] think everything, everybody should be equal, and I don't think that's right, cause if one person goes to school till sixth year, another person leaves in first year they shouldn't get the same pay. (*You reckon they should get different pay?*) Mm, higher standard of wages.

BOY, 15: Well, there's nothing wrong as long as there's, like everyone earns some money to live comfortable and all that, you know like they don't go starving. . .like over in Vietnam or whatever.

GIRL, 16: The poor, don't have to be poor, I mean like they can, oh there's not very poor, there might be poor because of their own rea, cause of their own, faults like, cause they can always earn money easily in Australia if they're prepared to work for it, and the rich are very prepared to work for it.

GIRL, 16: If they work for it, why not? If you work hard all your life you should have something to be able to, look back on and say, 'Well I've worked hard I've earned this'.

Loud and clear, the same message comes through: reward

should be proportionate to effort. But here it is observed that reward *is* proportionate to effort, and inference from this pre- miss leads to the conclusion that the present class structure is just. These two findings – which were quite unexpected – make it very clear that the gospel of work is more widespread among the children, and more fundamental in their outlook, than any doctrine of egalitarianism or social hierarchy.

Thus we would not expect to find much pressure for a basic reordering of society to do away with inequalities. The older children and teenagers, as a group, do not have strong feelings about class, and are mostly satisfied with the structure as it is. Asked what should be done about the position of the poor, or about inequality, their answers mostly run to charity, or the provision of more jobs, some older teenagers arguing that nothing can be done. None of them suggests activity by the unions; and few have any conception of the class bases of political parties or an idea that parties might differ over class issues. Most children, this is to say, do not see class as a problematic issue or feel themselves engaged in any kind of class conflict. This is clearly reflected in their self-classing. The older children and teenagers, almost without exception, and regardless of their class scheme, put themselves in a 'middle' position in the social scale.[9] But there are two groups whose feelings about, and perceptions of, class are sharper than this disengaged consensus. The reasons for their heightened awareness of class are extremely interesting.

In five cases there was evidence in the interviews (volun- teered by the children) of a recent upheaval in the financial position of the family. In all five cases there was unusual affect in the material on class. In one case, a 7-year-old girl, the mother had won a lottery, and the child proudly described herself as 'kind of rich' and recited details of the improved family position, additions to the house, etc. In four cases there had been a loss of income because of industrial accidents, a strike, or a demotion. All four (ages 11 to 16) made bitter comments about the rich, and two of them had class schemes involving an embattled dichotomy. The important points are that the affect is realistic from the point of view of the family's financial position, and that in the four cases of loss of income, the affect arising from a specific incident is generalized to the class structure as a whole.

The second group with heightened class consciousness was the teenagers in the lower-status district. There were no differences between districts in the propensity to judge the class system unfair (the question in Table 3); but there were differences in party preference and preferences for party leaders. Most children were not aware of the class bases of party support (though they exemplified it themselves); but the lower-status teenagers were. They identified Labor as the party of the working class, Liberal as the party of the affluent. Their answers show sometimes clearly and sometimes faintly, the working-class tradition out of which the Labor Party itself arose:

BOY, 14: The Labor're for, poor, mainly, the Liberal, well they, look after the rich, and they *try* to, they get all their votes from the rich, and they try to influence the poor, from the papers you know, the Liberal, I mean Labor they just, for the poor people. (*How does this happen?*) Oh I don't know...just their, they get all their votes from the poor people, want to help them...(*What are the differences between rich and poor?*) Oh...higher class, they want to you know keep things on their side, and the lower class, well they want more, more help and jobs. (*Who is it that's in the higher class?*) Oh, mainly, businessmen, you know, rich people. (*And what about the lower class?*) Oh, we're [or possibly, 'well they're'] the, just the plain working people.

No doubt the same kind of mechanism is at work here as in the first group, though here it operates collectively; the greater instability of jobs and precariousness of income among manual workers helping to heighten the class consciousness of those of their children soon to move into the labour market.

Children's class consciousness as social knowledge
Children are constant observers of the social world, and from their observations they construct interpretations of how it is organized and how it works. Of course they do not see it all at once, and their power to understand it only gradually develops. With regard to class, as far as the evidence from this study goes, the first impressions are of the crude difference between wealth and poverty. Then, in sequence, they learn of the occupational hierarchy, patterns of segregation between classes, alternative career patterns, and finally (for some by 16) the nexus between class and party politics.

The sequence, running from the simple and conspicuous to the complex and subtle, is intelligible; and the constructions that the children at any given stage place on the class structure are likewise intelligible when we know their cognitive possibilities and the kinds of information they are getting from the adult world. This leaves little room, as major determinants of beliefs about class, for the unconscious forces stressed by Davies, except perhaps at the stage where a choice is available between traditions current in the adult world.[10] Certainly these choices did not seem to be strongly constrained by the children's own class position. The interviewees were drawn from three suburbs of contrasting status levels, a distinction which was confirmed by the types of their fathers' jobs. There were no consistent differences between the three districts in attitudes to inequality, or self-classing, or class schemes.

These children are of course still at school; they are to that extent insulated from the workings of the labour market. A point which looms large in adult class schemes, the social location of one's own job, is necessarily lacking. Yet there are other evidence that simply leaving school and taking a job does not produce a notably higher level of class awareness. Table 4 presents results from a mass survey of Sydney teenagers in 1969 and 1970,[11] who were asked in a forced-choice question which class they thought they belonged to, but were given two options to *refuse* self-classing. Large numbers did so; and among both girls and boys, those out of school refused somewhat *more* often than their age-mates in school. (The same is true of choices of political parties.)

In this larger survey some relationship (though not a strong one) did appear between teenagers' social position, judged by district or fathers' jobs, and their class choices and opinions on matters such as trade unions. And in the interviews already discussed, there are pockets of class consciousness which can be seen to have some basis in economic events. In these cases the insulation between the child and the workings of the economic system has broken down; the relationship between the causes and effects of class position, to use Weber's phrase, has become transparent;[12] and a heightened consciousness of class results.

But most of the children's material about class comes to them indirectly. The most class-conscious groups in the interviews,

Table 4. Self-classing and refusal among Sydney teenagers, 1969–1970

	% Chose class	% Refused	Number of cases
Girls, 15–16			
In school	59	41	1150
Out of school	57	43	92
Girls, 17–18			
In school	65	34	200
Out of school	62	38	284
Boys, 15–16			
In school	64	36	1300
Out of school	59	41	69
Boys, 17–18			
In school	72	27	500
Out of school	64	36	256

the working-class teenagers, were reproducing elements of a historic tradition of working-class–Labor solidarity that stems from the situation of urban workers over nearly eighty years. In the mass survey, a nicely symmetrical pocket of upper-class consciousness was found among private school pupils.[13] Other traditions can be seen at work in the interviews – Christian charity and legendary tales of wealth and poverty among the younger children, the idea of Australian classlessness and the wider western 'gospel of work' among the older. Obviously, class schemes do not simply arise from the personal experiences of their owners. They encapsulate material from the experience of generations past, and this process is well advanced before the growing person enters jobs, unions, yacht clubs, etc. There is a kind of generational lag in mass class-consciousness, which must moderate the impact of changes in the industrial and occupational structure.

For this to happen, of course, requires that there must be some ambiguity in the class structure itself. Surveys such as those by Broom, Jones and Zubrzycki have shown that though there is a connection between their scales of income, education, type of occupation, and self-classing, it is not a very tight one.[14] To the extent that these reflect the criteria used in everyday life in making judgments about class position, judgments can diverge widely without being demonstrably wrong. It is possible for different people within the structure to entertain, quite reasonably, different images of the whole. (At a purely phenomenal level, of course; this is not to say that constructing a *theory* of the structure is impossible.)

The ambiguity of class has two sides, the ambiguity of the overall pattern, and the ambiguous position of people in it. It is here that the deepest uncertainty of the children lies. Very few of them, very few indeed, have a firm consciousness of their own class position. The constant 'middle' self-classing among the older children and adolescents is much less a claim to membership of a middle class than it is a denial of being either wealthy or poor. Class is not salient as a frame of reference for judging the self: the children do not answer the question 'who am I?' in class terms. They do not have that shared consciousness of class membership which is basic to class politics; and not surprisingly their political attitudes, and their party and candidate choices, are with few exceptions entirely free of class considerations.

It would be a mistake to infer that therefore class politics is on the way out, as a generation innocent of it grows to maturity; 1975 is enough to refute that idea. But there is a significant detachment here, not only an emotional detachment of the children from class issues, but also a detachment of knowledge and belief from social context. The most striking finding, overall, is that the children develop a detailed interpretation of class without a firm consciousness of class membership, and that the patterns of their beliefs are for the most part independent of their families' class positions. There are important elements of class consciousness which are now – whatever may have been the case in the past – detached from the industrial structure and communicated as traditions in other contexts.

In considering the communication of social knowledge we may distinguish between information which is tied to specific social position, in the sense that one must be in a certain position to get it, and information which is free-floating, available to all regardless of their position in a structure of social relationships. A paradigm of tied information would be the specific theology communicated only to the catechumens of one church; a paradigm of free-floating information, in a country such as Australia, would be the main items in the television

news. The assumption of much thinking about class consciousness has been that information about class and class relationships is tied information, that knowledge of class relationships
is closely associated with specific position in the class structure. On the contrary, the information about class which these
children use in building up their class schemes is almost wholly
free-floating information. There are many possible reasons.
The social mobility of families over one or two generations has
spread past experiences of class situations (e.g. unemployment
in the Depression) widely across the present structure. The
sheer physical mobility of contemporary teenagers, the rise of
comprehensive schools and the nomadism of their families,
widens the range of their contacts and experiences. And finally,
there is the heavy reliance of children at all ages on mass media,
the paradigm source of free-floating informaton, for their knowledge of society.

In this context, the extreme vagueness of self-classing among
the older children and adolescents can be seen to be of a kind
with their class schemes: for the data from which the schemes
are built up carry no messages that the receiver is of such-
and-such a class. The children are subjectively classless in a
class society, informed and ignorant at the same time.

Class and personal socialization

When interviewing the group of children and teenagers discussed in Chapter 7, I asked in passing what job they might get
when they left school. The younger ones said nurses, doctors,
policemen, pilots, air hostesses and ballet dancers, much as
expected. But the older ones surprised me. A good quarter of
those aged eleven to sixteen answered something like this:

GIRL, 12: Oh, I couldn't do it but I'd like to do, something to do with
science. [Laughing] I'm not brainy enough to...(*What would you
need to do to get into that kind of job?*) Oh...more brains [laughs],
ah, suppose you need a lot of money; I don't know...I'd like to
do astronomy or, archaeology or something like that.

GIRL, 13: Well, myself I'd like to be a kindergarten teacher. I've got
four brothers and sisters younger than me and I get along with them
real good, play games with them on weekends and that. I can get along
with children. I'm very patient with them, not like me sister she goes
off her rocket [laughs], bashes into them or screams or something.
That's what I'd like to be. Or if I couldn't do that, which I don't think
I've got the brains really, the intelligence, you know you've got to go
all through school and then university and college and such, then I
think I'd like to work either in some sort of shop, or then I'd go in
for a factory...

BOY, 15: I want to join the Air Force and be an electrical engineer but,
I don't think I'll be able to do it. (*Why not?*) I haven't got the
intelligence, I'm a bit behind in me studies. I went to the Vocational
Guidance Bureau about five weeks ago, and they said I should go to
the School Certificate, cause they reckon I'd pass it but my parents
don't think I will, so I'll be leaving at the end of this year.

Here are children and teenagers who have learned what the
'good jobs' are, and who have picked, often with some im-
agination, ones that would suit their own interests; but who are
convinced, before they have really begun, that they are not able

to get them. Not able – that is the crunch. For in fact they would be able to manage these jobs, given half a chance. They were selected for the survey as being children of normal intelligence and school performance.[1] The trouble with them is not that they are subnormal, simply that they are working-class. They live in lower-status suburbs, their fathers are tradesmen, drivers, factory process workers, and so on. And their estimate of their chances of getting the 'good jobs' is deadly accurate.

By contrast, the common experience of children from upper-status homes, with fathers in business or in professional jobs, is of a fairly smooth progress through school, fairly open access to whatever kinds of jobs they want, and lots of personal encouragement to do well in school and beyond. As an extremely interesting survey of students in Melbourne has shown, it is the parents of high occupational status who do most to encourage their children to go to university.[2] And something of this came through in interviews I conducted with other children, this time from upper-status suburbs:

BOY, 12: Well, I'd like to – my mother wants me to go to the university, and I want to go myself, and I want to say be an engineer kind of, my mother thinks it's too hard, but my mother wants me to be a doctor, and I'm not that keen on that. I'd like to do something more exciting...my mother said an engineer gets one of the most salaries in the world.

GIRL, 15: I'd like to be a teacher, I think they do a lot better than some people do...I'd like to teach either primary or infants I'm not sure at the moment, I'd only have to go to Teacher's College. Dad wants me to go to uni. and get a Bachelor of Arts degree but I don't think I'm clever enough for that, I'd just rather become an ordinary primary or infants' teacher. I'm going in for a test on Friday to the Guidance Department for an interview about occupations and you have to name the three that you'd like to do. (*Which ones did you?*) I put teaching first, and then if I couldn't do that, I wouldn't mind being a child welfare officer or a social worker, cause I like children...

BOY, 16: I haven't really decided, I'd like to go into fifth and sixth form for a start, I get my School Certificate this year...I think I'd like architecture or draughtsman. (*What training do you need for that?*) Well an architect, Sydney Uni., I go to any university, and draughtsman I think university too, I haven't investigated this...

The atmosphere is quite different, and the expectations too. Even where the girl here suspects she is not clever enough to become a teacher, her alternatives are other semi-professional jobs. (Compare the working-class girl's alternatives of a shop or a factory.) The confidence these children have, and the support from their families, is obvious.

This was a small study; but the finding is by no means isolated. A series of much larger surveys, by Connell *et al.* (in Sydney, 1969), Taft (Victoria, 1967 and 1969), Edgar (Victoria, 1971–2), and Rosier (national, 1970),[3] all give evidence of higher educational expectations among teenagers from higher-status backgrounds, or in schools where the general level of social status is high.

To explore the reasons for this, and other relationships between class and personal socialization, requires the study of a good deal of survey research. It will be useful to comment first on the kinds of social distinctions typically recognized in the surveys. The commonest procedure, as noted in the discussion of recent sociology in Chapter 2, is to classify people by occupation. People are divided into groups (from two up to about seven, depending on the survey), according to the prestige and typical income of their type of job or the job of the 'breadwinner' (i.e. usually the husband/father). This gives an occupational scale which is used as a measure or index of position in the class structure, and which is often enough called 'class' or 'status' itself.

The commonest distinction recognised in these scales is that between white-collar (non-manual) workers and blue-collar (manual) workers. Broadly, this yields a distinction between those who do well out of the economy and those who don't; and between those who support the Liberal and those who support the Labor parties. Yet the distinction is blurred: for instance some skilled tradesmen (manual) get substantially higher incomes than some clerical workers (non-manual). Women's jobs do not fit this classification at all well: the routine typist-cum-office-dogsbody kind of job that in pay, training, interest, etc., is often nearer semi-skilled factory work than anything else among men, is still often classified as 'white-collar'. Yet where survey evidence is available only in this form, we must simply accept the manual/non-manual classification as a general estimate of prestige and wealth.

Other classifications make finer distinctions within the white-collar and blue-collar groups. For instance they commonly recognize a grouping something like 'owners and managers of companies, and professionals', as their top occupational category. People with these occupations are by far the largest owners of shares, have the highest incomes, occupy the top positions in the hierarchies of organisations, and are overwhelmingly supporters of the Liberal and Country Parties; though an occupational category cannot be equated with a class, this one certainly includes many of the consciously privileged. White-collar jobs below this level, owners of family businesses, semi-professions like teaching and nursing, lower administrative and clerical workers in private companies and public service, are variously classified in occupational scales. Most people here are employees, but some own small businesses or have small shareholdings. The general politics are conservative – these groups form the mass base of the Liberal Party – though employee status is recognized in the development of 'white-collar unions' and their occasional militancy, for instance in the teachers' strikes of the last decade.

'Skilled' workers are the top category usually recognized in the 'manual' section of occupational scales. This too is a diverse group, varying from self-employed tradesmen who are little distinct in most regards from owners of family businesses, to fully-unionized and militant employees in heavy industry. A majority supports the Labor Party, but the balance is close. Below them come semi-skilled workers (drivers, factory operatives) and unskilled (labourers), often lumped together in one bottom category. These are generally unionized and relatively low-paid workers, the traditional differences in wages within the 'manual' categories having been preserved by the system of 'margins for skill' in the awards of arbitration courts. There is a large majority of Labor Party supporters at this level, and their unions are, broadly speaking, the more class-conscious and militant ones. In some parts of the country there is a marked concentration of migrants in semi- and unskilled jobs.

The arbitration system and the country's full-employment policy are supposed to put a floor under the incomes even of these lowest occupational categories, and their families in general live without ease but in a permanent financial crisis. What the occupational classifications do not take account of is a further set of people who have fallen through this 'floor'. These are the semi-destitute elderly, civilian widows and deserted wives with children, families hit by illness, unemployment or injury, migratory workers, alcoholics, and of course those who never had a floor under them to start with, fringe-dwelling Aborigines. These people in no sense constitute a group with any organization or sense of solidarity, but they are numerically important estimates of their numbers in Australia, in the various 'poverty' studies, range up to half a million people. They usually do not appear in surveys.

The discussion which follows is mainly based on surveys that use a classification of this kind. Some also use a classification in terms of family income, or a measure of the wealth or prestige of the suburb a person lives in. These are not equivalent, but they are of course all related.

Success in school and access to jobs

I remarked earlier that the working-class children in the Sydney interviews were justified in their poor estimate of their chances of getting the 'good jobs' they wished for. There is massive proof that this is so.

At various points the school system selects from all its clients a smaller number to go on to 'higher' training, or to enter programmes which normally lead to higher training. The main means of selection are formal examinations and standardized tests of abilities and skills. There is extensive evidence that children from upper-status backgrounds do better in these paper contests than children of lower-status backgrounds. In a study of the records of high schools in Adelaide in the 1960s, Wiseman showed that children whose fathers had professional and managerial jobs did best in the Intermediate exam, while children whose fathers were unskilled workers did worst. A similar investigation of high schools in Geelong by Balson also found differences in exam performance, though not for all school subjects. A large national survey of mathematics skills among 13-year-olds in 1964 found scores on these tests correlated with father's occupation; and a large national survey of 14-year-olds in 1970 found a clear connection of father's occupation with science test scores. Keeves, in a survey of high school entrants in Canberra, found scores on both mathematics and science tests correlated with a measure of the 'structural dimension' of homes (compounded of fathers' and mothers' occupations, fathers' education, etc. – which rather confuses interpretation).[4] Taking the school rather than the individual as the unit of analysis, a study of Adelaide primary schools in 1967 found differences in reading skills between schools at the extremes of a 'socio-economic ranking' of the districts they drew on.[5] The only study which did not find a relationship with occupational background is that by Everett, on Newcastle candidates for the Higher School Certificate in 1969.[6] This may be due to the strongly working-class character of the area, or to the fact that the study deals with students right at the top of the school system, after a very severe selection has occurred (about 78% being already lost). Some details of other studies (Wiseman's, and the national mathematics study) also suggest status differences in performance have mostly washed out by the end of high school, no doubt under the influence of selective dropout.

Closely related to differences in test scores, though whether as cause or effect is hard to say, is the fact that children of different backgrounds are unequally distributed among streams within schools. The studies by Balson and Wiseman, the national mathematics survey, and a study in Western Australia by Wheeler,[7] all confirm that children of higher status backgrounds are more likely to get into the academic streams in high schools.

Before the children can even sit for their exams they have to get into a secondary school. In the past, secondary education was a privilege effectively confined to the children of the wealthy. The vast expansion of secondary education in the past generation has changed this. Practically all children now go to a secondary school – but not all to the same one. Within the state school system there are wide variations in the concentration of occupational groups in different schools, which result mainly from the regional bases of recruitment to schools and the social differentiation of regions within cities, but also, as a survey by Toomey suggests, from a tendency by parents of higher status to choose the more academic types of schools for their children. Wheeler's survey in Western Australia, and a massive study of Melbourne schools by Hunt, show the marked social differences that exist within the state systems; and it appears that the schools with the higher-status groups of parents have the better academic results.[8] There are also private schools, which cater for a minority of students – but a very distinctive minority. There is a modest tendency for Catholic schools to draw higher-status children than the state schools. There is a very immodest tendency for Protestant schools to do so. Surveys by Hunt in Victoria, Prince in Western Australia, Connell *et al.* in New South Wales, Blandy and Goldsworthy in South Australia, and Radford and Wilkes nationally, all give recent statistical proof of what is historically obvious, that these schools cater for an occupational and economic élite.[9] Hunt for instance reports that 94% of the students in Melbourne 'independent' (i.e. Protestant private) secondary schools came from white-collar backgrounds; Blandy and Goldsworthy report that average incomes in the South Australian examples are about *double* the average incomes of state school children's parents. The structure of the school system thus serves as a streaming system on a grand scale, which sorts children in very large measure on class criteria.

One of the most important consequences of different performances and backgrounds is that children leave school at different ages. There are five types of study that give evidence of a link between occupational background and staying on in school. Surveys of the population of high schools in a given year – e.g. Wheeler in Western Australia, Connell *et al.* in New South Wales, Blandy and Goldsworthy in South Australia, Choppin nationally – show that the occupational status of parents of upper-form pupils is (on average) higher than that for children in lower forms.[10] The inference is that a greater percentage of children from lower-status backgrounds have dropped out in between. Surveys of those *leaving* in a given year – Radford nationally in 1959–60, Taft in Victoria in the late 1960s – similarly show the leavers from upper forms to come from higher-status backgrounds or schools with a higher-status clientele.[11] Karmel *et al.* in South Australia, and Fisher *et al.* in Wollongong, show ecological correlations between the occupational composition of schools and their retention rates: for example, the 5th year retention rate for schools in the uppermost of the five status categories used in the Karmel report was 44%, and that for schools in the lowest was 17%. An analysis by the Schools Commission of data from the 1971 national census, covering teenagers in and out of the educational system, shows that those with fathers in upper occupational brackets are more likely to be in school or higher education at ages 16, 17 and 18.[12] Finally, studies which follow a 'cohort', i.e. a group of children entering in one year, through their school careers, give the most direct and dramatic demonstrations of earlier leaving by children of lower-status background. Wiseman divided a cohort in an Adelaide high school into four occupational-status groups: in the top group, 83% were still in school in their fourth year, 57% in their fifth year; in the three lower status groups, about 50% were still in school in fourth year, and about 20% in fifth. Moore *et al.* did the same for a sample of state school entrants across New South Wales, dividing them into three status groups (by a composite of father's occupation and parents' education): at the Grade 12 (Higher School Certificate) level, 76% of the top group were still in school, 41% of the middle group, and 15% of the lower group.[13]

Some people might have thought differences like these would be reduced by the award of government scholarships to the talented poor. They would be sadly wrong. The bulk of evidence (in the studies by Taft, Hunt, Blandy and Goldsworthy, and the Karmel report on South Australia) shows Commonwealth secondary scholarships going in higher proportions to the *upper* occupational groups. Hunt's very large survey of Melbourne shows this pattern in each year from 1964 to 1970, and not only that; the percentage going to schools of lower occupational background, low to start with, *fell* markedly through this period.[14] The working class, it seems, bore the brunt of a declining (relative to total school population) provision of government scholarships. How this will have been changed by the introduction of means-tested scholarships in the mid-1970s remains to be seen.

At the top of the educational tree, these gaps yawn wide indeed. The graceful prose of the Martin Committee distilled the situation as it was at the beginning of the 1960s:

Table 42 shows the data collected on 114,000 students of the estimated 145,000 who left Australian schools between 1st April 1959 and 31st March 1960. The 11 categories of 'father's occupation' shown in column A are indicative of socio-economic and related circumstances in the families of school leavers. It will be noticed that of the school leavers whose fathers were in the category 'unskilled or semi-skilled', and who totalled 33 per cent of the fathers of male leavers, only 1.5 per cent entered university. In contrast, only 2 per cent of the fathers of male school leavers were classified as 'university professionals' but 35.9 per cent of their sons entered university.[15]

The repeat of this survey by Radford and Wilkes in 1971–2 showed a very similar situation. Of the children of unskilled and semi-skilled workers who were leaving school, 3% of the boys and 2% of the girls went to university; of the children of professionals, 29% of boys and 21% of girls did so.[16] Studies of the intake in individual universities and states (Karmel *et al.* on Flinders University, Blandy and Goldsworthy on South Australian entrants; Dow *et al.* on Melbourne University, Gilchrist and Hammond on Victorian entrants; Dufty on the University of Western Australia) confirm this. The general picture is that about 50% of university entrants come from the professional and managerial backgrounds that account for around 15% of the workforce; and this pattern has remained very stable. As Dow *et al.* observe:

despite the increase in retention rates in secondary schools and in numbers of university undergraduates in Victoria during the 1960s, there has been virtually no change in the social composition of students entering the University of Melbourne.[17]

This is not to say that universities are the exclusive preserve of the ruling class. There has been an increased demand for technically-trained people for the professional and semi-professional occupations that the universities feed, and some bright working-class youth have been drawn in with the rest. And perhaps there are some institutions in Australia which are harder for working-class people to get into: the Melbourne Club and the Royal Sydney Yacht Squadron spring to mind. It remains true that the universities are powerfully class-biassed in their intake and output. The Colleges of Advanced Education which have multiplied in the last decade are less so, as Dufty in Western Australia and Champness and Taylor in Victoria have shown; but even here there is a distinct skew towards upper occupational groups.[18] Both types of institution can thus influence the inheritance of class position.

One 'inherits' class position in various senses. A child may ascriptively (i.e. without his or her own effort) acquire the status or prestige accorded the family as a whole, merely by choosing the right parents. This is most likely to be true of families in relatively stable and relatively small settlements, i.e. in the countryside, as Martin has suggested.[19] In the cities, things are more impersonal; and there are some forces that act across the whole social structure. In a class structure based on property, one can inherit property, and with it a claim to the benefits and privileges available to money. This is a means of transmission quite independent of personality and the process of personal socialization. But there are other kinds of entitlements to privilege and other ways of getting money that are related to personal socialization. If these too can be made to depend on the class position of the older generation, they will also lead to the inheritance of class position by the younger. Among the vast majority of Australians who are not property-owners on a large scale – i.e. not owners of property one could live off – this revolves around access to jobs (entitlements to money) and qualifications (entitlements to jobs).

That the chances of getting higher educational qualifications are related to differences in the occupational position of parents, we have just seen. We can follow these differences back into the occupational world in surveys of teenagers who have just left school. The two very large national surveys by Radford in 1959–60 and Radford and Wilkes in 1971–2, each covering more than a hundred thousand school leavers, found sharp differences in occupational destination. In the first survey, among the sons of unskilled or semi-skilled manual workers, about 50% had gone directly into manual jobs; less than 2% had gone to university and hence might be bound for the professions. Among the sons of professionals and managers, about 10% had gone into manual jobs, but about 30% had gone on to university. The pattern in the second survey was similar. In the second survey fewer girls went directly into 'home duties', but class bias in the types of jobs they got persisted. The 1970 survey in Sydney by Connell *et al.* found similar patterns among teenagers who had recently left school: working-class boys concentrated in apprenticeships and manual jobs, working-class girls in shops and secretarial jobs rather than the semi-professions.

There seems to be no Australian research which follows a cohort of school leavers through their first jobs and along the line of their occupational lives. But there are surveys of the adult population from which the pattern can be reconstructed retrospectively, which compare adults' present jobs, incomes, etc., with their parents' jobs, education, etc. These are commonly called 'social mobility' studies – equivalent to a study of the inheritance of social position with the assumptions reversed – and though there are traps in interpreting them they can yield useful information. There are of course good reasons why peoples' jobs, incomes, etc., should not match their parents'. People get promoted, demoted and sacked, they move or decide to try something new. Quite apart from this, the types of jobs available to one generation differ from those available to the next. Some jobs disappear or shrink (e.g. housemaids, coachbuilders, corset makers), and some new jobs appear as civilization progresses (computer punch operators, disc jockeys, security police). Nevertheless the surveys do show a general correspondence between the type of job a man has and the job his father had (the information is lacking for women). The most important of these studies is a 1965 national survey reported by Broom and Jones. Of men in this survey who said their fathers had white-collar jobs, 60% themselves had white-collar jobs, 35% blue-collar; while among men who said their fathers were blue-collar workers, 31% had white-collar jobs and 65% blue-collar.[20]

There are various ways in which occupational inheritance can occur. It can follow from a literal inheritance of the basis of the trade, for instance a farm – it is notable that farmers and graziers have a relatively high level of occupational inheritance. It can follow from a direct stimulation of the child's interest and skills in the trade. The most important example of this is girls' early training for the trade of housewife, which is normally carefully undertaken by their mothers. Among boys in suburban settings this is more difficult, as fathers usually work away from the home; but some types of male jobs can be observed by boys, and again it is notable that occupational inheritance is relatively high in two types of occupation where this kind of contact is easy, farmers and craftsmen. Finally, occupation or occupational level can be 'inherited' via qualifications, and these are most formally specified in crafts (via apprenticeship and certification) and professions (via higher education and certification). The sons of professional men and managers are markedly concentrated in similar types of jobs; among some élite groups, such as doctors, occupational inheritance is very high indeed.[21]

There is certainly not exact correspondence between the

generations; there is mobility, possibly more in Australia than in some other capitalist countries. Yet even mobility, according to an ingenious three-generation study by Allingham, is affected by social background, the children of downwardly-mobile parents being more likely to be upwardly mobile than their peers.[22] It is clear that there are occupational-inheritance effects that reach out over the adult life-span affecting the general occupational level entered, sometimes the specific occupation; and it seems that the class-biassed filtering that occurs in the education system is an important reason for this. Why then does this filtering occur?

'Brains', intelligence and language

The working-class children themselves have an explanation; they haven't got the brains. This is well worth examining. The idea of 'having the brains' or 'being brainy' is almost universal among Australian schoolchildren. It is their basic explanation of success and failure in the procession of tests that the school system confronts them with. 'Brains' are understood as a fixed quality of the person: you either have them, or you don't. If you have the brains, you can do well in exams. You will not necessarily do well, as you can 'have the brains' but 'not do the work'; but often enough having the brains will make up for being lazy anyway. If you don't have the brains, you can't do well.

The idea of 'brains' thus serves as an ego-protector for the children – necessarily the majority – who do not come out on top in tests. The examination system implicitly locates the reason for success or failure in the person, in the individual child; the idea of 'brains' accepts this but takes the sting out of it. You can't blame a child for doing poorly if he or she didn't have the brains to do better. In constructing this interpretation the children are of course drawing on the general culture: the 'brain' is a recognised social type, celebrated in the ever-popular television and radio quiz shows. But its force comes straight from their intimate environment in the schools. Australian education for generations has been riddled with competitive examination to a really extraordinary extent. Constant pressure is put on school children to perform well in them. And there is no doubt that (however much psychologists may question them) the exams are accepted as valid tests by the children.

163

Table 5. Studies of the relationship between social status and intelligence

Study	Date	Sample	Measure of intelligence	Measure of class position	Finding
Collins, 1950	1947	2758 10-year-olds, Tasmania	Unspecified group test	Father's occupation divided into 5 groups (farmers excluded)	**Occupational group** I II III IV V 62 56 53 50 41 Mean score
Middleton, 1954	1949	128 6th grade boys and girls ages 10–13, Melbourne	Otis Intermediate	Father's occupation	'Significantly related to class of origin' for boys, but not for girls
Porcheron, 1955	1953	267 4th grade children, Sydney	ACER Junior B verbal group test	Combination of father's occupation and suburb of home	**Status group** I II III 36 29 26 Mean score
Hammond and Cox, 1967	1957	519 boys aged 10–11, Melbourne	ACER Junior non-verbal; verbal classification test	Social class factor in factor analysis of various measures	Verbal classification test loads +0.27 on social class factor. Non-verbal tests not reported, but evidently load less than 0.20, if at all
Balson, 1965	1964	177 Form 3 boys and girls, Geelong	Otis Higher A verbal group test	Father's occupation	'Intelligence test scores significantly favoured children of parents in the upper occupational levels'

Wiseman, 1967

			Father's occupation divided into 4 groups	Occupational group			
				I	II	III	IV
1961	188 Form 1 boys and girls	Unspecified group test		Mean IQ 120	110	113	107
1966	473 Form 1 boys and girls	Unspecified group test		Mean IQ 116	111	111	108
1967	612 Forms 1–5 boys and girls, Adelaide	Unspecified group test		Mean IQ 115	110	110	106

Connell et al., 1975

1969	C. 2000 secondary school boys and girls, Sydney	Otis Higher B verbal group tests	(a) District classified by drop-out rate	'Different levels of measured intelligence are associated with both parental occupation and living area in Sydney'
			(b) Father's occupation divided into 6 groups	Occupation and intelligence $r = 0.32$ in subsample of 13–14-year-olds

Blandy and Goldsworthy, 1975

			Father's occupation divided into 4 groups	Occupational group	
				I	II
1970	3805 Form 3, 4, 5 boys and girls, Adelaide	School records – unspecified group tests	(a) Father' occupation	Mean IQ 114	107 (3rd year)
				118	115 (5th year)
			(b) Family income	'The fathers and parents of the high IQ children tend to be wealthier, on average, than the fathers and parents of the low IQ children'	

165

Failure forces them to doubt their own powers; repeated failure
convinces them they don't have the brains. And failure is the
common experience of lower-status children. The convictions
about their poor occupational chances stem from their actual
experience of school life, and what they understand as objective facts about themselves. There is no need to bring in heroes
and villains among teachers and parents to explain class
differences in self-confidence and occupational choice among
the children. Given the present institutional setting, their own
experience will do the job.

The children's ideas about brains can be seen as a defensive,
ego-protecting interpretation of reality – an ideology, in a
simple form. This is not to say that they are wrong. After
all, many teachers have the same idea, though they call it
'intelligence'.[23] What is the actual relationship between social
class and basic ability?

It is plain at the outset that there is a close link between
general intelligence (as measured by conventional intelligence
tests) and success in examinations.[24] The connection is not
quite perfect, but it is indeed very close. Further, there is
conclusive evidence, from a number of surveys, that class
background is correlated with intelligence among Australian
children. This is an important point, so I will document it in
detail. Since the 1940s a number of surveys have been done
using measures of status and standard intelligence tests. They
are abstracted in Table 5.[25] It is abundantly apparent from them
that children from upper-status homes, on average, score
higher on conventional group tests of verbal intelligence than
children from lower-status homes. There can be no argument
about the fact.

There can be argument, however, about its meaning. Have
we succeeded in explaining the class differences in 'achievement' by finding class differences in basic ability? The answer
to this I believe is no, or at least not yet, and not by means
of the conventional intelligence tests used in these studies.
For these group verbal intelligence tests are not making a
separate kind of measurement of some underlying ability that
influences examination performance. They are making essentially the same kind of measurement as the examinations themselves. The 'intelligence' measured by these tests is a general
measure of the ability to take this kind of test; in essence, an

index of probable exam performance with accidents of curriculum and teaching ruled out.

Where does this test-taking ability come from and how do class differences in it arise? This is an extraordinarily complex problem, which has been the subject of a great deal of dispute, and rather less solid research, in a number of Western countries. An influential school argues that IQ is largely genetically determined; an equally influential school argues that it is not; and some daring souls have suggested that the question is insoluble. Both the technical and political sides of this argument have become too complex to thrash out here. I will simply record my opinion that the hereditarians have had rather the worse of the argument; that as Kamin argues, it can even be considered that 'There exist no data which should lead a prudent man [or woman – RWC] to accept the hypothesis that I.Q. test scores are in any degree heritable.'[26] At the least we may assume that the conditions in which children grow up have an important bearing on the matter. This can be argued on purely logical grounds: IQ is not a thing, it is a standardized description of certain acts, and these acts necessarily have reference to, and take their meaning from, a social situation. And it can be argued, if more cautiously, on experimental grounds: such as the findings of Lemercier and Teasdale in a small study of the impact of 'Sesame Street' on the cognitive skills of working-class children, and those of Gilchrist and Hammond on the circumstances connected with a rise in relative standing on intelligence tests over the high school years.[27]

One of the most influential hypotheses about the way the social situation of children is linked to cognitive capacities and school performance, developed by Bernstein in England, holds that characteristic patterns of interaction in the families of working-class and middle-class children lead to differences in the structure of their language.[28] Specifically, working-class children are thought to develop a restricted speech code and middle-class children an elaborated code; the latter is closer to the language of school instruction, and develops skills (e.g. of abstraction) that are drawn upon in school testing. This is an attractive hypothesis, which has been accepted as true of the local situation by some Australian educators[29] – though it has come in for criticism abroad. What is the local evidence?

Two studies of young children, by Gunn and Teasdale, report

167

class differences in linguistic skills. Teasdale's study of children aged about 5, using a standard test of psycholinguistic abilities, suggestively finds that the audio-vocal subtests were more closely related to the children's social background than the visual-motor subtests, and this points in the direction of the speech patterns hypothesized by Bernstein. But these studies do not address the core of the theory, which is about the structure of utterances. An ingenious study of university students by Poole, comparing utterances of students from working-class and middle-class backgrounds, is more relevant, and some of the predicted differences do show up, though they are not very marked and many of the tests show no difference.[30] This of course might result from the social selection in university entrance. The most pertinent Australian research on the problem comes to a stronger conclusion. In a carefully-designed study of high school students, Owens tested for the syntactic differences predicted by Bernstein's theory, and concluded:

In general, these predicted differences were *not* found, thus raising numerous questions about the sufficiency of the theorizing about 'elaborated' and 'restricted' language codes and their socio-economic bases. Overall, given a writing task with explicit directions and clear structure, pupils with low socio-economic backgrounds responded with syntax indistinguishable from that of pupils with high socio-economic backgrounds.[31]

This is not a large body of evidence, and no doubt more will become available. But so far as it takes us at the moment, we cannot rely on differences in language structure to explain the class patterns in intelligence testing and school success.

Let us come back to the concept of intelligence itself. IQ testing treats 'intelligence' simply as a dimension (or set of dimensions) of differences between people. The dimension is taken to represent some underlying trait, and it is more or less assumed that the character of this trait and the extent of differences are much the same at different ages. The approach to intelligence taken by Piaget is rather different: there are supposed to be differences in the nature of intellectual activities at successive stages of growth; everyone (barring a small minority of the 'mentally defective') goes through much the same stages of development and arrives, or in principle could arrive, at much the same intellectual powers at the end. But some children certainly go through the course at a faster pace; and it is plausible to suggest that the initial acceleration might be produced by a richer and more stimulating early environment. Given that the children, in the context of Australian schools, are subjected to repeated competitive testing, those who develop faster are going to be classified as 'better' by the tests at any one intermediate age. Hence they are likely to be put in academic streams, given more encouragement and recognition, etc.; and what was originally just a difference in pace may be converted into a real difference in final achievement.

This is speculation; plainly, a crucial question is whether there are in fact social class differences in the pace with which children move through Piaget's stages. I know of only two Australian studies giving evidence on this. The larger is the Sydney study of teenagers by Connell *et al.*, which used a written test of the achievement of formal thought, the last of Piaget's stages. This measure is indeed related to father's occupation and district for the 13–14 age group; more of the children from upper status backgrounds have reached the level of formal thought. (The relationship weakens in the older age-groups, as might be expected from selective dropout.) The smaller study, of 6 to 10 year old children by de Lacey, has better measures as it used individual rather than group tests, in this case tests of classificatory ability. De Lacey too found significant differences between white children of high and low occupational status.[32] This does not amount to a large body of research, but it makes a pace-of-development argument at least plausible.

This argument, however, assumes that test-taking skill depends on some more general intellectual qualities, at least in the early stages of schooling. And this need not be true. It is possible that test-taking involves a rather specific skill without much connection with other spheres of life – except the connection that the school system itself builds in. Two Australian surveys, by Taft and Dewing, have looked for a relationship between examination success and 'creativity', and found none.[33] The question would then become, why upper-status children on the whole specialize in this kind of skill while lower-status children on the whole do not.

Values and material conditions

The explanation often given is that working-class children are 'culturally deprived', or at least culturally different in ways that affect their schooling. There is a good deal of rather woolly writing on this subject, which suggests that working-class families are different in language, in aspirations and motivation, in 'norms' concerned with educational success and getting on in the world, etc.; all of which make working-class homes less 'educationally supportive' than middle-class homes[34] – given, of course, a middle-class education system. In an earlier version of this chapter I suggested that this argument, for all its popularity, was wrong; that what Australian evidence there was, ran against the view that 'different classes hold different values which could account for different achievement levels'; and hence one should look to the material conditions of life at different class levels as the crucial explanation of educational differences. A detailed criticism of this argument has been offered by Toomey, who raises objections to the view that income is an important direct determinant of success in school, and suggests that the 'style of life' of families – understood mainly as the attitudes and behaviour of parents, their level of education, etc. – is the crucial influence.[35] This approaches, though it does not fully adopt, the view that there are different class cultures which influence educational outcomes.

We have already seen that the evidence for class differences in language structure in Australia is not persuasive – if there are such differences, they are not sufficiently marked to show up in the most careful research that has been done. What of differences in attitudes and values relevant to education – the 'norms' that are supposed by some to be more easily accepted by middle-class children, to explain differences in occupational expectations, etc.? There is now a moderate amount of Australian survey research on this. It has to be treated with care, as the measures used in some of the surveys are technically fairly weak – for instance in the study by Katz which is often cited as evidence for class differences in values – and the measures of class position are sometimes confused. It is also rather important to distinguish between attitude studies of different generations. The results of these surveys are shown in Table 6, for school pupils, and Table 7, for adults.[36]

The results abstracted in Table 6 are broadly consistent with the view argued before: there are not marked differences in children's attitude to education according to occupational background. Rosier's study seems to provide the strongest opposition; but he reports only an ecological correlation, which is not directly comparable, and includes things like the number of books in the home in his measure of home background, a point which will be taken up below. On the whole, the differences that do occur are mostly small and not always consistent in direction. Put the other way around, we can say that children from different status groups show much the same range of values connected with education, show on average similar attitudes to their schooling. There are certainly no signs of differences that are powerful and pervasive enough to account for the marked differences in educational outcomes that we know occur.

What then of attitudes in the older generation – the parents and other adults whose pushing and persuasion might have this effect regardless of the children's views? In Table 7 there is rather more evidence of differences – not completely consistent, but still rather stronger. There are however real difficulties in interpreting this evidence. The strongest support for the idea of status differences in attitudes comes from the studies by Toomey and Keeves. Keeves' measure of status is a composite one, which is not easy to interpret. Both Toomey and Keeves include questions on the educational *hopes and expectations* of parents in their measures of attitudes. People may realistically have different hopes and expectations for children's educational success regardless of the *value* they place on it. This is clearly shown by Connell *et al.*, who found a stronger correlation of father's occupation with teenagers' expectations of staying in school ($r = 0.33$) than with their liking for school or beliefs about its relevance. The same point is made in the survey of adults by Vinson and Robinson. Their evidence of status differences in expressed desire for higher education for children, confirmed by Parsler, is clear enough. But this still cannot be directly interpreted as evidence of 'difference in the belief in the *value* of higher education' (to quote Parsler – my italics); given the other things besides values, e.g. considerations of cost, that might enter such a judgment. The most direct study of values among adults, by Feather, finds few differences

Table 6. Studies of the relationship between social status and attitudes to success and education among school pupils

Study	Date	Sample	Measure of attitude	Measure of class position	Finding
Cox, 1962 Hammond and Cox, 1967	1957	C. 400 boys aged 10–11, Melbourne	(a) Projective test of need achievement (b) Projective test of success orientation	Social class factor in factor analysis of various measures	(a) No relationship (b) No relationship ($r < 0.20$, hence not reported)
Katz, 1964	?	819 boys and girls aged 14–16, NSW	(a) Question on what defines success (b) Question on how success is achieved	Father's occupation, 3-fold classification	(a) No differences in mentions of wealth, personality, security, family; upper status group mention status more often (b) Majority of all groups say 'hard work'; upper status boys more often; inconsistent pattern among girls
Keeves, 1972	1969	C. 230 Grade 6 boys and girls, Canberra	(a) Liking for school scale (b) Liking for maths scale (c) Liking for science scale (d) Academic motivation scale	Composite measure including parents' occupations, father's education, religion, size of family	(a) $r \leqslant 0.13$, n.s. (b) $r \leqslant 0.13$, n.s. (c) $r = 0.15$ (d) $r \leqslant 0.13$, n.s.

Connell *et al.* 1975	1969	C. 600 boys and girls aged 13–14 with Australian-born parents, Sydney	(a) 'Dislike for school' scale (b) 'Relevance of education' scale	Father's occupation, 6-fold classification	(a) $r = -0.19$ (b) $r = 0.16$
Rosier, 1973	1970	5243 14-year-olds, national	Attitude to science	Composite measure of father's occupation, parents' education, etc.	Ecological correlation across schools = 0.43
Maddock, 1975	?	345 high school students, Adelaide	'Orientation to learning' scale	Father's occupation	No correlation
Edgar, 1974	1971–1972	1214 high school students, Victoria	(a) Question on competence: mention academic competence (b) Desire to stay at school (c) Ideal aspirations for higher education	Father's occupation, ANU 6-fold classification	(a) Significant relationship: upper status higher (b) Curvilinear (c) Significant relationship: upper status higher

Table 7. Studies of the relationship between social status and attitudes to success and education, among adults

Study	Date	Sample	Measure of attitude	Measure of class position	Finding
Toomey, 1968	1964	1042 Parents of entering high-school students	(a) Preference for certain type of high school regardless of proximity (b) Aspirations for children and preference for academic-type subjects (c) Tendency to discriminate school types according to children's ability	Property values in area of school	(a) Non-manual stronger (b) Non-manual higher (c) Non-linear pattern
Vinson and Robinson, 1968	1967	1455 adults, Sydney and Melbourne	(a) Stress education in advising child about future	Occupation, 6 groups based on Congalton	(a) No trend

Author	Date	Sample	Measure	Class index	Finding
Parsler, 1971	1967	621 adults, Melbourne	(b) Mention education as means of mobility (c) Desire higher education for children	Occupation, 3 groups	(b) No trend (c) Monotonic positive relationship
			Level to which they 'would like' or ' would have liked' their children to continue education	Occupation, 3 groups	Upper groups more often nominate post-secondary, for both boys and girls
Keeves, 1972	1968	C. 230 mothers and fathers, Canberra	Rating scales of attitudes to child's education	Composite measure, as above	Mothers: $r = 0.39$ Fathers: $r = 0.46$
Feather, 1975	1972 1973	(a) 587 adults (b) 667 adults, Adelaide	Rokeach Value Survey: relative stress placed on 18 terminal and 18 instrumental values	Income	Most values show no differences – including being 'self-controlled' and 'ambitious'. However 'sense of accomplishment', one of few that show higher-income groups consistently higher

between income groups; and the value placed on 'ambition' is not one of them.

On the available evidence, then, we may infer that there are status differences in educational expectations and hopes or wishes, but not on educationally-relevant values or attitudes in the strict sense. This is not a matter for surprise, as studies of attitudes on other topics have generally found few relationships, or only modest ones, with occupation.[37] But this leaves us more or less where we began. How are the differences in hopes and expectations produced?

A partial answer is suggested by the difficulty that occurred in interpreting Rosier's study, that his measure of home background included, along with father's occupation, items on the parents' education and books in the home. Toomey has rightly pointed out that parents' level of education has widely been found to correlate with children's success in school, and this includes the education of non-employed mothers. It is a plausible inference that a child's specializing in the kind of intellectual performance fostered and tested by the schools will be aided by having adults around who have themselves had some success at it, who can show how to do it. Such adults are of course commoner in upper-income and upper-occupation homes.[38] Here we are on the territory of the differences in behaviour that are the second component of Toomey's suggested differences in 'lifestyle'.

Is it the case that parents of different status levels, who (on average) hold different expectations for their children, do offer different levels of support for it? The main evidence on this comes from two studies of teenagers, in Sydney and in Victoria; and unfortunately they contradict each other. The Sydney survey by Connell *et al.* finds no substantial differences between status groups in the extent of parents' reported help with homework, the slight differences if anything favouring the lowest. Similarly, there are no substantial differences in the teenagers' expressed desire for guidance from parents about schooling. Edgar, however, reports from his Victorian study occupational differences in the tendency to use fathers as an aid on homework (though there are some inconsistencies here), the amount of praise offered by parents (but not in perceptions of the parents' desire for the child to stay in school), and in their use of more intellectual types of reading matter and encouragement of discussion in the family. The measures used in these two studies, particularly the former, are fairly crude, and a real understanding of the matter will need a rather different, closer-up, method of research. It is possible, but not certain, that there is a kind of tradition of educational practice handed down within many families, which presumably originated a couple of generations ago when mass education systems were being constructed, and which must be largely independent of the general attitude to education spread across the population.

Some of the things that parents can do are of course related to their wealth, such as buying a house that is big enough for the school child to have that staple of advice on 'How to Study', a separate room for the student. The Sydney survey did find systematic differences here: among 13–14 year olds, for instance, the numbers with a room of their own ranged from 41% in girls from state and Catholic schools in the lowest of three status categories (41% also for boys), to 56% in the uppermost category (54% for boys), and 80% among Protestant private school girls (77% for boys). Reports from social welfare agencies, such as O'Neill and Paterson's *The Cost of Free Education*, show the difficulty that the poorest families have in providing such basic materials as school books and equipment and adequate clothing. Schools in some low-income districts, such as run-down inner-city areas, are notoriously badly off in terms of adequate buildings, space and equipment – a point that is now fairly well recognized, but remains the subject of teachers' protests.[39] Under the system, which has been widespread, where school equipment has been financed by parents' contributions and government grants proportional to what is raised locally, differences in the wealth of districts are likely to be reinforced. The Karmel committee looked into the incomes of primary schools in Adelaide, and found those in the lowest-status areas depressed below the general level. The contrast with the profusion of equipment, facilities and space in the wealthier private schools, as described for instance by Smolicz, is marked.[40] It is debatable how far differences in parents' purchasing power are converted into differences in educational environment in schools across the middle of the spectrum of income; but there can be little doubt about the impact at the two extremes. How far the 'needs' policy in funding schools adopted by the Labour government – bitterly opposed by sections of the ruling class at the time of its introduction – has gone towards changing this, remains to be seen.

We seem to have come out of this extended review of evidence with a fairly meagre haul of positive conclusions. There are class differences in educational success, and in expectations of it, in the cognitive skills making for it, and in some of the equipment useful for it; but not, it seems from the principal evidence, in the language structures or attitudes that have often been thought to underlie it.

Social hierarchy, alienation, and the pattern of values

So far this chapter has discussed differences among children that can be traced back to the social positions of their families. This is the most obvious influence that class structure has on personal growth, but not the only one, nor even necessarily the most important. All such differences in personal socialization could be wiped out, and the class system would still roll on. The reason can be found by analysing the similarities among Australian children and youth that derive from the class system.

A clear example of this is the shared beliefs that children hold about the class structure and social hierarchy itself. This was explored in Chapter 7, where it was seen that there are no marked differences between children of different social backgrounds in the development of such ideas as the scale of occupations. The 'good jobs' that the working-class youngsters discussed earlier have in mind, are very much the jobs their upper-status agemates would like. A general agreement was found in earlier studies of Australian children's judgments of the status of occupations, by Middleton, Taft and Dufty. In this the children match their elders. There appears to be a broad consensus among adults from different social classes about what are the most and the least desirable jobs.[41] Both adults' and children's judgments of course reflect actual differences between types of jobs in wage rates, qualifications, and opportunities to command.

Conventional scales of occupational prestige, even measures of income, are simplified abstractions from a context. They are useful for some summary purposes, but if we want to understand their whys and wherefores we must go back to the context from which they were taken, the structure of relationships among people engaged in work. Within a capitalist social order this structure centres on the relationship of employer to employee, and the power of the employer to direct the activity of the employee. Given the techniques of mass production and distribution, and modern methods of communication, this power can be extended over large numbers of people at once, indeed has to be. As firms grow in size, they come to adopt bureaucratic structures where the personal power of control is crystallized into regular rules of conduct and formal hierarchies of command. In these respects the relationships inside privately-owned companies converge with those inside government departments.

What is important for an analysis of socialisation is the way these general features of the structure affect the individual job and its performance. The job, in such a system, becomes something which is externally defined. Rules of procedure are laid down to be followed, instructions come down from hierarchical superiors, work comes in channels from other points in the organization. The pattern is often analysed in terms of role theory. It is mistaken to think, as some role-theorists do, that roles are governed by sets of norms which lay down the actions that are to be performed. That can be true only for the most mechanical of performances. Most sanctioned performances (or roles) are governed rather by *criteria* which must be met by action as each new situation arises and each new task is performed. And in privately-owned industry the criteria to be met are essentially alien to the person who has to meet them. They are laid down without his or her participation, in the service of goals such as corporate growth and profit that have no reference to him or her except as a means. The ultimate criteria may in fact be unknown, except in the most shadowy sense, to the worker.

In Australia, this alienated structure of performance derives from the historic fact of imported capitalism; its ideological underpinning is paradoxically a doctrine of individualism. The way in which people are trained for this kind of working life is plainly very important, and the mass education system would seem to be central to the process. It has been said in joke that we should not carry the reform of education too far, or schools will no longer prepare children properly for the boredom of adult life. The point of the joke applies even where the adult reality is not boredom, but more subtle forms of alienation. The day-to-day round of classroom life is different in content, but in form is a model for the most important features of life at work. As D'Urso has recently argued, in a forceful statement of what is now a widespread criticism of schools,

Contrary to popular belief, it has been argued, the primary function of schooling is a latent one. It is not the cultivation of cognitive abilities which, 'objectively assessed', determines the adequacy of school-leavers to perform a variety of jobs in industry, business or public service. Instead, the experience of schooling within a bureau-cratic system shapes the personalities of the young as future job holders within a mass-technocratic society. The 'hidden curriculum' of the school leads the young to internalise such norms as the hier-archical disposition of power and acquiescence in one's own power-lessness, compliance with authority, job fragmentation and extrinsic job motivation, external direction and evaluation of one's work and worth.[42]

This is stated in very general terms, and there are points one could disagree with, such as the idea that 'norms' of com-pliance are thoroughly internalized – what research we have on high schools suggests that the characteristic attitude of the pupils is rather cooler and more sceptical than this might suggest, and they stress autonomy more than conformity in their value judgments.[43] But it is certainly true that they are trained in the *practice* of compliance, whether they like it or not; and I think D'Urso is generally correct in his view of the effects of the characteristic patterns of social relations in formal education. We simply lack, in Australia, the close-up portraits of schools as social units which would give more insight into the processes involved and the forces that sustain them.

The class structure does not exist, and probably could not long exist, as a system of naked power. It is based on a system of property rights, and these are much more readily enforcible if they are widely believed to be legitimate. Common beliefs surrounding the subject of private ownership are thus important to the stability of the class structure. If a system of mass belief compatible with private ownership is successfully maintained, the bases of ruling-class power are effectively unassailable. If important divisions appear in mass beliefs concerning these issues, the class structure is in danger: and if a cleavage of opinion on this issue comes to match the divison of society along the lines of class position, a good old-fashioned socialist revolution is in train.

What can we say about the formation of mass beliefs in this area? Issues of such weight require strong direct evidence to determine, and that is lacking. But there are several studies which have some bearing, and it is possible to form an opinion on two important issues.

The first is the question of consensus and cleavage. For technical reasons the conventional survey methods of opinion and value measurement make it difficult to test the presence of consensus *per se*. But they readily allow a test of whether the division of opinion that does exist is related to class position. And the general trend of results suggests that it is not. We have already seen that there are only minor differences between children of different backgrounds in their estimation of jobs, in desire for success or conceptions of it. My interviews with Sydney children found no class differences in attitudes to inequality, nor even (surprisingly) in self-classing or class schemes, i.e. ideas of what the classes are. Some further evidence on self-classing has shown that group differences do emerge in the later teenage years, with working-class identifications more common among early leavers and signs of upper-status consciousness in the Protestant private schools.[44] This however is as far as it goes; there are no signs of major class differences among teenagers in attitudes bearing on the class structure. Unfortunately none of the available research bears on the issue of private property.

The second point follows on from this very imperfect indication of consensus, or lack of class-patterned dissensus. What *are* the dominant values among youth? A survey of adolescents and young adults by a market research firm in Victoria, asking what was liked and disliked about jobs, elicited answers overwhelmingly often in terms of the advantages to the individual person. (Compare the older children's ideas of a 'good job' in the interviews at the start of this chapter, and contrast the younger children's ideas.) Open-ended questions asked by Wheeler about what adolescents would most like in life, what they would wish for, elicited answers mainly for private fulfilment. Little's sensitive interview study of university students in Melbourne agrees with results from a group of adults in South

Australia in finding a value-pattern centring around individual, personal realisation or development. A poll-type study of values in Queensland secondary schools remarks on the prevalence of individualistic values making for success in the urban middle-class life for which the students are heading.[45] It is amusing to see that Katz's study, which could have given important information on the issue – asking what a sample of adolescents understood by success – already pre-judged the issue of individualism. The key question was phrased: 'Is there anybody that you actually know who has done well *for himself?*' (my italics), and the study naturally got private-benefit answers to the following question: 'What makes you say that he has done well?'

The common drift in these scattered findings is clear: by adolescence a commitment has developed to private goals and private fulfilments rather than collective ones. At the least, the private goals are nearer the surface and more accessible to common research techniques. But a more recent and systematic analysis of young people's personal values, with a more sophisticated method, qualifies this picture. The questionnaire designed by Stroobant distinguishes things valued from the criteria on which the valuing judgments are based; and shows for instance that criteria of personal autonomy and reciprocity with other people affect the value placed on such things as affection and the self. The general picture is still one of a generation whose concerns are mainly personal – interestingly this concern is stronger among those who have left school and have experience of work – but there is rather more suggestion of idealism in value judgments than the earlier surveys had shown.[46]

We have, then, some rather contradictory implications about the relationship of personal values to the class structure. The tendency to individualism and the focussing of concerns on private life are plainly compatible with the continuation of a class structure based on private property and relying on the absence of organized mass resistance. So is the widespread acceptance of a 'gospel of work' noted in Chapter 7. But the concern for autonomy, and the person-centredness of youth that comes through in the recent values research, are in some tension with the demands of mass production and the character of alienated labour. It seems that there might be a base for opposition and resistance here. But apart from a minority who have experimented with counter-cultural forms of life, the opposition remains latent. Youth in jobs are poor unionists: their rate of union membership is well below that of the adult workforce, and they show no great enthusiasm for the union principle of the right to strike.[47]

Class and personal socialization: theoretical reflections

A class structure is not a thing, a static object or system of categories. Class is a kind of event, occurring in history; a class structure is created, and changes through historical time. To persist, it must in some way be reproduced from day to day and generation to generation. The process of its reproduction is one of the critical points where change may emerge.

There are two kinds of 'reproduction' which must be distinguished, corresponding firstly to processes which distribute people among positions in the class structure, and secondly (and more fundamentally) to processes by which a structure of positions and relations among them is maintained in its everyday working. 'Occupational inheritance' and 'social mobility' are concepts that refer to the first of these forms of reproduction, presupposing the second. The concept of the 'reproduction of the relations of production' in Marxist theory refers to the second, and is independent of the first. There can be stability or change in one without the other. The ascendancy of particular families can survive changes in the structure within which that ascendancy occurs: see for instance the history of the Churchills in England over the last few centuries; or, less dramatically, the Macarthur-Onslows in Australia. Conversely a structure can persist despite the circulation of families from generation to generation within it, or indeed the rise of 'new men' within a lifetime. This is important to note because evidence of inter-generational mobility has sometimes been taken to be evidence of the absence or weakness of a class structure, or evidence of egalitarianism, which it emphatically is not.[48] It remains true that changes in the structure of relations have commonly coincided with the rise of new families to power, as shown for instance in the rise of new groups of capitalists in the recent period of industrialization in Australia.

Personal socialization has a part to play in both processes; but in neither case is the relationship simple. To the main-

tenance of the pattern of distribution of families across positions in the class structure, it contributes the differences in
'educational achievement' and 'occupational attainment' that
were documented earlier in this chapter. How are we to understand this pattern? – given that explanations in terms of
differences in values and attitudes and the structure of language
do not seem to be supported by the Australian evidence.

It is necessary to go back to some more general considerations about class and education, and some of the complexities
of class structure that were passed over before. The fundamental feature of class structure under capitalism, the existence
of a labour market organized by a system of private property,
can be thought of as having both remote and direct links with
the pattern of educational inequality. The remote links are
through the formation of a particular occupational structure
within this class framework. This is a very complex process,
and only the outlines of an analysis can be suggested here. With
the growth of industrial capitalism some historic features of the
European (and colonial) social order are reshaped. A form of
the state arises which is committed to the interests of the
owners of capital and provides both technical–economic and
ideological services for them. The occupations of the people
change with the advance of industrial production and its
increasing need for large-scale organization and 'tertiary'
services. Occupational groups become differentiated – among
other ways – in their relationship to the state and to the internally similar large-scale organizations that characterize mature
capitalist production. Administrative and professional groups
in particular come to have very close links with the higher-level
operations of these organisations.

One of the most important of the activities of the capitalist
state is the creation of a large-scale system of formal education.
The education system itself is not simple. The respectable and
propertied in the nineteenth century created their own schools
for the transmission of a literary culture and genteel manners
along with a dose of religion, and these have persisted. Mass
state education was introduced for a number of reasons – social
control, the raising of productivity by making the workforce
literate, and a missionary notion of spreading enlightenment.
It became more specialized with the development of technical
education around the end of the nineteenth century, for the

purpose of supplying the skilled workforce needed for industrial production. Universities were created at first with very little reference to the state provision of mass education, mainly to supply local finishing to the products of the private schools; but in the twentieth century were re-integrated through the development of state secondary schools as a pathway towards administration and the professions. Occupational groups become differentiated in their relationship with the educational structure as they do in their relationship with the administrative structure of the state – indeed the two processes are related.

It is often remarked that the schools have a middle-class culture – this is the insight behind the 'cultural deficit' theories of educational inequality. But to say that says little unless the character of middle-class culture is specified. Some features of school life, especially high-school life, draw on quite general features of middle-class life – for example their competitive individualism and their stress on respectable public behaviour. But other features of the schools seem to represent a much more specific selection: their literariness and 'paperiness', to coin a term; their highly formal organization of work and means of judging achievement; their regular and predictable system of promotion. These are not much like the occupational world of the capitalist entrepreneur, but are like the world of the administrator, the bureaucrat and professional. There is a continuity of social practice between the high school and a specific part of the occupational structure developed under capitalism; and it is notable that if we examine the fine detail of the patterns of educational inequality, within the privileged groups it is the children of administrators and professionals rather than the children of entrepreneurs who have the highest rates of 'educational success' at points such as entry to universities. Technical education, by contrast, has a more informal and task-oriented teaching practice; and technical schools and institutions draw more heavily from the middle levels of the occupational structure.

The notion that the practices of everyday life in occupational groups affect the use they and their children make of a differentiated education system of course implies that there is some carry-over into home life, and there is practically no research on this process. There are perhaps some clues in the fragmentary information about differential use of books and approach to conversation in some of the surveys. But most surveys have concentrated on the study of easy-to-measure expressed attitudes, which now looks increasingly like a blind alley. The notion of some specific types of educational traditions, that emerged rather mistily from the earlier discussion, may well have more to do with the pattern of everyday activity in the home than with the conveying of beliefs and values.

The discussion of educational 'opportunity' and inequalities in it has usually conceived the educational system as a single market. We are now, I think, obliged to conceive of it rather as a strongly segmented market, with different occupational (and other – e.g sexual) groups having a standing relationship with different segments of it. It is also a decidedly imperfect market, and here the direct links of the property system and distribution of income come into play. Some groups, the poorest, have difficulty getting into a bargaining position at all; their children struggle with hostile circumstances and get out of school in large numbers as soon as legally possible. Other groups, the richest, are able to buy their way into favourable segments if they wish. (A majority in all occupational groups send their children to state schools; but Hunt's study in Melbourne shows that nearly half of the children of professionals and managers go to private schools.)

Any attempt to remove 'educational inequality' by trying to compensate for some of the imperfections of the market is likely to fail if it does not tackle the basic character of the market itself; still more so if it attempts to compensate by doing such things as training up parents in more favourable attitudes. Any attempt at reform *within* the market can be – and in the past always has been – absorbed or outflanked. If it is correct that the educational market in its basic features and mode of operation is created by class processes in the ways sketched above; if, to put it bluntly, the class structure is the cause of the trouble; then there is in the final analysis only one way to cure it: by removing the cause.

This of course is made more difficult by any forces that promote the reproduction of the class structure in the second sense: the maintenance of a structure of social positions and relationships. To this, personal socialization contributes the training in alienated performance that makes possible the continuance of capitalist production. This is not a kind of perfor-

mance people are born with. It is an acquired skill, and needs
a considerable amount of training. The process of socialization
also contributes the formation of a pattern of values which in
important respects is compatible with the persistence of class
relations. The value-pattern of possessive individualism is a
classic form of ideology, characteristic of bourgeois social
consciousness and of societies under bourgeois domination. It
is of course promoted by business-backed propagandists and
expressed politically by the Liberal Party (and more energetically by some right-wing fringe groups). But, except in emer-
gencies such as the 1947–9 political crisis, this is obviously not
regarded as a matter of high priority. The ruling class does not
normally *rely* on organized propaganda to counter the dangers
of socialist socialization.

Indeed the discussion in this chapter has repeatedly cast
doubt on the supposed importance of attitudes and values in
this whole area; and, by implication, on the importance of the
'agencies' that in much of the literature on socialization are
supposed to pass on attitudinal 'norms' to the rising generation.
What seems more important is the learning of social practices,
such as a specific style of work, and a prudential respecting of
(rather than an attitude of respect for) authority and private
property. The 'agency' of socialization here is, in a sense, the
whole social structure which provides the rationale of these
practices; and perhaps, more specifically, some reified social
relationships that exist in the context of that structure. The
most important agency of socialization to class relations is, very
simply, money – fundamentally a symbol of social relationships, which in a property-based economic order takes on the
character of a thing, independent of men and women and
capable of controlling them. The whole pattern of social relationships constituting the class structure confronts growing
children as facts, which they duly learn, much as they learn
about the weather or school bus schedules. Their own inesca-
pable participation in the network of class relationships is their
educator, and this real experience, I am convinced, is far more
powerful in shaping them than any second-hand experience of
class that may be passed on by familiar adults.

Where attitudes and values are important is in a negative
sense: in what does not happen, or at least not on any scale.
The development of an effective opposition to the ruling class

does require the articulation of an oppositional world-view and alternative social values, and their adoption by large sections of the working class. The crucial feature of the cultural defence of capitalism is not so much the inculcation of middle-class values through the whole society (though that would do the trick), as the prevention of the formation of an oppositional working-class culture.[49] And that may be achieved with less effort, by the maintenance of social and political patterns which divert or disorganize opposition.

Experience may produce opposition as well as acquiescence, and it was the traditional assumption of socialist theory that the experience of working-class life would do so. Are there signs of a class-socialized politics among Australian youth? The best *prima facie* evidence for it comes from studies of political party preferences which indicate that lower-status children more commonly support the Labor Party, and those from upper-status backgrounds more commonly support the Liberals.[50] But closer examination suggests that we cannot take this as a sign of a polarization of attitudes being generated from the children's own experience of their class position. In the first place, there is good reason to think that the party preferences expressed by youth are weak preferences, expressing little in the way of personal commitment. In the second, the idea that class politics are here being generated by class situation requires that the adolescents should have a clear consciousness of their own class position. They are certainly able to pick a class, but often in a way that itself is a refusal to commit themselves; and again, when given a good chance to disclaim class membership, large numbers do so.[51] It appears that the class pattern in party preference found among youth is more a matter of a tradition handed on by their parents than a consequence of their own experiences of class; and of course there is serious doubt that support for the Labor Party normally implies anything much in the way of social radicalism.

The most visible signs of radicalism among Australian youth at present are in counter-cultural and sexual liberation movements. The relationship of these movements to the class structure is tangled. Their main strength so far seems to have come from middle-class dissidents, and counter-cultural activities are often marked by an extreme individualism, anti-bourgeois in intention but still contained within the boundaries of the dominant ideology. Other activities, however, have involved attempts to work out methods of cooperative labour and communal living, and sections of the women's movement especially have developed a strong socialist orientation. Some important breaks with the patterns of everyday life under capitalism are occurring here. Though these movements have a long way to go, they have opened up country that will need to be occupied in a more general movement towards socialism.

The media and middle-class culture

The utility of a PAPER in the COLONY, as it must open a source of solid information, will, we hope, be universally felt and acknowledged. We have courted the assistance of the INGENIOUS and INTELLIGENT:– We open no channel to Political Discussion, or Personal Animadversation:– Information is our only Purpose; that accomplished, we shall consider that we have done our duty in an exertion to merit the Approbation of the PUBLIC, and to secure a liberal Patronage to the SYDNEY GAZETTE.

Thus the statement of aims in volume 1, number 1 of Australia's first newspaper.[1] The author-editor did interpet the 'no politics' rule strictly when it came to criticisms of the colonial government, as was appropriate to a semi-official publication censored by the governor's secretary, but a trifle less so when it came to the convicts. Any who showed a spirit of resistance immediately became, to the paper, 'ruffians', 'desperados', 'atrocious criminals', 'banditti', and 'villains' of the deepest dye.

When an opposition press appeared in the 1820s, not only able but energetically willing to criticize the colonial government, the official monopoly of mass communication ended. The social assumptions, however, changed little: respectability, public order, and private property continued to be basic. Such themes can be traced, with variations in detail but an overriding harmony, through all the great organs of the colonial press, the *Sydney Morning Herald*, the Adelaide *Register*, the Melbourne *Age*. Editorial policy remained in the hands of the educated and respectable, and usually affluent, proprietors. They had their differences, of course, the *Argus* and *Age*, and the *Register* and *Advertiser*, being celebrated pairs of rivals. Some arose from factional conflict among bourgeois politicians, some from clashes of economic interest; but they were internal conflicts in the ruling class, sometimes shaped, but not generated, by class conflict.[2]

Beyond the major papers there was a significant fringe of radical press activity in the nineteenth century, especially in periods of heightened social conflict. The 1840s produced a press directed mainly towards working men, with ideas influenced both by the Chartist movement in England and the contemporary struggle for land in Australia. The last decades of the nineteenth century produced a trade union and regional labour press of quite surprising scale and vigour; a socialist-influenced city press of which the early *Bulletin* was by far the most important product; and a feminist press, notably the *Dawn*. The labour movement of the twentieth century continued to produce some vigorous journalism, notably in the *Australian Worker* for a period under the radical journalist H. E. Boote. But most union and Labor Party papers degenerated into house organs distinguished either by stupefying dullness or factional bitterness. The radical press lost its information-gathering function and came to depend almost wholly on the capitalist press for its news, restricting itself to selection and commentary in an attempt to counter the editorial bias of the mainstream press.[3]

That the editorial policies of the major papers reflect the interests of property owners is a truism; but it is more obvious at some times than at others. Mayer, in *The Press in Australia*, has a lot of fun demolishing left-wing pamphlets attacking the press;[4] it is notable that most of them come from the late 1940s and early 1950s, a period of heightened class conflict, while his own book was written in a period of quiescence. It is also true that the newspapers will sometimes turn to a safe-looking Labor government as an alternative to conservatives in disarray. The *Sydney Morning Herald* supported Curtin, and Murdoch supported Whitlam in 1972; even the Hobart *Mercury* gradually became resigned, in the 1950s, to an apparently permanent but not very terrifying state Labor government. One must allow for the fact that some papers will conduct an intelligent defence of capitalism.

But to say that editorial policies reflect capitalist interests is not, in the final analysis, very important. Few readers, especially at an age when they are likely to be forming their political commitments, pay much attention to editorial arguments. In the

1969 survey of Sydney teenagers discussed in the last two chapters, a series of questions was asked about the media. Most teenagers said they read papers regularly, but gave very different attention to different parts of them. As may be seen from the following percentages who said they read these sections 'almost every day', editorials rate very low:[5]

	Girls	Boys
Headlines	66	66
Comic strips	50	54
Personal advice columns	48	30
Sport	23	52
Political news	13	15
Editorials	12	13

And from studies of adults, we may doubt that editorial arguments have much persuasive effect on those who do read them.[6] Indeed it is quite likely that those who do are already the most interested in politics and typically partisan themselves, thus least likely to be swayed. A good deal of the argument about 'press bias', then, misses the point.

The critic who offered the most persuasive alternative analysis of the political role of the Australian press was A. E. Mander. In *Public Enemy the Press*, a 1944 pamphlet that deserves more attention than it has got, he argued:

Among all the chief newspapers the differences in policy are striking but superficial. On what may be considered fundamental matters they are unanimous...[and] the great majority of the people also are unanimous. It is in regard to those matters that the power of the press is most strongly felt, especially as, in those matters, it is usually not recognised as such.

What are the 'fundamental' sentiments and beliefs which all newspapers support? They are, essentially, those sentiments and beliefs which justify the social-economic system under which press proprietors and their friends flourish. The prestige of the Royal Family; the prestige of wealthy people; the prestige of 'free' newspapers; the assumption that commercialism is essential to civilisation; a belief in the inherent sanctity of capital-investments; and a vague notion that ordinary Australians somehow are more 'free' when the great industrial companies are owned by private shareholders, than they would be if the shareholders were the nation.

In support of those basic sentiments and beliefs, the whole power of the press is continuously exerted.[7]

In this passage Mander was groping, without much in the way

of theoretical guidelines, towards an analysis of the hegemonic role of the press and the politics of popular culture; even, perhaps, towards a theory of intellectuals. And that is the direction in which analysis of the media must move to achieve an adequate account of politics itself. Here, as in the more general analysis of Australian class structure, it is necessary to pick up in the 1970s where the socialists of the 1940s left off.

Organizing and ideology-making

In its support of the conservative parties against Labor, the press has performed a role that is more organizational than persuasive. The Labor Party, rising to challenge middle-class parliamentarians around the turn of the century, was able to draw support from a mass organization in the trade unions, which were rapidly expanding in the same period. Their opponents had no such mass organization. Though attempts were made to create one in the branch structure of the Nationalist parties, and the farmers' organizations provided an effective base for the country parties, it remained a fragile achievement in most parts of the country until the heyday of Menzies' Liberal Party.[8] In this situation it was the press, very largely, that formed the link between the conservative leadership and its mass base. This was not through any particular bias in argument, but through the normal functioning of its news services, reporting the speeches and activities of public men, and a certain amount of political advertizing at election time.

In periods of crisis the thing might be more consciously arranged. A striking account of this is given in a memoir by A. Grenfell Price, the academic who became chairman of the 'Emergency Committee' that coordinated the conservative campaigns in South Australia in the depression election of 1931. Scattered through this remarkable document we get a number of insights into the coordination of the press. (The *Advertiser* and *News* are Adelaide dailies.)

On my return to Adelaide we faced three lines of work: First the committee had to raise funds; second we had to organise the State for the Federal election; and thirdly we had to choose a combined team of Federal candidates.

The first job was to raise funds. On May 14th I spoke to the Business Men of Adelaide in the Wool Exchange putting the need for funds as strongly as possible. My speech is fully reported in the 'News' of that day...

Our second job was that of organisation...As time went on we built up our organisation of the country districts...We also got out a tremendous lot of country publicity by means of the 'Advertiser' and the Country Press. Hogben organised an excellent city press section which fed the 'Advertiser' as the newspaper which circulated everywhere, and I boiled down the publicity articles sent out by Martin Threlfall from Canberra, and the Country Press published a great deal of this work...

[The Emergency Committee runs the campaign with a staff of seventy. The committees include:] *Press* – Parish and Martindale from the Advertiser with a permanent salaried man – Sexton of the Advertiser.[9]

Plainly, sophisticated public-relations operations are no novelty in Australian politics. Note the way in which the *Advertiser* participated – not only printing the material put out, but also supplying people for the campaign. (So, one might note, did the University of Adelaide, which gave Price leave from his teaching for the duration of the campaign.) There is no way of telling how effective it all was, apart from the fact that the conservatives won a smashing victory in the election. But if the argument here is correct, the persuasiveness of the propaganda is not enormously important. The key thing is that there is a mass of people who, for reasons largely of class consciousness, are predisposed to vote for conservative leaders. The media pass on to them the necessary information. 'Owing to the splendid services of the press', Price remarked in a speech in July 1931, 'it has been unnecessary for us to do a great deal of publicity work.'[10] Plainly the 1931 campaign was exceptional. The press has not normally been so coordinated, nor played so important a mobilizing role. But we see here in dramatic form something that continues unobtrusively in more 'normal' times. The function of conveying the flow of information necessary to sustain conservative politics continues, and has carried over from the press to the electronic media.

This still gives the media controllers a persuasive role, but more in the internal politics of the ruling class than in the mass arena. As suggested in Chapter 3, press proprietors (and now television proprietors) have maintained the mixed business and political role that other groups of businessmen have long since dropped. Proprietors, and sometimes journalists, have played important roles in the factional struggles of the conservative parties in the twentieth century, as they did in the middle-class parliaments of the nineteenth. From one point of view the metropolitan press over the last two generations can be regarded as a part (and sometimes as the major part) of the organizational wing of the conservative party of the day. Its owners and managers can be regarded as political functionaries in their own right.

Though the effect of editorial persuasion on elections is dubious, there can be little doubt of the importance of a much more general kind of persuasion. As Mander argued, the press continuously promotes 'those sentiments and beliefs which justify the social-economic system under which press proprietors and their friends flourish'. The media more generally work in such a way as to create the ideological conditions for the success of conservative politics. Again I would like to stress this is not a matter of 'bias' or partisan reporting or conscious distortion of the truth; no evil-minded capitalistic plotters need be assumed.[11] It is an outcome of the normal, regular processes by which commercial mass communications work in a capitalist system, producing and reproducing an ideological interpretation of the world.

This has many facets, but it can perhaps best be shown through the category of 'progress'. Modern conservatism is different in a number of ways from the aristocratic and religious European conservatism of the nineteenth century. It is secular, optimistic, and ties its defence of private property to a doctrine of prosperity and progress. This is nowhere more clear than in those countries, like Australia, which were colonies of settlement in the nineteenth century. 'Progress' was almost the condition of their existence: killing off the blacks and filling up the country with whites and their buildings was the process with which local politics began. The media are involved in maintaining an ideology of progress both through their commercial role as advertisers, and in their manner of representing things as news.

The maintenance of a high-consumption economy depends on mass marketing techniques. This requires not only the stimulation of artificial wants and the turnover of fashions, as many critics of advertising have argued, but more generally the standardization of tastes and what may be called the levelling-up of interests, i.e. the tendency for people to become all-round consumers. The advertising, news, and entertainment elements of the mass media all play a part in this. Indeed it is not easy to separate them, in cases like the daytime television quiz shows directed to housewives, where the entertainment involves frequent mention and awarding of prizes which are brand-named consumer products, which in themselves constitute news about what is available to buy.

The media are thus agents in the care and maintenance of a growth economy – their profits, largely derived from advertising revenue, depend upon it. Their representation of the world in orthodox news happily matches commercial need. Consider a number of familiar types of news story: the building of schools, highways, factories, and shops; their openings; the breaking of records in transport, production, export, sports; the growth of population; and so on. All are common news items; and what makes them 'news', typically, is the assumption of progress – that here is something bigger, better, faster or more than we had before, and that people want to know about that. The assumption on which much of the world is interpreted in the media is that of the equivalence of progress, prosperity, and the social good. Disaster stories are a nice inversion of this; for disasters register in the news as the effects of human or cosmic error, rather than integral consequences of a social system.

There are of course some exceptions to these points, such as the development of environmental reporting. But though this has produced some nice muck-raking in occasional feature stories, it has hardly touched the elemental assumptions of the reporting of progress. The most prominent example in the Australia news media, the frequent and prominent reporting of the 'road toll', illustrates the way it can be absorbed. For the regular tale of bloodshed is regularly accompanied by interpretations (usually provided by a politician or police official) putting the blame on the carelessness or drunkenness of the individual drivers, rather than the insanity of the whole car-based transport system.

On a much grander scale, the ideology of progress has justified the fact of violence. Progress originally meant the invasion of the Australian countryside and the replacement of blacks by farmers, sheep and cattle. This meant killing off large numbers of the blacks, and the press of the day mostly followed through its assumptions by supporting the settlers in this process; reinterpreting it, by a spectacular leap of logic, as self-defence against the barbarous and treacherous natives. The ideology of progress and private property in fact has helped to provide justification for all the major episodes of internal violence in Australian history: the genocide with which it began; the repression of convict resistance and bushranging; the resistance on the goldfields (where progress and property for once clashed with established authority); the intimidation of unions and a long series of official strike-breaking activities; and the constant undercurrent of official violence through police, courts, and prisons by which the property system is upheld.[12]

The argument here has moved some distance from the media, but I wanted to point out some of the ramifications of an ideological process. Here we have something more than a doctrine which contributes to the stability of a capitalist order: we have a way of looking at the world which facilitates its development in a certain direction.

How, more precisely, can the facilitation occur? There has been a lot of speculation on the impact of mass media on the values and attitudes of their audiences. They are said to stimulate violence in children, produce a consumption ethic, and so forth.[13] There are often interesting ideas in this literature; but there is something odd about a general line of reasoning that formulates the impact of the media basically in terms of attitudes or traits of character. Chapter 8 suggested that this might be a blind alley in the analysis of socialization, and the argument may be reciprocally applied to the mass media as one of the 'agencies' concerned. For the media are literally *media*, means of communication. Their most important effects should be at the level of communication, of symbolic interaction and symbolic thought. To understand their impact we should examine their content as a system of symbolization; as, in some sense, a language with a structure and constraining power of its own.

Media iconography

Most people who follow an author like Agatha Christie would probably agree that there is a distinct set of types who populate her novels: the ageing financier, the faithful retainer, the ingenuous young man of independent means, the elderly gentle-woman in reduced circumstances, and so forth. One can speak of 'the world of Agatha Christie', and the phrase will conjure up a set of characters who certainly existed in the real world but equally certainly are a highly selected sample of it. In the same way one can speak of 'the world of the mass media'; and it has an equally select membership.

Journalists would probably agree that it is easier for some people to get into the news than others: ministers, pressure group spokesmen, etc. But they hardly realize how sharp the social selection becomes in the final product. This can be seen in Table 8, which shows the occupations of the people who appeared in a week's run of the two Adelaide daily papers, compared with the national distribution of occupations in the 1966 census.[14]

It is obvious how overwhelmingly middle-class is the world as seen by the press. 81% of people in the *News*, 87% of people in the *Advertiser*, are from white-collar occupations. The pre-dominance of these groups would be even greater if we counted numbers of mentions rather than numbers of people, for some politicians, businessmen and senior civil servants reappear in successive stories and issues. It is hardly going too far to say that there are only three ways for a working class man to get into the paper: to become a jockey or horse trainer; to suffer a catastrophe, preferably bizarre; or to commit a rape. A working class woman has only the second way.

It is not only the people who are selected. Of the few blue-collar workers who get into the paper, it is only the profes-sional sportsmen who get in by virtue of carrying on their daily work. In other cases it is a man who happens to be a labourer who is indicted for rape, or a woman who happens to be a housewife who is killed by a car. (It is of course true that working-class people are disproportionately likely to be ar-rested and appear in court;[15] but this is hardly part of their normal occupation.) Even union officials, who are reasonably often in the news, are rarely there by virtue of their ordinary work. The daily paper does not normally report that such-and-such a factory has now been organized, or such-and-such grievances pursued and resolved. But it does report splits in unions, controversies they are involved in, and the like. In contrast, it is the normal work of politicians, company direc-

tors, entertainers, etc., that counts as 'news' in the conceptual
vocabulary of the media; or at least episodes in the normal work
that epitomize its processes and register its progress. We
regularly read of the issuing of the company report, the
conduct of the annual general meeting and the content of the
chairman's address; the opening of installations and the tour
of inspection; the policy statement and the performance.

Thus the striking selectivity of the media in their representation of the social world by a narrative of events involves not

Table 8. Who's in the paper? Occupations of people mentioned in the Adelaide *Advertiser* and *News*, 26 January–
2 February 1974, compared with 1966 census figures

Occupation	Advertiser Number	%	News Number	%	Census %
White-collar					
I	139	37 ⎱	142	38 ⎱	12 ⎱
II	154	41 ⎰ 87	115	31 ⎰ 81	11 ⎰ 42
III	35	9 ⎰	46	12 ⎰	19 ⎰
Blue-Collar					
IV	18	5 ⎱	10	3 ⎱	16 ⎱
V	4	1 ⎰ 13	0	0 ⎰ 19	22 ⎰ 59
VI	28	7 ⎰	58	16 ⎰	21 ⎰
Total	378		371		

NOTE: The analysis covers editorial matter, excluding letters to the editor,
overseas events, and overseas visitors to Australia. Persons appearing in more
than one story are scored only once. Groups (e.g. police, directors of a
company) scored once per story in which they figure. Organizations *per se* (e.g.
the Weather Bureau) not scored; nor 'spokesmen', presidents of associations,
etc., where actual occupations not clear. The categories, based on those
devised by Broom, Jones and Zubrzycki, are as follows.

I. Upper professional, graziers and big farmers, lower professional: in-
cluding judges, professors, entertainers. MP's included here.
II. Managerial, self-employed shop proprietors, other farmers. Company
directors included here (N.B. *Advertiser*).
III. Clerical and related workers, armed services and police.
IV. Craftsmen and foremen. Blue-collar union officials included here.
V. Shop assistants, operatives and process workers, drivers.
VI. Personal, domestic and other service workers; miners, farm and rural
workers, labourers. Professional sportsmen such as jockeys included
here (N.B. *News*).

only a selection of persons, but also a selection of social processes. The media present by implication a definite inter-pretation of the way the world operates, in which the ordinary activity of the bourgeoisie and certain types of public figures is defined as being what counts, what is worthy of attention; spiced for entertainment with aberrations in the life of the working class.

For the bulk of the population, the world of events is defined in this way as alien, somewhat strange and portentous, even dangerous. Within the media a counterbalancing kind of mat-erial appears, based on familiarity – news that has no news value, a kind of anti-news that serves to reassure rather than inform. Thus the 'Queen's Life at Home' kind of reporting, the elaboration of the homely details of the lives of famous people. Perhaps the most striking examples of this are in the achingly sad *Daytime TV* kind of magazine addressed to housewives, packed with stories about television stars under headlines such as 'My Husband is First with Me, Always', 'Star in the Kitchen', and 'My Future is Built Around My Family'.[16] But note it is not strictly the familiar – Mrs Jones around the corner – that is written about; it is the familiar refracted through the lives of media stars and public figures. The familiar must be mythologized in order to be brought within the category of public event, and serve as symbolic reassurance.

Within the world of the movers and shakers, of course, not everything counts as news. Indeed much of the most important activity goes unreported. As noted in the discussions of the business leadership in earlier chapters, this applies to most of the politics and policy formation in companies. By almost any criterion, the investment decisions of the steel monopoly BHP are major public-policy events; but the processes by which they are determined very rarely, and then very briefly, enter news reporting. This poses problems for the study of the companies; but here we are more concerned with the consequences of this gap for the events that *are* selected to be news. They are in effect cut off from their own history. They are transformed, not into a connected account of the working of the social system, but into type-events, into symbols; and that is a pro-cess with wide implications.

Barthes, whose writings on popular culture provide some

brilliant insights into the working of the media in a class society, has pointed to this separation of the event (or image of a person or event) from its history as one of the key features of the process of mythologizing reality. In this process events, things, and people are emptied of their specific historical reality, and transformed into carriers of meaning, the terms in a language of myth.[17]

Again it will be useful to study a concrete example. The myth that perhaps plays the greatest part in politics is that of leadership, or more precisely, to coin an even more horrible term, leaderliness. There is a highly stylized and limited[18] set of images through which individual leaders are represented – the familiar photographs of the leader leaning forward into the platform microphones, the leader signing the document at the desk, the leader on the steps of the aeroplane, the two leaders clasping hands. The imagery is independent of particular persons, and can be translated out of the big-time if necessary – as witness the *Australian* house ad current in 1974, a drawing of a slightly pained young executive on the steps of a plane, with the caption 'His *news*paper – his *business* paper'. At a slightly more complex level, there are stylized images of deliberation and command such as the photographs of the board gathered in its polished room, and be-suited managers inspecting the plant, through which the major companies commonly present themselves in advertisements, handouts and annual reports.

The thing signified in all this is not so much a particular person and act – which would be the literal meaning of the photograph or the accompanying news report – as the quality of being a leader. And in the mythical world created by this and similar processes, leaderliness is one of the fixed components of the world, one of the things eternally present, unquestionable. The crude political payoff is the subliminal message: be satisfied, the world is in good hands; though we have problems, there are decisive, competent men making investigations and taking decisions in your best interests. So mythologized, the imagery of leadership becomes part of the cultural defences of the *status quo*.

That the key process here is at the level of meanings and implications a step behind the literal meanings of the media content, at the level that Barthes calls myth, was nicely shown in the Liberal Party leadership struggle in 1967–8. Mayer and

Curnow give an amusing account of newspaper editorialists' struggles to define the nature of national leadership in the distressingly concrete language of job-advertisements.[19] This is not to imply that myth lacks power. It can certainly cause trouble for those who attempt to instance it, but who for various reasons fail. By any rational calculation of the public good, the country was about as well (or badly) governed under Gorton and McMahon as it had been under Menzies: their administrations were for all practical purposes the same, being middle-class, technocratic, pro-American, and mildly welfarist. Yet it was widely believed that the later two Liberal Prime Ministers were disasters, and this no doubt helped the party's slight electoral decline in 1972. McMahon's efforts to hook himself into the myth of leadership through a pretence of decisiveness were particularly comic and politically damaging.

The process can have much broader implications than the fate of a conservative politician. Let us consider another example. Over the page from the picture of a 50-year-old politician climbing into a plane is a picture of an 18-year-old blonde leaning forward to show her cleavage. Sex is mythologized in the capitalist mass media just as leadership is, but far more extensively, as it is standard fare in advertising as well as entertainment and photo-journalism.

Once again, there is a marked stereotyping in the images and texts. There are fixed formulae for the sexy photo and its flippant caption, as for the sexy delivery of a song. Such formulae make an issue of *Man* magazine from the 1970s almost identical to an issue from the 1950s (and not very different from cheesecake publications of half a century before); and make the swayings of one 'female vocalist' in front of the variety-show camera almost identical to those of every other. The sexiness of the mass of advertisements, television shows and cheesecake pictures is much more stylized even than pornography. It is not merely inhibited sexuality, it is frozen sexuality. Once again, the substratum of historical fact has been cut away; the meaning of sex has been somehow withdrawn from the message of sexiness.

Middle-class culture has traditionally been sexually repressive, and the apparent sexual liberalization of middle-class-controlled media, especially in the last generation, represents an important change in taste and style. But it has been achieved by a process in which sexiness has been divorced from sex. The latter is a part of the world of sweaty bodies; the former is a term in a language of myth. It is a term that can stand on its own, or be joined with others to form sentences of persuasion (the 18-year-old blonde showing her cleavage on a rock by the stream slowly draws on her menthol cigarette . . .) according to commercial need.

This allows an apparent liberalization to remain repressive. Marcuse's account of the process as one of 'repressive desublimation', allowing through the new hedonism a personal release that serves to stabilize the whole social order,[20] overestimates the release. In much of the media there is simply a new form of control: the representation of sexuality has been placed in the service of a new meaning at the level of myth, a meaning that is in fact narrower, more restricted, than the actual biological and emotional realities. Sexuality is transformed from act into language, and a thin, undernourished language at that.

The divorce of people from their context, of events from their history, of objects from their making, is one of the fundamental processes by which the media operate as an ideological force. Perhaps the most striking feature of this is that the social process, as represented in the contemporary media, practically excludes the processes of production.[21]

In the case of news columns and news programmes, as we have seen, this occurs through a selection of people and events. The products of the processes missing from the news do appear, in advertisements. But here they are equally divorced from the processes by which they have been made. They are represented in another way: by a brand name. This, on reflection, is quite an important ideological device. It conceals the actual relations of the workplace and attributes the product to the owner of the workplace. This car is said to be 'by Chrysler', that mixer 'from GE'. (The thing reaches a mighty pitch of absurdity when, as in the case of refrigerators and petrol, goods produced in the one plant are marketed under rival brand-names by rival companies.) Sometimes workers enter brand-name advertisements, but then as types – the company's happy family, or the wizened old watchmaker, or the grocer-philosopher slicing his old-fashioned cheese.

Conclusion

In a sense it is wrong to have a chapter called 'the media and middle-class culture', as if the one were external to the other. The media *are* middle-class culture, or at least a very important component of it. The processes through which they work, the transformations that their materials undergo, are central processes in the production of an ideology. I have stressed that it is not 'bias', in the sense of conscious choice of material to serve a particular point of view, that is the main point. It is rather the normal functioning of the media in a commercial context and a class society, which produces a selective and eventually mythologized version of the daily history of the social order. To recall the *Sydney Gazette*, the Australian media have indeed acquired the assistance of the Ingenious and Intelligent, in the sense of being a base for a local intelligentsia engaged in producing and disseminating an approved ideology; and they have, it would seem, merited the Approbation of the Public, which continues to buy. In the final analysis one must look to processes outside of culture to destroy the Liberal Patronage that they have undoubtedly secured.

The pattern of hegemony

The problem of control

Socialists of the nineteenth century, though disagreeing in every conceivable way about how it should happen, were reasonably agreed that the collapse of capitalism would happen, and probably in their own lifetimes. A system so morally ugly could not last long. Marxists believed that it would be torn apart by its economic contradictions; syndicalists believed that it would be shattered by the militancy of organized labour; Laborites in Australia widely believed it would be ended by moral means, as the majority of people saw the obvious superiority of socialism.

And by any reasonable expectation, the capitalist system should have collapsed by now. It has stumbled into two frightful world wars and a disastrous depression, while working class parties have come to power, by revolution or election, in most of the countries that have been the centres of capitalism. But it has not collapsed. The hosts of Israel have compassed the city seven times, the economic trumpets have blown and the politicians have shouted with a great shout; but for some reason the walls have not fallen down. World capitalism is more productive, as vigorous, and arguably as well entrenched, as in the days of Marx and Engels. Even worse, the workers' movements have become infected with diseases that they once thought belonged to capitalism itself, ranging from bureaucratic inertia and a taste for minor privilege all the way to the police-state terror of Stalinism.

Through this rather chilling experience, twentieth-century socialism has been forced to recognize in a much sharper way the resilience of capitalism and the strength of its non-economic defences, on the one hand, and the ambiguities and internal weaknesses of working-class movements on the other. Some

205

of the most important developments in socialist theory have been attempts to analyse these problems: the theories of Lukács, Gramsci, and Althusser on ideology, consciousness and cultural control; the anarchist, Trotskyite, and now Maoist critiques of revolutionary parties' corruption in power; and the many attempts to bring Freud to the aid of Marx in explaining mass support for a repressive social order. The two issues are of course closely related; and I would suggest that, given the history of the twentieth century, they must now be seen as the central problems of socialist theory. To give them a name, they can be seen as parts of the general problem of hegemony.

The term 'hegemony', as is well known, comes from Gramsci, specifically his attempts to extend Marxist concepts to analyse the situation facing Italian revolutionaries in the era of fascism. Gramsci sometimes used the term simply to refer to the leadership role in an alliance of parties or classes for a specific struggle. But he also extended it to cover situations where a kind of permanent alliance existed; where a general solidarity between oppressors and oppressed had developed, with cultural processes reinforcing the political and economic domination of the ruling group. The type case, analysed by Gramsci in a famous essay, was the southern region of Italy, which was the poorest and most oppressed but remained tightly controlled by conservatism.[1]

The kinds of mechanisms Gramsci identified as producing a hegemonic situation are plainly important; his discussions of the role of intellectuals are particularly suggestive. But it seems necessary to extend his concepts, particularly to get a grip on the problem of stability in highly industrialized regions with well-developed working-class groups; and to take account of other mechanisms of control. Theorists such as Reich and Marcuse have argued that the defence of advanced capitalism has shifted in a major way to psychological mechanisms, which mostly act at an unconscious level and require the concepts of psychoanalysis to grasp.[2] Whether or not their specific hypotheses are correct, it does seem important to bring into account the psychological forces that act to stabilize the social order.

Hegemony as a *situation*, a moment in history in which control is effectively exercised, can thus be distinguished from the *mechanisms of control* that operate in it. Situations can vary in the mechanisms that are active, and in the depth of control that is achieved. The latter point is important because there is a strong tendency in the literature, understandable but dangerous, by the mere fact of formulating a concept of cultural or psychological control to exaggerate it into a concept of total control. Control is never total – even in Nazi Germany at the height of war there were circles of resistance – though it can be pretty thorough. Hegemonic situations range from a strongly established pattern of direct controls with only marginal dissidence, through situations where a working class has formed as an economic and social category but its mobilization is being aborted, to situations where mobilization has occurred though only within decided limits. The last of these situations arose relatively early in Australia, and much of the history of the labour movement in the twentieth century has concerned battles over the limits of mobilization.

To speak of cultural control presupposes some notion of 'culture', and this is a difficult idea to pin down. In the development of socialist thought it has often served as a kind of tactical reserve, called in to do battle when orthodox economic and political analyses have failed. Or it has been seen as a soft part of social analysis, an epiphenomenon of economics and politics, lacking a rigorous theory and perhaps incapable of having one. This attitude has now begun to change, partly under the influence of the women's movement whose arguments have established processes such as personal socialization and sexual interaction, and structures such as the household and family, as central rather than marginal features of an analysis of oppressive social structures. What follows is not based on a really systematic theory of culture, but does at least sketch a framework for discussing cultural and psychological control.

There are a number of distinct levels at which one can analyse hegemony; or, to use another metaphor, different ways of slicing into the complexities of a hegemonic situation. They are illustrated severally by works of some of the theorists already referred to. When Gramsci speaks of a sociopolitical bloc, he is referring (among other things) to a commitment to particular parties, and the failure of other parties to attract support. This defines one level of possible analysis, that of personal politics, social attitudes, individual consciousness. In Reich's account of fascism, and Marcuse's account of the

American working class (and for that matter in Freud's *Civilization and its Discontents*), there is an attempt to analyse the contribution of repression and displacement to social order. This defines another level at which hegemony can be analysed, the level of the unconscious. In Althusser's theory there is an attempt to specify the operation of ideology as a system of social practices, as regular patterns of action by which people are constrained.[3] This identifies a third level, that of routine interactions, which may be analysed independently of the first two.

Plainly this is not a catalogue of all ways of applying the analytic knife. But these are at least well-considered cases that have received some theoretical development. And they do, I think, correspond in a meaningful if rough way to issues that have been raised, unsystematically, in discussions of culture and mass psychology in Australia.

The postwar hegemonic situation

An analysis of hegemony may usefully start with the event that set the pattern of postwar politics in Australia. In the late 1940s a conservative political mobilization occurred, on a scale unprecedented since the first world war. A coordinated, expensive and dramatic propaganda campaign was launched against the Labor government by the business and political leadership of the ruling class. In 1949 the conservative parties swept back to federal office, where, with a temporary interruption by the Whitlam government, they have remained ever since. In the 1950s and 1960s the remaining state Labor governments were picked off one by one; for a short period at the end of the 1960s there was no Labor government anywhere in Australia, a situation that had not been known for half a century.

The reasons for this period of decline of political Labor have mostly been sought in changes in the party images and class consciousness of the electorate – i.e. at the first of the analytic levels just set out. This is natural, as this kind of discussion is the stock in trade of politicians themselves, journalists, and others whose daily business involves parties and parliaments. Arguments range from suggestions that the working class has disappeared, to more modest ones that with increasing affluence, its outlook has become more moderate or more complacent; that Labor as a class-identified party has lost out in a period of declining class consciousness; that the expanding

208

groups of white-collar workers have a different political outlook from that of the workers they are replacing, among other things a greater consciousness of their own social status, and refuse to identify with a specifically working-class party.[4]

It certainly is true that, as polls and surveys measure it, the sense of class membership and class division declined in the postwar decades. Comparing Oeser and Hammond's survey in Melbourne in the late 1940s with his own in the early 1960s, Davies observed signs of 'evaporating proletarian conscious-ness', looser definitions of class, and a much less solid sense of one's personal position in the class structure. Union mem-bership as a percentage of the workforce, an important long-term index of working-class organizational strength, stopped growing in the middle 1950s, and indeed went into a slight decline. The Labor vote did not decline as drastically as some discussions suggested, but the clear connection between occu-pational grouping and support for a particular party weakened through the 1950s and 1960s. There are indications that the differences between occupational groups in attitudes on econ-omic issues also weakened after the 1940s.[5]

The last two observations do not imply that there was less (or much less) support for radical views, but they do suggest that the social trends of the postwar period made it more difficult to mobilize. With occupational groups less solid in their outlook, occupation-based organizations like the unions would be less able to transform radical opinion into effective action. At the height of the Vietnam struggle there were indeed some union attempts to block the shipment of war supplies, but they were never remotely comparable with the Port Kembla 'pig iron' strike of 1938 or the wharfies' blocking of supplies to the Dutch in Indonesia in the late 1940s.

The polls from the Vietnam years, as well as the landslide in the 1966 election, show that for some years at least there was widespread support for the Liberals' interventionist policy among groups who normally did not vote Liberal. The 1966 campaign is almost as interesting as 1949, though it confirmd an existing government in power rather than created a new one. And it is interesting partly for the extreme traditionalism of the two main symbolic appeals that were made by the winning side. The threat, on the one hand: foreign, Asian, communist, supposedly engaged in a 'thrust' towards Australia–even the propaganda maps were traditional, showing red arrows slashing downwards toward Australia, greatly assisted by gravity. The appeal to affiliation, on the other: the need to show solidarity with the nation's mentor and protector, in this case the United States, so that it would keep faith in future. It is possible that the top policy-making levels of the government in the mid 1960s were themselves so ignorant that they believed these arguments, but it seems most unlikely.[6] They have a mythic quality about them, and tap into a long tradition of threat images in Australian popular consciousness.

The conscious anticommunism that was a large part of the 'threat' symbolism in 1966 goes a long way back, in a tradition of ruling-class fears of anarchy and uprisings that can be traced as far back as the convict era. Explicit anticommunism emerged in the 1920s as a confused but potent brew of anti-Bolshevik, anti-foreign, anti-working-class and anti-Labor sentiment. The Communist Party of the day being only a tiny sect, the main political payoff at the time was simply a new means of attacking the labour movement at large. But in the 1940s the Communist Party did become a real political force, controlling a number of important unions, sweeping up much of the socialist left of labour politics into its own expanded membership, and at one point, in a fit of bravado, thinking it could challenge the ALP for political leadership of the working class.

The reaction that was unleashed by this began inside the labour movement, with the emergence of an anti-communist grouping based on the Catholic church's lay organisations – the famous 'Movement' which became the basis of the DLP – at a time when the ruling-class leadership was still pre-occupied with its own internal reorganization. But its circle rapidly widened; by 1949 the Chifley government was locked in conflict with the communist-controlled mining unions, and the conservatives under Menzies were using anticommunism as a major rhetorical weapon, berating Chifley, who was doing quite well in the repression line, for not taking stronger action. Once they had defeated the ALP the conservatives moved on to attack the Communist Party, and socialism and dissidence generally under the rubric of communism. A series of offensive measures was launched: the Communist Party Dissolution Bill, state and federal Royal Commissions into communism and espionage, government control of union elections, sedition prosecutions, withdrawal of passports, enquiries and surveillance by security police (the federal arm of which, ASIO, had been newly established by the Labor government). Little organizational damage was done to the Communist Party; a cynic might remark that its preservation in some form was decidedly useful to the Menzies government. But if, as seems likely, the main purposes were electoral appeal and intimidation of radicals, these were certainly achieved. The modest flowering of socialist thought and reforming optimism that had occurred in the 1940s was brought to a sudden end. The cultural initiative passed to conservative intellectuals; and Menzies continued to win elections.[7]

The effect of all this at the level of attitudes might have been trivial, had it not been for the economic changes that made the positive side of conservative propaganda plausible. A rising level of real incomes made their equation of free enterprise and prosperity credible; the swelling flow of consumer goods made their rhetoric of progress practically materialize in every house. The completed industrialization of the Australian economy, which had been going on for a long time but was greatly accelerated around the 1940s, made a rhetoric and iconography of 'modernity' plausible. It is not necessary to suppose that this kind of change translated directly into votes for the Liberals – who until the late 1950s were running neck and neck with Labor in the popular vote – but it probably did so eventually, and it also shaped the outlook of the opposition. The actual policies propounded by Evatt in the 1950s were very close to those of Menzies; under Calwell the Labor Party leadership began to get twitchy about its image and to seek for modernity and style; under Whitlam, who had both, the federal leadership droppped even gestures towards a working-class identification and ironically promoted themselves as better free-enterprisers than the Liberals.

This is only a sketch of the process of legitimizing the ruling class and domesticating the opposition in this period. A fuller account would have to look at the role of mass media in creating understandings of the world in which conservatism appeared to be commonsense; a classic case would be the newspapers' reporting of strikes. It would look at the ways advertising and public relations attempt to popularize particular companies and as a by-product legitimize capitalism in general

– e.g. in the corporate invasion of Australian sport in the last decade. But perhaps enough has been said to show how the hegemonic situation can be approached, if not completely explained, at the level of conscious attitudes. Let us now consider another level that was obviously relevant to the discussion of threat campaigns, the level of unconscious processes.

There are two senses in which one can speak of the unconscious. In the first, what is unconscious is simply what a person is unaware of about himself or herself – as for instance the rules of grammar which are not called to awareness, though they are obeyed, in everyday speech; or, more pertinently, the set of categories through which the social world is interpreted. The threat schema is a useful example of this. Most people would hardly be aware of carrying in their heads a system of social categories which gave prominence to a threatening alien and opposed it to a nurturant relative, though that is plainly the categorical structure that was widely activated in the Vietnam years. Threat schemata can be found widely in popular fiction, comic books, etc., from the period.[8]

But there was obviously something dynamic in the threat schema, not just an implicit set of categories for interpreting the world. This involves the second meaning, where what is unconscious is so because it has been repressed, and retains an active motivational power – the classic Freudian concept of the dynamic unconscious. The force of the threat schema, in a situation where invasion is by all realistic criteria ridiculously unlikely, presumably arises from its assimilation to repressed material which is totally inaccessible to political argument or ridicule. (Arthur Calwell vastly amused Labor Party audiences in 1966 with his sketches of the powerful Chinese invasion fleet of motorized junks and sampans setting sail for Australia; but arguments about the actual intentions and military capacities of Asian communism got no response from the electorate at large.) To be more specific, one might suggest that rape and castration anxieties are at work in the political threat schema. But, though some plausible support for this could be offered from cultural material such as the rich garbage-bin of Australian racism, the crucial evidence could only come from clinical life-histories which are not locally available.[9]

On another line of argument, we are not so shy of data.

Marcuse argues that advanced capitalism is able to relax many of the psychological repressions which had been imposed in an era of greater scarcity and need for accumulation; and further is able to turn that relaxation to account, by doing it in a way that preserves social discipline. There are a number of lines of evidence that there has indeed been a relaxation of moral constraints in postwar Australia. (The existence of the Festival of Light is not one of them: a White Cross League with the slogan 'Keep Thyself Pure' can be found in the 1930s, Bands of Hope in the nineteenth century, and evangelical denunciations of a decline in morality among Australians can be traced without a break back to the year 1788; such things are simply part of the stock in trade of ministers and priests.)[10] The relaxation of censorship, easy circulation of pornography, the more direct sexuality of literature and films and sometimes performing art, are one line of evidence. Changes in divorce laws and the much easier social acceptance of divorce, which do not seem to have affected the popularity of marriage but have weakened the constraints in it, are another. In some survey material, such as the two large Sydney studies of teenagers in 1952 and 1969, there is direct evidence of a shift of popular attitudes towards acceptance of dancing, kissing, and other minor liberties among the young.[11]

The argument proposes that this relaxation has occurred in ways that tend to stabilize rather than disrupt the capitalist system. Here it seems likely that there have been tendencies in both directions. The mention of teenagers raises one very clear case of absorption, the development of the pop industries – records, fashions, pop radio and magazines, etc. – which have turned teenage sexuality into a highly profitable business. (The mass entertainment industry more generally does this; though its characteristic products for adults, such as television variety shows and women's magazines, are much more inhibited than the material addressed to teenagers.) Here the relaxation of repression is both controlled and exploited in the same action. But there are also ways in which a weakening of repressions has led in an anti-capitalist, counter-hegemonic direction; most significantly in the sexual liberation movements that took shape in the early 1970s.

The women's movement, to the extent that it has not been simply anti-male but has sought the sources of the oppression of women in the specific history of this society, has been very much concerned with the way a social order hooks private motivation up to the maintenance of a social structure. It has shown, particularly through its analyses of femininity, how women come to be dependent on, indeed actively want a situation in which they are subordinated. Not only does this provide a useful model for the analysis of the psychology of social subordination in general, but it has a direct relevance to this case, for the 'sex-role' pattern is an important part of the cultural structure of capitalism.[12]

This may be seen, for instance, in the consuming side of the main growth industry of the postwar period. The motor cars that were manufactured and sold to a really mass public for the first time in the 1950s were not simply sold to 'the public' – they were sold specifically to men. Their design and use has been closely integrated with a sexual division of labour, and their marketing has freely used male fantasies of power and potency. Cars quickly became a major goal of working-class boys – their sexual success largely depending on access to them – and set up pressures to maximize their short-term incomes in order to pay off hire-purchase obligations. The very structure of the car market, with an almost infinite regress of speed and price, presented men with an endless pursuit of more and more automotive prestige and, at least in fantasy, more and more elegant and expensive women.

On the other side, household consumption is repressively organized through the pattern of femininity, an organization of character and sexuality which by adulthood is practically outside conscious control. The mechanism is evident in the distinctive mass media addressed to women, the women's magazines and daytime TV shows. It is not so much that the advertisers who finance these media are directly promoting femininity: they are on the contrary promoting their products. But they do this by using the 'feminine' structure of motives, self-images, etc., to arrange sales. It is the media themselves (capitalist enterprises, but generally distinct from the advertisers) which promote – and to the extent that they fill a gap and control aspirations – enforce femininity.

One of the senses in which we can speak of a hegemonic situation, perhaps the most common in advanced capitalism, is where there exists a working class in the economic sense which is inhibited from mobilizing. It is a banal, and probably mistaken, view that affluence leads to complacency and apathy. But I would suggest that the specific kind of affluence that countries like Australia have experienced, has meshed with much older patterns of sexual organization in ways that strongly inhibit class mobilization, both in terms of unconscious dynamics and patterns of daily activity.

This now involves the third of the analytic levels mentioned earlier, that of routine patterns of interaction. The sexual distinctions and patterns of motivation just discussed are sustained by a division of labour that is most clearly expressed in the daily life of suburban households where the wife–mother stays home and does the housework and child care while the husband–father drives daily off to a paid job.

Social critics have dwelt heavily and long on the postwar expansion of suburbs and the character of the suburban lifestyle; as Rowse suggests, 'suburbia' became a symbol of the whole society for a certain kind of social criticism. A fine example is Patrick White's play *The Season at Sarsaparilla* (1961), in which he bitterly caricatures the crassness of suburbanites. Suburbia was perhaps the most canvassed cause of the decline of working-class militancy: a house, a hausfrau and a Holden were supposed to take all the sting out of life.[13]

The pattern of suburban living is indeed historically important, but it must be understood in context, in terms of the forces that persuaded or pushed large groups of the working class into the outer reaches of the cities. There was no lemming-like rush to spiritual death beyond the reach of the sewerage. There were good reasons why people should move. Governments in the grip of the 'populate or perish' syndrome, or more realistically seeking a labour force for industrial expansion, raised population pressures in the cities by large-scale immigration and incentives for breeding. As the volume of motor traffic increased (an end of petrol rationing was part of Menzies' 1949 platform) the inner-city working-class areas, now stigmatized as 'slums', became more unpleasant and dangerous to live in, especially for families with young children. Even such relief measures as the rent controls imposed by NSW Labor governments resulted in a lack of maintenance by landlords, who no longer found it profitable to keep houses in good condition, and the decay of physical conditions in the centre (until owner-occupation later spread back).[14]

Beyond these material reasons, there was a systematic attempt to sell suburban living as the most desirable way of life. In the decade or so after the war real-estate developers, builders, consumer goods manufacturers and retailers mounted a massive campaign in the media promoting the suburbs and all the equipment of suburban living. Much of it was directed to women, playing on their sense of themselves as social managers as well as their femininity and motherhood. A fascinating example is the architectural soap opera 'Joanna Plans a Home' that ran as a serial in the *Australian Home Beautiful* in 1946. Joanna was supposed to be a young serviceman's bride, and, in successive episodes, was weaned away from her traditional tastes to a belief in modern design and 'new ideas' in living, or at least the equipment for living. Rather delicately, the sense that the reader might know her own mind about her environment was undercut, and models of the formation of taste under the guidance of experts – architects, a wealthy friend with 'a very modern house', and of course the magazine itself – were substituted.[15]

The significance of this is not so much at the attitudinal level, as in committing the newly-forming families to a pattern of life that absorbed an increasing share of their energies in private activities and bound them economically to the system. To buy the 'little piece of earth with a house and a garden' that Menzies apostrophized in a famous wartime speech,[16] normally sent a man into debt for most of his working lifetime. To fill the house with appliances and buy the car that derisory public transport often made necessary, meant a further debt load. Merely to sustain the basic way of life the husband was locked into his job. The wife was still locked into unpaid household labour (with a slowly growing tendency to add a part-time or unskilled job to it), now in a situation where the labour was much more isolated than in the higher-density inner districts. The routines of interaction that in the interwar years had provided a basis of working-class solidarity, mutual aid and sometimes mobilization were altered, and mobilization correspondingly made more difficult.

One of the features of suburb-building was the differentiation of the housing market, the range from treeless fibro developments to brick mansions in wooded hills. The differences, which were not only widely known but forced upon people's attention by estate agents, reflected marked differences in credit rating and purchasing power that in turn reflected social differentiation in the workforce. The segmentation of the working class and the emergence of privileged groups within it has been recognized as a block to working-class mobilization as far back as the time of Marx, who with his contemporaries spoke of an aristocracy of labour. There are reasons to think that the segmentation of the Australian working class increased after the mid-century. Calculations based on award wage rates indicate an increased inequality of wages from about the middle 1950s, after a period in which the dispersal of wages had fallen. The institutional recognition of differences among groups of workers was reinforced by events such as the Engineers' cases of 1961–2, of which Encel remarked that the Arbitration Commission had practically legislated to establish a profession. The informal segregation of workers was of course increased where members of non-English-speaking migrants entered, notably in heavy industry. Though more women entered the paid workforce, and to that extent reduced the greatest of all divisions in the working class, they entered segregated employment for the most part, characterized by different (and more boring) work, or simply separate work groups, and almost always unequal pay.[17]

The existence of different groups of workers is of course a technical necessity of production. What is at issue here is not the division of labour, but the embedding of that technical necessity in an elaborate structure of status distinctions, income differences, customary privileges and differential recruitment. As was remarked earlier, these are not 'soft', epiphenomenal and ephemeral matters. On the contrary, as the women's movement is finding in the case of sex segregation in employment, and as the industrial unionists found half a century before in their attempt to end craft exclusiveness in union organisation, they are extremely tough and resistant patterns of customary interaction. It is difficult to say whether a change in these patterns is a condition of general mobilization or can only be achieved by it. But either way, the fact that they were generally reinforced rather than reduced in the postwar period of industrialization and affluence was an important feature of the hegemonic situation.

217

Agents and opponents

The argument so far has sketched ways in which this situation can be analysed, and some of the mechanisms of division and control that can be seen at work. Assuming that hegemony is a specific historical situation and not a permanent condition, it must be produced by processes that are identifiable in history. Gramsci's own analyses suggest that the identification may revolve on specific groups of people, notably the intellectuals.

Ministers and priests seem to be of much less importance in the Australian situation than in Catholic Italy, though some influence can be seen. The Catholic church was important in sustaining the Movement though it was laymen rather than priests who were most active. Protestant clerics, as Wolfsohn observed in a biting essay on 'ideology makers', helped to maintain the miasma of bourgeois respectability in public life.[18] Of late the mist seems a little clearer, and protestant ideologists more concerned with fighting the pornographers than calling for national purpose and social discipline.

Teachers and journalists seem likely to have been of more importance in terms of the size of their audience and continuity of contact. Both are highly unionized occupations, but both have longish preparation and qualifying periods, a claim to semiprofessional status, and a clearcut internal hierarchy of prestige and promotion. Both, moreover, work under strong constraints from superiors with well-defined traditional expectations about their activity. Understandably then, the content of the communication they engage in is for the most part perfectly compatible with the *status quo*. Is it more than compatible: can these groups be seen as active agents in the creation of a hegemonic situation?

Certainly the content of their work, if we go back to the time of the first world war and before, was so; in a period when working-class mobilization was occurring, the content of the papers was mostly hostile, while the directly political content of school lessons was nationalist and imperialist to a marked degree.[19] But that evidently did not prevent mobilization then, while in the last generation in teaching at least, the flagwaving and ethnocentrism has considerably declined. There are other kinds of influence than direct persuasion: as in the case of journalism discussed in Chapter 9, so with teachers the influence may have more to do with the concepts in which people think about the social world than with their attitudes. In some ways, also, while the propaganda content of teaching has declined, the organization of the school system has moved in a more socially integrative direction. The most notable case of this is the development of comprehensive secondary schools, in place of the sharply segregated systems of the prewar period. In practice there are inequalities within them, as shown in Chapter 8, but the comprehensive school with its general-education programmes is still an important symbol of 'community' solidarity and social integration.

So also is the army of social workers, now commonly organized in departments with titles like 'Community Welfare' that are almost banners announcing their ideological function. Administering private or state relief to the poor, traumatized, or incompetent, social workers simultaneously announce the benevolence of the system and the oddity of not succeeding in it. How far they serve as controllers of potential dissidence is unclear; certainly there is now some shift among them towards the view that they should be aiding the mobilization of their clients. But it is not hard to see the ideological effects of their activity in terms of legitimation, in terms of the definition of poverty and suffering as aberrations, on the fringe of an otherwise contented community, rather than an integral product of an integrally divided social order.[20] In this they are not alone, though they are certainly the clearest example. The state in its benign aspect, its welfare service, and general uplift departments, must be seen as an important force in the construction of hegemony. In the postwar case, an important extension of this kind of state activity occurred shortly before the conservatives took state power. Though previously quite enterprising in denouncing the extension of bureaucracy, the federal Liberals took over the welfare apparatus and ran it on much the same lines as before. They were not stupid.

Social workers are less clearly intellectuals than teachers and journalists, though there may be important elements of persuasion in their daily work. If the discussion earlier in this chapter is accepted at least as asking some of the right questions – whatever may be thought of the answers – it indicates the importance in the creation and maintenance of hegemony, of other groups who are decidedly not intellectuals. To make the point only one case is needed – that of parents, who are plainly the social category most closely involved in the creation and transmission of sex differentiation. As we penetrate to levels byond that of political consciousness, the need to extend the account of agents becomes sharper. The idea of agency also must change, as one moves into the realm of unintended or unconscious effects. Some intellectuals are hirelings of the ruling class, though not all are; but it makes little sense to think of any parents that way, though their due performance of expected tasks may be in fact more crucial to the interests of the ruling class than the scribblings of any number of journalists or academics.

In defining hegemony as a situation, I wanted to stress its historically contingent character; or to put in plainer English, the fact that cultural control can be opposed, weakened, and overcome. It may be difficult, but it is possible. In an analysis of hegemony there should always be a consideration of counter-hegemonic activity.

Again it is useful to consider intellectuals. Though in a weak position, groups of socialist intellectuals continued to be active in the 1950s and 1960s, a number of them splitting from the old Communist Party and concentrating their activity on magazines such as *Outlook* and *Arena*. Intellectuals, especially staff and students in the universities, were an important early base for the sexual liberation movements, and a vigorous literature analysing the oppression of women sprang up alongside a revived socialist literature of class analysis in the 1970s. The most important example of counter-hegemonic activity was the campaign against the Vietnam war in the late 1960s: counter-hegemonic as well as directly political, because it involved a violation of the dominant ideological view of Australia's place in the world, it involved symbolic law-breaking in demonstrations, and in the later stages a highly effective campaign of ridicule against the conscription authorities. The campaigners were a very interesting alliance of new intelligentsia with traditional working-class militants; an unstable alliance, as it turned out, though both groups were later incorporated with others in the Whitlam coalition of 1972–4, and a similar alliance was created in the 'green ban' movement against urban redevelopment in the early 1970s.[21]

The most consciously counter-hegemonic movement, though

it recruited very largely from students, has had more than a tinge of anti-intellectualism. This is the counter-culture or alternative society, the groups of fulltime or part-time dropouts who have attempted to reconstruct their lives outside the labour market around a system of collective, mainly rural, production and a sharp redirection and simplification of personal consumption. It is interesting, as a sign of the persistence of some pre-capitalist and anti-capitalist popular sentiment, that these groups have often been able to make effective use of rural traditions and win acceptance from country people who in terms of sexual morality, dress, speech, party preference, and general squareness, are polar opposites.[22]

That there is also latent anti-capitalist feeling in urban contexts can be seen from episodes such as the Ford strike discussed at the beginning of this book. The riot on the day of the abortive return to work, though played up as a violent episode, did not actually involve many attacks against persons; the strikers mainly directed their energies towards smashing or at least marking things that symbolized the company and its system of control-gates, signs, a wall, the administration block. That was a flash flood, but it is not the only event of its kind. There is a regular undercurrent of sabotage in large industrial plants; that this worries management is sugggested by GMH's sacking of an Adelaide shop steward in February 1975 on the grounds that he sympathized with saboteurs. Attempts have been made in the last few years to blow up a BHP oil installation in South Australia, and a pipeline in Melbourne, the latter being part of a green-ban campaign. The Builders Laborers in Sydney in the period of their recently-deposed radical leadership even experimented with the occupation of building sites, though they did not attempt to work them.

This survey can end, then, on a more discordant note than was sounded earlier. The system does not have it all its own way, even with the apparatuses of control that have been sketched. There is opposition and conflict, within cultural institutions as well as job sites, as has been shown in high schools in the last few years. There are people, and there are forms of action, that have escaped the net; though in the last few decades they have mostly been fairly isolated or have been deflected from a confrontation with the core of the capitalist system. One of the most important things that intellectuals can do through their proper work is to overcome that isolation and prevent such deflections. Being counter-hegemonic is not enough. One must be relevantly counter-hegemonic, and in sufficient masses to do real damage, and be able to carry through to the actual construction of a human society. In both critique and construction socialist intellectuals have a massive work to do.

NOTES

CHAPTER 2

1 V. G. Childe, *How Labour Governs* [1923], 2nd edition, Melbourne, MUP, 1964, with introduction by F. B. Smith.
2 B. Fitzpatrick, *British Imperialism and Australia* [1939], reprinted Sydney, SUP, 1971; *The British Empire in Australia* [1941], 2nd edition 1949, reprinted Melbourne, Macmillan, 1969; *The Australian People*, Melbourne, MUP, 1946; *A Short History of the Australian Labour Movement*, Melbourne, Rawson's Book Shop, 1940; *The Rich Get Richer*, Melbourne, Rawson's Book Shop, 1944. For a sketch of his life see G. Blainey, 'Brian Fitzpatrick (1906–1965) and his works', *Business Archives and History*, 1966, vol. 6, 77–81; for a very useful account of his programme and ideas, and a corrective to critics, see H. Bourke, 'A reading of Brian Fitzpatrick', *Labour History*, 1974, no. 27, 1–11.
3 T. Irving and B. Berzins, 'History and the new left: beyond radicalism', in R. Gordon, ed., *The Australian New Left*, Melbourne, Heinemann, 1970, 66–94; H. V. Evatt, *Rum Rebellion* [1937], 6th edition, Sydney, Angus and Robertson, 1947, e.g. 85.
4 The basic economic revision is by N. G. Butlin, *Investment in Australian Economic Development 1861–1900*, Cambridge, CUP, 1964; for a clear recognition of class formation in the city (though not a model of how to analyse it) see R. Lawson, *Brisbane in the 1890s*, St Lucia, University of Queensland Press, 1973; and the excellent short history by P. Nagel, *North Adelaide 1837–1901* [1971], Adelaide, Austaprint, 1974.
5 T. Rowse, 'The conspicuous consumption of ideology: George Johnston's *The Australians*', *Australian Studies Booklist*, no. 2, 1974–5, 3–12; review of Docker, *Australian Left Review*, no. 46, 1975, 45–50.
6 M. Kiddle, *Men of Yesterday*, Melbourne, MUP, 1961; D. B. Waterson, *Squatter, Selector and Storekeeper*, Sydney, SUP, 1968; G. Serle, *The Rush to be Rich*, Melbourne, MUP, 1971, 86–123.
7 I. A. H. Turner, *Industrial Labour and Politics*, Canberra, ANU, 1965, xvii.
8 R. A. Gollan, *Radical and Working Class Politics*, Melbourne, MUP and ANU, 1960, *passim*; for the Legislative Assembly, 51.
9 *Ibid.*, 33.
10 *Ibid.*, 104.

11 *Industrial Labour and Politics*, xiv.
12 R. A. Gollan, *Revolutionaries and Reformists*, Canberra, ANU Press, 1975, 284.
13 *Radical and Working Class Politics*, 213.
14 *Industrial Labour and Politics*, 9.
15 M. Dixson, 'Stubborn resistance: the Northern New South Wales miners' lockout of 1929–30', in J. Iremonger *et al.*, ed., *Strikes*, Sydney, Angus and Robertson, 1973, 128–42; P. Cochrane, 'The Wonthaggi coal strike, 1934', *Labour History*, 1974, no. 27, 12–30; L. Richardson, 'Dole queue patriots: the Port Kembla pig-iron strike of 1938', in Iremonger, *Strikes*, 143–58.
16 *Industrial Labour and Politics*, xviii, xx.
17 *Revolutionaries and Reformists*, 288.
18 R. Ward, *The Australian Legend* [1958], Melbourne, OUP, 2nd edition, 1966, 45 n. 36 on social attitudes; 17, 65 on children; 94–100 on sexuality; *cf.* E. H. Erikson, *Childhood and Society* [1950], revised edition, Harmondsworth, Penguin, 1965, 13.
19 *Australian Legend*, 228.
20 *Ibid.*, 13.
21 *Ibid.*, *passim*, esp. 184.
22 *Ibid.*, 19, 40–1. His argument is rightly criticized by H. McQueen, *A New Britannia*, Melbourne, Penguin, 1970, 124.
23 *Australian Legend*, 184; *cf.* 242–5. The importance of environmental explanations to earlier Australian intellectuals has been pointed out by W. Osmond; for an interesting illustration of their political impact in the form of an acceptance by the Labour Party of physical planning as a means of social change, see P. Spearritt, 'The Consensus Politics of Physical Planning in Sydney', B.A. Hons. thesis, Department of Government, University of Sydney, 1972.
24 E.g. *New Britannia*, 90.
25 *Ibid.*, 126. The argument was announced in McQueen's 'Convicts and rebels', *Labour History*, 1968, no. 15, 3–30.
26 *New Britannia*, 124–5, 177.
27 *Ibid.*, 153, 180.
28 *Ibid.*, 13; *cf.* his reply to critics in 'Australo-marxismus: on some reactions to *A New Britannia*', *Politics*, 1972, vol. 7, 48–54.
29 C. M. H. Clark, *Select Documents in Australian History*, Sydney, Angus and Robertson, vol. i, 1950; vol. ii, 1955; *Sources of Australian History*, London, OUP, 1957; *A Short History of Australia* [1963], revised edition, New York, Mentor, 1969; *A History of Australia*, Melbourne, MUP, vol. i, 1962; vol. ii, 1968; vol. iii, 1973. For the chapter cited, *History*, ii, 81–109.
30 His formal definition of civilization (*History*, i, 3 – 'a people brought out of a state of barbarism') is exceptionally vague; I am taking it in the sense in which he develops his major themes in general remarks later on – e.g. i, 380. *Cf.* the dicussion of the problem in V. G. Childe, *Social Evolution*, London, Watts, 1951.
31 *History*, ii, 290–1; i, 254–5.
32 *Select Documents*, ii, xvi–xvii.
33 *History*, i, 235. Cf. the startling 'in the meantime', *Short History*, 229: what was happening in the mean time was urbanization and industrialization.
34 For the latter instances, *History*, iii, 245–68; *Short History*, 221, 223, 248–9.

35 R. G. Collingwood, *The Idea of History*, Oxford, OUP, 1946, esp. 274ff.
36 A striking case of this is the comment on convict women, *History*, i, 246 – typical of historians' treatment of the issue.
37 *History*, ii, 82, 86, 90, 166; iii, 115, 306; *Short History*, 259.
38 *History*, iii, 284.
39 Since I have been mainly concerned with the concept of class and its connection with method, the discussion has largely ignored the actual propositions about the history of the class structure put forward by these writers and others such as Martin, and the argument over their claims. But for an example of Clark's formulation of a position about bourgeois dominance at the end of the nineteenth century later adopted by McQueen, see *Select Documents*, ii, xii.
40 See W. Osmond, *The Dilemma of an Australian Sociology*, Melbourne, Arena Publications, 1972; J. Zubrzycki, 'The teaching of sociology in Australian universities, past and present', in J. Zubrzycki, ed., *The Teaching of Sociology in Australia and New Zealand*, Melbourne, Cheshire, 1970, 1–32.
41 M. Ancich, R. W. Connell, J. A. Fisher and M. Kolff, 'A descriptive bibliography of published research and writing on social stratification in Australia, 1946–67', *ANZ Journal of Sociology*, 1969, vol. 5, 48–76, 128–52. There is a persistent myth that such research is very rare or very new, which says more about sociologists' self-images than about the real state of affairs. For an illuminating example, that totally ignores the socialist tradition, see K. B. Mayer, 'Sociology in Australia and New Zealand', *Sociology and Social Research*, 1964, vol. 49, 27–31.
42 O. A. Oeser and S. B. Hammond, ed., *Social Structure and Personality in a City*, London, Routledge and Kegan Paul, 1954, ch. 17 esp.; O. A. Oeser and F. E. Emery, *Social Structure and Personality in a Rural Community*, London, Routledge and Kegan Paul, 1954, chs 1–3.
43 E.g. *City*, 101–2, 249ff.
44 *City*, 261ff.
45 A. P. Elkin, ed., *Marriage and the Family in Australia*, Sydney, Angus and Robertson, 1957, introduction; and for its wider context in his thought and teaching, 'Anthropology: its study and use in Australia', *International Social Science Journal*, 1955, vol. 7 no. 2, 234–44.
46 J. I. Martin, 'Marriage, the family, and class', in Elkin, *Marriage and the Family*, 25, 31.
47 Notably in 'An analytical approach to the theory of social stratification', reprinted in *Essays in Sociological Theory*, revised edition, New York, Free Press, 1954, 69–88.
48 'Marriage', 32.
49 *Ibid.*, 36.
50 *Ibid.*, 49.
51 M. Kiddle, *Caroline Chisholm*, abridged edition, Melbourne, MUP, 1969, 57.
52 A. F. Davies and S. Encel, ed., *Australian Society*, Melbourne, Cheshire, 1965, 1 – they include the census as a type of social survey.
53 P. Lafitte, *The Person in Psychology*, London, Routledge and Kegan Paul, 1957, 133ff.

54 A. A. Congalton, *Status and Prestige in Australia*, Melbourne, Cheshire, 1969, 5.
55 J. D. Allingham, 'On the measurement of occupational prestige', *ANZ Journal of Sociology*, 1965, vol. 1, 53–61; P. Morrison, review in *Australian Quarterly*, 1969, vol. 41 no. 4, 120–2; R. J. Stimson, 'Perceived status and residential desirability in Adelaide suburbs', ANZAAS Congress, Sydney, 1972; R. J. Stimson and E. A. Cleland, *A Socio-Economic Atlas of Adelaide*, Adelaide, Flinders University, 1975.
56 *Status and Prestige*, 49–51.
57 L. Broom, F. L. Jones, and J. Zubrzycki, 'An occupational classification of the Australian workforce', supplement to *ANZ Journal of Sociology*, 1965, vol. 1 no. 2; F. L. Jones, 'Occupational change in Australia, 1911–66', *Indian Journal of Sociology*, 1971, vol. 11, 123–36.
58 F. L. Jones, 'A social profile of Canberra, 1961', *ANZ Journal of Sociology*, 1965, vol. 1, 107–20; 'A social ranking of Melbourne suburbs', *ANZ Journal of Sociology*, 1967, vol. 3, 93–110; *Dimensions of Urban Social Structure*, Canberra, ANU Press, 1969; *cf.* p. 35 for a 'bootstraps' definition of class.
59 L. Broom, F. L. Jones, and J. Zubrzycki, 'Social stratification in Australia', in J. A. Jackson, ed., *Social Stratification*, Cambridge, CUP, 1968, 215.
60 *Ibid.*, 229–30.
61 F. L. Jones, 'Social stratification in Australia: an overview of a research program', *Social Science Information*, 1974, vol. 13, 99–118.
62 For a summary of the attitude literature see M. Goot and R. W. Connell, *Social Patterns in Public Opinion*, forthcoming.
63 R. R. Alford, *Party and Society*, London, Murray, 1964, 176, 337; 'Class voting in the Anglo-American political systems', in S. M. Lipset and S. Rokkan, ed., *Party Systems and Voter Alignments*, New York, Free Press, 1967, 67–93.
64 C. Burns, *Parties and People*, Melbourne, MUP, 1961; A. F. Davies, *Images of Class*, Sydney, SUP, 1967; for a biting critique see R. Thompson, 'Class as fiction', *Arena*, no. 13, 1967, 62–8.
65 H. Stretton, *Ideas for Australian Cities*, Adelaide, the author, 1970; Urban Systems Corporation, *City of Adelaide Planning Study: 2nd Progress Report*, Adelaide, City Council, 1973; see p. 25 for a typically fatuous set of 'possible priorities for action' to achieve this.
66 R. A. Wild, 'Social stratification or statistical exercises?', *Politics*, 1971, vol. 6, 169–77; *Bradstow*, Sydney, Angus and Robertson, 1974; P. Hiller, 'The subjective dimension of social stratification: the case of the self-identification question', *ANZ Journal of Sociology*, 1973, vol. 9, 14–21.
67 L. Fox, *Wealthy Men*, Sydney, Current Book Distributors, 1946; G. R. Trenoweth [?], *The Money Monopoly in Australia*, no publication details but possibly Melbourne *c.* 1934; E. W. Campbell, *The 60 Rich Families Who Own Australia*, Sydney, Current Book Distributors, 1963; L. Fox, *Australia Taken Over?* Sydney, the author, 1974; for Fitzpatrick see n. 2 above. S. Encel's discussion of this literature, in *Equality and Authority*, Melbourne, Cheshire, 1970, 327, is a little misleading in calling pamphlets such as Rawling's *Who Owns Australia?* (Sydney, 1937) simply 'left-wing' – this is anti-bank more than anti-ruling-class and has affinities with the social credit position.

68 The principal works are E. L. Wheelwright, *Ownership and Control of Australian Companies*, Sydney, Law Book Co., 1957; E. L. Wheelwright and J. Miskelly, *Anatomy of Australian Manufacturing Industry*, Sydney, Law Book Co., 1967; J. Playford, *Neo-capitalism in Australia*, Melbourne, Arena Publications, 1969.

69 Notably Osmond, *Dilemma of an Australian Sociology*.

70 *Equality and Authority*, 39.

71 *Ibid.*, 101–8.

72 See R. G. Brown, 'Poverty in Australia', *Australian Quarterly*, 1963, vol. 35 no. 2, 75–9; 'Poverty in Australia – the evidence', *British Journal of Sociology*, 1964, vol. 15, 150–64, for the origins of this literature.

73 R. F. Henderson, A. Harcourt and R. J. A. Harper, *People in Poverty*, Melbourne, Cheshire, 1970.

74 For an illuminating discussion of these essays see W. Osmond, 'Toward self-awareness', in R. Gordon, ed., *The Australian New Left*, Melbourne, Heinemann, 1970, 192ff.

75 K. Rowley, 'Pastoral capitalism', *Intervention*, no. 1, 1972, 9–26; 'The political economy of Australia since the war', in J. Playford and D. Kirsner, ed., *Australian Capitalism*, Melbourne, Penguin, 1972, 265–324.

76 Some examples of this were cited in n. 15; see now A. Curthoys, S. Eade and P. Spearritt, ed., *Women at Work*, Canberra, Australian Society for the Study of Labour History, 1975.

77 E.g. M. Indyk, 'Establishment and nouveau capitalists', *ANZ Journal of Sociology*, 1974, vol. 10, 128–34; and work on the ruling class between the wars by P. Cochrane at Adelaide University.

78 L. Sandercock, *Cities for Sale*, Melbourne, MUP, 1975.

79 E.g. *Papers from the National Women's Conference on Feminism and Socialism*, Melbourne, Women's Conference Committee, 1974.

CHAPTER 3

1 There were 198 407 companies recorded in *Taxation Statistics, 1971/2* (the most recent available). The number of shareholders is a very rough estimate, based on outdated Gallup Poll figures; there is urgent need for a good study of this.

2 J. Playford, 'Who rules Australia?', in J. Playford and D. Kirsner, ed., *Australian Capitalism*, Melbourne, Penguin, 1972, 113.

3 P. Karmel and M. Brunt, *The Structure of the Australian Economy*, Melbourne, Cheshire, 1962; P. Brown and H. Hughes, 'The market structure of Australian manufacturing industry, 1914 to 1963–4', in C. Forster, ed., *Australian Economic Development in the Twentieth Century*, London, George Allen & Unwin, 1970, 169–207, esp. p. 195.

4 E. L. Wheelwright, *Ownership and Control of Australian Companies*, Sydney, Law Book Co., 1957; E. L. Wheelwright and J. Miskelly, *Anatomy of Australian Manufacturing Industry*, Sydney, Law Book Co., 1967; T. Sykes, 'In a few hands', *Australian Financial Review*, 12 February 1973 to 16 February 1973.

5 H. Rolfe, *The Controllers*, Melbourne, Cheshire, 1967.

6 S. Encel, *Equality and Authority*, Melbourne, Cheshire, 1970, 303–7, 376–2.

7 Wheelwright and Miskelly, *Anatomy*, 38–45; J. Playford, 'Myth of the sixty families', *Arena*, 1970, no. 23, 26–42.

8 E. L. Wheelwright, *Radical Political Economy*, Sydney, A.N.Z. Book, 1974, 116–22; Playford, 'Who rules?', 120; Encel, *Equality and Authority*, 4.

9 Wheelwright, *Political Economy*, 116.

10 Playford, 'Who rules?', 123–48, and *Neo-capitalism in Australia*, Melbourne, Arena Publications, 15–32; Encel, *Equality and Authority*, 364–75.

11 B. McFarlane, *Economic Policy in Australia*, Melbourne, Cheshire, 1968; R. Catley and B. McFarlane, *From Tweedledum to Tweedledee*, Sydney, ANZ Book, 1974.

12 Playford, 'Who rules?', 112, 123, 125–6.

13 Encel, *Equality and Authority*, 322.

14 B. Fitzpatrick and E. L. Wheelwright, *The Highest Bidder*, Melbourne, Lansdowne, 1965.

15 Commonwealth Treasury, *Overseas Investment in Australia*, Treasury Economic Paper No. 1, Canberra, Australian Government Publishing Service, 1972.

16 Encel, *Equality and Authority*, 339; Playford, 'Who rules?', 113.

17 B. L. Johns, 'Private overseas investment in Australia: profitability and motivation', *Economic Record*, 1967, vol. 43, 233–61.

18 Wheelwright, *Ownership and Control*, 82.

19 For an up-to-date summary see J. S. Western, *Australian Mass Media*, Sydney, AIPS, 1975.

20 J. R. Poynter, *Russell Grimwade*, Melbourne, MUP, 1967.

21 A. Marshall, *The Gay Provider*, Melbourne, Cheshire, 1961.

22 Wheelwright, *Political Economy*, 130–1.

23 See G. McCarthy, *The Great Big Australian Takeover Book*, Sydney, Angus and Robertson, 1973.

24 R. S. Parker, 'Power in Australia', *ANZ Journal of Sociology*, 1965, vol. 1, 85–96.

25 A. L. May, *Battle for the Banks*, Sydney, SUP, 1968. For this interpretation, see R. W. Connell and T. H. Irving, 'Yes, Virginia, there is a ruling class', in H. Mayer and H. Nelson, ed., *Australian Politics, a Fourth Reader*, Melbourne, Cheshire, 1976.

26 See Chapter 1 of *Class Structure in Australian History*.

27 For surveys of executive rakeoff, which indicate bonus payments alone can add around 20% to the salaries of top management, see C. Braybrook, 'Executive salaries, bonus payments and fringe benefits in 145 manufacturing firms', *Personnel Practice Bulletin*, 1969, vol. 25, 184–211; and D. Gunzburg, 'Executive salaries and benefits in non-manufacturing firms', *Personnel Practice Bulletin*, 1971, vol. 27, 11–45.

28 Occupational breakdowns of shareholders are few and far between; but for interesting early examples see R. K. Yorston, 'Some accounting implications arising from the corporation viewed as a social unit', *Australian Accountant*, 1952, vol. 22, 41–54, 77–87, esp. Appendix A; and C. Turnbull, 'The diverse ownership of C.S.R.', in A. G. Lowndes, ed., *South Pacific Enterprise*, Sydney, Angus & Robertson, 1956, 271–83 – which mendaciously claims that the shareholders' list is 'indistinguishable from a "sample" of all but the most unfortunate or feckless sections of the community' (unless the unfortunate and feckless are the majority of the population!).

29 See the detailed account in A. R. Hall, *The Stock Exchange of Melbourne and the Victorian Economy*, Canberra, ANU Press, 1968.

30 Senate Select Committee on Securities and Exchange, *Australian Securities Markets and their Regulation*, Canberra, Australian Government Publishing Service, 1974.
31 For biographies of these figures (mostly bad) see C. Edwards, *Bruce of Melbourne*, London, Heinemann, 1965; D. C. Kemp, *Big Businessmen*, Melbourne, Institute of Public Affairs, 1964; D. Nicholas, *The Pacemaker*, Adelaide, Brolga Books, 1969; K. Perkins, *Menzies, Last of the Queen's Men*, Adelaide, Rigby, 1968.
32 For a development of this distinction see Chapter 7 of *Class Structure in Australian History*.
33 Encel, *Equality and Authority*, 66–70, 268–74.
34 See W. D. Forsyth, *Governor Arthur's Convict System*, London, Longman, 1935; N. G. Butlin, *Investment in Australian Economic Development, 1861–1900*, Cambridge, Cambridge UP, 1964.
35 Playford, 'Who rules?', 133–8.

CHAPTER 4

1 For Wheelwright's work, see the citations in Chapter 3; K. Sheridan, *The Firm in Australia*, Melbourne, Nelson, 1974.
2 This figure for 1967–8 is given in Department of Trade and Industry, *Report of the Committee on Small Business* (1971), Canberra, Government Printers, 1974.
3 H. Rolfe, *The Controllers*, Melbourne, Cheshire, 1967.
4 *Kompass Australia*, Melbourne, Peter Isaacson, 1973, 3rd edition, vol. 2; *Jobson's Year Book of Public Companies of Australia and New Zealand*, and *Jobson's Mining Year Book*, Sydney, Jobson's Financial Services, 1973.
5 See the discussion of internal financing in Sheridan, *Firm*, 128–31.
6 The outline of BHP's history is in H. Hughes, *The Australian Iron and Steel Industry 1848–1962*, Melbourne, MUP, 1964; B.H.P., *Seventy-five Years of B.H.P. Development in Industry*, Melbourne, 1960; G. Blainey, *The Steel Master*, Melbourne, Macmillan, 1971. For recent developments see Jobson's *Year Books* and BHP's *Annual Reports*.
7 For the history of RTZ, see R. West, *River of Tears*, London, Earth Island, 1972; not reliable in detail, but a fascinating account of the overall pattern. The Australian history is detailed in CRA's *Submission to the Senate Select Committee on Foreign Ownership and Control*, July 1972.
8 Collins House still awaits its biographer – or perhaps team of biographers. But an outline of the group's formation and operation can be gained from G. Blainey, *The Rush that Never Ended*, Melbourne, MUP, 2nd edition, 1969; and W. S. Robinson, *If I Remember Rightly*, Melbourne, Cheshire, 1967. There are also some bad house histories of particular companies in the group. For recent developments see Jobson's *Year Books* and *Mining Year Books*, and *Annual Reports* of the companies named.
9 For an account of these relationships see R. A. Witton, 'The corporate connection', *Dissent*, 1972, no. 29, 28–41; for the growth of motor manufacturing see P. Stubbs, *The Australian Motor Industry*, Melbourne, Cheshire, 1972; for a useful general survey of the Australian oil industry and its history, R. Murray, *Fuels Rush In*, Melbourne, Macmillan, 1972.

CHAPTER 5

1 See the very useful analysis of this tendency in T. Irving and B. Berzins, 'History and the new left', in R. Gordon, ed., *The Australian New Left*, Melbourne, Heinemann, 1970, 66–94.

2 N. E. Long, 'The local community as an ecology of games', *American Journal of Sociology*, 1958, vol. 64, 251–61.

3 Since it would be very laborious to cite references for every step in this tangled tale, I will give a general citation here.

Business operations are normally conducted in a fair degree of privacy, often deliberate secrecy. A study of these events is immensely aided by the coincidence of the Minsec collapse with a vigorous Senate enquiry into stock-market scandals. Evidence given to this enquiry, widely reported in the press at the time, and now published in the report of the Senate Select Committee on Securities and Exchange, *Australian Securities Markets and their Regulation*, Canberra, Australian Government Publishing Service, 1974 and 1975, yields very important information about both investment groups and the inner history of the Nabarlek companies. Unless otherwise specified, the following account of events up to August 1971 is based on the evidence published by this committee and the conclusions stated in its own report. It is a pity that the committee's analysis is not up to the standard of its detective work. It is written wholly from the point of view of protecting the outside capitalists (variously called 'the public' or 'the investor') from the inside ones. Apart from proving again the gullibility of small capitalists, and the ingenuity of the bigger ones in finding ways of gobbling them up, it adds nothing to our understanding of the basic processes.

My account of Patricks and its strategy leans heavily on the excellent paper by M. S. Indyk, 'Establishment and nouveau capitalists: power and conflict in big business', *ANZ Journal of Sociology*, 1974, vol. 10, 128–34, based on published evidence and interviews. There is a useful six-part resume of the other group's history by J. Byrne, 'The Minsec affair', *The Australian*, 23 April 1973 to 28 April 1973 – the liquidator's remark quoted later in the text is reported in the last of these articles; and a very good account of its early career by G. Souter, 'Rise and fall of the House of Minsec', *Advertiser*, 24 February 1971 to 26 February 1971, which naturally does not cover the liquidation. Neither gives very much detail on the market operations by which Minsec made its money; some more, though still not a great deal, is in T. A. Nestel's evidence to the Rae Committee. The brokers at flood tide are sketched by R. Ackland and K. Graham, 'The Brokers', *Business Review*, 30 July 1970, 11–13, 23. Few economists seem to have studied the boom. There is useful background in P. J. Rose, 'Aspects of financing the mineral industry in Australia', *Australian Economic Review*, 1969, no. 4, 7–18; and *Australian Securities Markets*, Melbourne, Cheshire, 1969. R. E. McKinnon, 'The 1969–70 Boom on the Australian Stock Exchanges...', B. Ec. Hons thesis, Flinders University, is the best account I have seen of the Poseidon boom, but does not carry the story beyond the Tasminex fiasco of early 1970.

4 The Rae Committee's account of Minsec, documenting its history and *inter alia* its dealing in shares of subsidiaries, is in Senate Select Committee, *Australian Securities Markets...*, Part 1, vol. 1, chapter

14; and for a summary of T. A. Nestel's *in camera* evidence on 'runs', see chapter 8, 7–14. Note that the 1969–70 profit quoted in the text is different from that quoted in Minsec's report and the press at the time. *Australian Securities Markets...*, Part 1, vol. 1, 14.39–14.44, concludes that a sum of about $3 million was quietly deducted from the profits declared for that year to conceal heavy losses incurred in trading of Poseidon stock early in 1970–1.

5 Indyk, 'Establishment and nouveau capitalists', 132–3.

6 There was a genuine rise in mining investment, dating from the early 1960s, and some of the bigger companies did begin mining operations about this time, notably in iron ore. And there was generally an expectation of long-term profits from mineral production, which made the whole show work. But if we focus on the share trading operations of 1969–70 these remarks hold true.

7 See the material on ownership cited in M. Goot and R. W. Connell, *Social Patterns in Public Opinion*, forthcoming.

8 The position before the mining share boom is discussed in B. Fitzpatrick and E. L. Wheelwright, *The Highest Bidder*, Melbourne, Lansdowne, 1965. The official survey of the position in the early 1970s, which gives this estimate, is Treasury Economic Paper No. 1, *Overseas Investment in Australia*, May 1972: see pp. 21–7. Economists have paid more attention to this issue than to the stock exchanges. There are some useful articles and a short bibliography in G. D. McColl, ed., *Overseas Trade and Investment*, Ringwood, Penguin, 1972. Wheelwright's re-analysis of the position is in 'Development and dependence: the Australian problem', *Australian Quarterly*, 1971, vol. 43 no. 3, 22–39. On the growth of American business in Australia, see D. T. Brash, *American Investment in Australian Industry*, Canberra, ANU Press, 1966; and M. Richards and R. Witton, ed., *The American Connection*, Melbourne, Macmillan, 1976.

9 The key policy statements by Gorton and McMahon, referred to here and later, are in *Hansard* (House of Representatives) for 16 September 1969 and 26 September 1972 respectively.

10 These takeovers were extensively reported and debated in the financial press at the time, which is my basic source for the following discussion, especially the *Australian Financial Review*. G. McCarthy, *The Great Big Australian Takeover Book*, Sydney, Angus & Robertson, 1973, is a useful if messy survey of them; his analysis does not get much deeper than a call for better national leadership.

11 For these interesting figures – notable for their demonstration of the role of nominee companies in concealing foreign shareholdings – see the report of the Senate Standing Committee on Industry and Trade, *The Proposed Takeover of Ansett Transport Industries*, Commonwealth Parliamentary Paper No. 35 of 1972. For the background to the political intervention see P. Blazey, *Bolte: A Political Biography*, Milton, Jacaranda, 1972.

12 It is interesting to note that 15% of BHP shares are owned by shareholders with foreign addresses, and that 24% of the registered shareholders are foreigners (*Annual Report 1973*, 41). The percentage of shares, if the Ansett and TNT figures are any guide, may be doubled when we take account of shares which are held for foreign owners by Australian nominee companies. There are three nominee companies among BHP's top four shareholders. BHP is of course a

joint venturer with overseas firms in several large mining and manufacturing operations in Australia, and increasingly abroad. And in August 1973 it was announced that the chairman himself (Sir Ian McLennan) had been made a member of the International Council of the Morgan Guaranty Trust Co. of New York, the heart of one of the two greatest American business empires.

13 *Report No. 1* of the Senate Select Committee on Foreign Ownership and Control of Australian Resources, 25 October 1972, 4.

14 A. Reid, *The Gorton Experiment*, Sydney, Shakespeare Head, 1971; L. Oakes and D. Solomon, *The Making of an Australian Prime Minister*, Melbourne, Cheshire, 1973; which with Reid's earlier and better book *The Power Struggle*, Sydney, Shakespeare Head, 1969, offer a virtually continuous narrative of the Liberal Party leadership from 1967 to 1972. K. West, *Power in the Liberal Party*, Melbourne, Cheshire, 1965, is essential background on the Menzies era.

15 In the series 'I did it my way', *Sunday Australian*, 8 August 1971 to 12 September 1971. These articles led to Gorton's fall from the ministry; they are an important corrective to Reid's account.

16 See N. Blewett and D. Jaensch, *Playford to Dunstan*, Melbourne, Cheshire, 1971, especially Chapter 10; D. Jaensch, 'Conservatism's last gasp', *Politics*, 1972, vol. 7, 82–6, and 'The split in the political right in South Australia', *Politics*, 1974, vol. 9, 87–91; and from the angle of the reformers, S. Hall *et al.*, *A Liberal Awakening: The LM Story*, Adelaide, Investigator, 1973 (not 1937, as the copyright statement in the book plausibly suggests).

17 Oakes and Solomon, *Making*, have the key information on campaign finances and the involvement of these businessmen. For estimates of expenses in press and radio advertising, showing a virtual parity of Labor with Liberal expenditure, see S. McLean and P. Brennan, 'Cheque book democracy', *New Journalist*, 1973, no. 7, 16–17. But it is clear from figures in the 1973 Annual Report of the Australian Broadcasting Control Board that when Country Party and DLP advertising is added to the Liberals', the conservatives had their usual heavy advantage in the electronic media at least.

18 A classic illustration of this is the Vernon Report of 1965, mentioned in Chapter 3, which called for central planning by experts. Sir James Vernon was general manager of CSR. In this as in other ways following the Menzies example, Whitlam too appointed a general manager of CSR to head his committee of enquiry into manufacturing industry.

CHAPTER 6

1 *Nation Review*, 10 May 1974. Compare the interesting arrangement under which Federation Insurance pays annual commissions to the Country Party: *Australian*, 30 May 1975.

Again, it would be tedious to cite references for every event mentioned in this chapter. Unless otherwise mentioned, information can be found in the financial and daily press at the times noted. Citations will be given for quotes, and for events not generally reported.

2 *Advertiser*, 23 July 1973. On the formation of research and policy groups for the party by businessmen, see *Australian Financial Review (AFR)*, 27 June 1973; *Australian*, 21 February 1974; *National Times*, 10 March 1975. For the influence of marketing experts in

Snedden's 1974 campaign see L. Oakes and D. Solomon, *Grab for Power*, Melbourne, Cheshire, 1974, 192, 244–6, 262–4, 366–7, etc.

3 On the Anthony–Budd connection, *Nation Review*, 10 May 1974.

4 *Advertiser*, 2 March 1974; *Australian*, 22 May 1974, 25 July 1975.

5 The most comprehensive pre-election statement of the Labor programme is in J. McLaren, ed., *Towards a New Australia*, Melbourne, Cheshire, 1972. This, interestingly, has nothing by Connor and little reference to minerals and energy; but has clear statements, especially in the chapter by Hurford, of the underlying developmentalism of the approach.

6 M. Mackerras, 'The swing: variability and uniformity', in H. Mayer, ed., *Labor to Power*, Sydney, Angus and Robertson, 1973, 234–41, argues that the 2.5% can be seen as a second instalment in a nearly 10% swing to Labor since 1966. But the 1966 vote was abnormally low; and the fact that Labor did not proceed to sweep the states argues that there was no general social shift underlying the 1972 result.

7 See B. McFarlane, *Economic Policy in Australia*, Melbourne, Cheshire, 1968; J. Playford, *Neo-capitalism in Australia*, Melbourne, Arena, 1969.

8 See e.g. *Advertiser*, 30 August 1973; *National Times*, 28 April 1975; *Australian*, 11 July 1975.

9 See for instance the register of consultant firms compiled by the Cities Commission (Circular of 3 June 1974), which claimed this was 'common practice'; and the *Final Report* of the Steering Committee for Murray New Town Research Project IV, SA Department of the Premier, Economic Intelligence Unit, 1973, for an example of incentives.

10 *Interprobe*, produced by Philip Luker and Staff, publishers (*inter alia*) of *Foodweek*.

11 *AFR*, 8 October 1973.

12 For an early outline of Connor's policy, see his statement in the House of Representatives, 12 April 1973, *Parliamentary Debates*, 1973, H of R 83, 1411–14. For application of the majority ownership rule, see *Advertiser*, 13 October 1973, 9 November 1973; in negotiations on lead smelting the government allowed a majority interest to the British-owned CRA but insisted on an Australian veto on decisions, exercised by the Australian company in consultation with Connor's department – *Australian*, 8 June 1974. For the iron-ore cartel negotiations, *Advertiser*, 1 June 1973; on uranium exports, Connor's statement in the House, 23 October 1973, *Parliamentary Debates*, 1973, H of R 86, 2513–14. For the fuel distribution policy, *Australian*, 27 March 1973 (SA–Sydney pipeline); *AFR*, 3 October 1973 (NW Shelf). For the end of exploration subsidies to private companies, *Advertiser*, 8 April 1973.

13 For a sample, see the abuse of Connor by the former Liberal M.P. and defender of public morality E. St. John, now managing director of a mining company, in a submission to the Industries Assistance Commission – *Australian*, 27 May 1975.

14 Examples of attempts at direct control of prices are meat (*Australian*, 19 April 1973), and petrol in the ACT (*AFR*, 3 October 1973), which proved abortive. On the tariff exercise, see the article by one of the economists who recommended it, F. H. Gruen, 'The 25% Tariff Cut; was it a mistake?', *Australian Quarterly*, 1975, vol.

47 no. 2, 7–20, who notes that price control was not its primary purpose. For details of the second manoeuvre see J. Rydon, 'Prices and Incomes Referendum 1973: the pattern of failure', *Politics*, 1974, vol. 9, 22–30.

15 Chairman's address to S. A. Brewing Holdings Ltd., *Advertiser*, 19 May 1973.

16 *AFR*, 19 November 1973; 26 July 1973.

17 Sir Ian McLennan, *Chairman's Address*, 24 September 1974. On the first enquiry, see *Steel Price Rises*, Parliamentary Paper No. 59 of 1973.

18 For the Treasurer's statement, *Advertiser*, 12 September 1973. The claim about market depression was made by Hawke of the Brisbane Stock Exchange – *Australian*, 14 April 1973. For the later fluctuations see *Australian*, 7 July 1975, 12 July 1975; compare the jump in share market activity caused by the mini-budget of November 1974.

19 *Australian*, 27 May 1971. Nor is it peculiar to Australia: see the attempts to blame the Japanese government for the collapse of Nihon, reported in *AFR*, 23 April 1974.

20 See for instance the attacks by P. Samuel in the *Bulletin*, 11 May and 18 May 1974; and by L. C. Brodie-Hall of the WA Chamber of Mines, *AFR*, 15 May 1974.

21 Company report in *Advertiser*, 26 April 1973.

22 The best account of this framework of ideas is in D. Aitkin, *The Country Party in New South Wales*, Canberra, ANU Press, 1972. For a fine rhetorical Labor version of it, see Grassby's chapter in *Towards a New Australia*.

23 *Australian*, 19 May 1973.

24 For examples of the cartoon images, see the leaflet advertising *Interprobe, Don't be got at by Government or caught by Consumers*, Sydney, 1973; the AMA leaflet *So What's Wrong with Nationalised Health?*, n.d. (1974?); and for a fine series, *IPA Facts*, various dates. In May 1973 the AMA set up a fund to fight 'socialized medicine', 'creeping nationalization', etc. – see *Australian*, 14 May 1973; *Australian*, 15 May 1973. The dispute over the AIDC is analysed by M. Indyk in 'Establishment and nouveau capitalists', *ANZ Journal of Sociology*, 1974, vol. 10, 128–34.

25 *AFR*, 4 February 1973, which has an interesting comment on a group of business ideologues; on the Singleton dispute, *Australian*, 9 May 1974, *AFR*, 14 May 1974, and Oakes and Solomon, *Grab for Power*, 272–5.

26 BHP *Chairman's Address*, 11 September 1973; *AFR*, 24 October 1973.

27 R. Carnegie in *Australian*, 5 June 1975; R. Jackson in *Australian*, 27 May 1975.

28 See *AFR*, 13 August 1973; and for the BHP–CSR struggle to dominate the cement industry, *AFR*, 16 August 1973, 4 October 1973, 19 October 1973. On the steel can story see G. Lafitte, *B.H.P.'s Public Relations Fraud*, Melbourne, 1973.

29 *AFR*, 25 June 1973; *Advertiser*, 9, 10 September 1973; B. Juddery, *At the Centre*, Melbourne, Cheshire, 1974, 229.

30 Prime Minister's press statement, 8 April 1974.

31 See e.g. *AFR*, 18 October 1973. It may seem odd to call the doctors 'businessmen', but that is strictly true – they are one of the

wealthiest groups of professional entrepreneurs in the country, and
the issue at stake here was precisely the question of their
entrepreneurial independence and the social costs of allowing it to
continue.
32 See statements by Wilcox (Victoria), *AFR*, 14 August 1973; Knox
(Queensland), *AFR*, 23 May 1974.
33 For the IPA (NSW), see ads in *AFR*, 4 September 1973, 22
November 1973 – address, 'Asbestos House', Sydney. For the other
NSW group see C. J. Puplick, 'The New South Wales Constitutional
League and the "Double No" Campaign', *Politics*, 1974, vol. 9,
31–4. For the Australian Chamber of Commerce, *Advertiser*, 8
September 1973. For the content of Singleton's campaign, see J.
Singleton and G. Alexander, 'These elections were genuine',
Quadrant, Jan–Feb 1975, no. 93, 36–96. For another rousing
summary of current anti-state ideology see the display ad
'Announcing a new political party for *Workers*', *National Times*, 27
January 1975.
34 See the AIDC controversy already mentioned; speech by R. B.
Prowse of the Bank of NSW – who had made his mark in the 1940s
bank nationalization campaign against Labor – *Australian*, 16
October 1974; *National Times*, 6 May 1974.
35 *Australian*, 14 March 1974, on the survey. 'Company profits and
finance', *Australian Economic Review*, 1975, no. 3, 21–6 is a very
useful account of the trends, especially the effects of inflation.
36 *Australian*, 20 March 1974.
37 For mining, see *Industrial and Mining Review*, September 1973; and
National Times, 31 March 1975, reporting a coordinated PR
campaign. The 'image' advertising of multinational companies has
already been mentioned in the discussion of nationalism. For
advertising, see ads of the Australian Newspapers Council, e.g. in
National Times, 17 March 1975. For the appointment of Polites as a
national spokesman for business, *Australian*, 14 December 1972; for
the NCI proposal, *Australian*, 11 June 1975.
38 For Singleton's fundraising, see Oakes and Solomon, *Grab for
Power*, 272; for Combe's statement, *Australian*, 13 April 1974.

CHAPTER 7

1 One of the earliest and best is C. B. Stendler, *Children of Brasstown*,
Urbana, University of Illinois, 1949. The literature has been
reviewed by A. F. Davies, 'The child's discovery of social class',
ANZ Journal of Sociology, 1965, vol. 1, 21–37. Davies' own
argument about the origins of class consciousness is developed in
Images of Class, Sydney, SUP, 1967.
2 Thus distinguishing it from the concept specified by G. Lukács,
'Class consciousness', in *History and Class Consciousness*, London,
Merlin, 1971, 73.
3 This project is described in more detail in R. W. Connell, *The Child's
Construction of Politics*, Melbourne, MUP, 1971.
4 'Ali Baba and Cassim were brothers who lived in a town in Persia.
Cassim was rich and famous, while Ali Baba was so poor that he had
to earn a living by cutting wood and selling it in the town...' – from
Arabian Nights, Glasgow, The Children's Press, n.d. (c. 1930).
Compare the sexist modern version: 'Once upon a time there were
two brothers, Kassim and Ali Baba. Now Kassim had married a rich

wife and he had become a wealthy merchant. But Ali Baba had married a poor wife, and his money was soon gone. It was all he could do to earn enough money by cutting firewood to sell.' From *Ali Baba and The Forty Thieves*, Sydney, Golden Press, 1967.

For children's oral culture see P. and F. Opie, *The Lore and Language of School Children*, Oxford, OUP, 1959; and for Australian parallels, I. Turner, *Cinderella Dressed in Yella*, Melbourne, Heinemann, 1969.

5 See for an outline of his theory J. Piaget, *The Psychology of Intelligence*, London, Routledge and Kegan Paul, 1950.

6 See Davies, *Images*; and S. B. Hammond, 'The self and society', in O. A. Oeser and S. B. Hammond, ed., *Social Structure and Personality in a City*, London, Routledge and Kegan Paul, 1954, 261–78.

7 S. Ossowski, *Class Structure in the Social Consciousness*, London, Routledge and Kegan Paul, 1963.

8 If the sample were random, this would pass a severe test of statistical significance. Omitting 'don't knows' and dichotomizing age between 10 and 11, $\chi^2 = 17.45$, d.f. = 2, $P < 0.001$.

9 The detailed findings on this point match those of Stendler, *Children of Brasstown*, remarkably closely.

10 A detailed examination of the material in the interviews on sib constellations in fact provides no support for Davies' hypothesis; nor, when critically examined, do the statistics in his *Images of Class*. See R. W. Connell, 'The Child's Construction of Politics', Ph.D. thesis, University of Sydney, 1969, 464–77, for details. It is only fair to say that neither of these studies has the kind of clinical detail that would be required to give Davies' ideas a thorough test.

11 For details of this study see W. F. Connell, R. E. Stroobant, K. E. Sinclair, R. W. Connell and K. W. Rogers, *12 to 20*, Sydney, Hicks Smith, 1975.

12 M. Weber, *Wirtschaft und Gesellschaft*, Köln, Kiepenhauer & Witsch, 1964, vol. 2, 681.

13 See Connell *et al.*, *12 to 20*, 281.

14 See especially L. Broom, F. L. Jones, and J. Zubrzycki, 'Five measures of social rank in Australia', paper presented to 6th World Congress of Sociology, Evian, 1966.

CHAPTER 8

(To avoid a great deal of repetition in the citation of surveys, the notes to this chapter normally omit studies referred to in the text but already cited.)

1 See the description of this survey in R. W. Connell, *The Child's Construction of Politics*, Melbourne, MUP, 1971.

2 G. Little, *The University Experience*, Melbourne, MUP, 1971.

3 W. F. Connell, R. E. Stroobant, K. E. Sinclair, R. W. Connell and K. W. Rogers, *12 to 20*, Sydney, Hicks Smith, 1975; R. Taft, 'The career aspirations of immigrant schoolchildren in Victoria', La Trobe Sociology Papers No. 12, 1975, and 'Aspirations of secondary school children of immigrant families in Victoria', *Education News*, 1975, vol. 15, 38–41; D. E. Edgar, 'Adolescent competence and sexual disadvantage', La Trobe Sociology Papers No. 10, 1974; M. J. Rosier, 'Some differences between Population II schools in Australia', IEA (Australia) Report 1972:4, and 'Home background

is major factor in school results', *School Bell*, 1973, vol. 28 no. 4, 10–11.

4 R. Wiseman, *A Study of Social Class Differences in Performance and Progress in a High School*, Adelaide, SAIT, 1967, 'Social class differences in school performance and progress', in F. M. Katz and R. K. Browne, ed., *Sociology of Education*, Melbourne, Macmillan, 1970, 223–33, and 'Secondary school and family background – a review of some recent Australian studies', *Australian Journal of Education*, 1970, vol. 14, 66–75; M. Balson, 'Culturally deprived children in Victorian schools', in Katz and Browne, *Sociology of Education*, 234–43, originally published in 1965 in the *Teacher's Journal*; T. Husen, ed., *International Study of Achievement in Mathematics*, Stockholm, Almqvist and Wiksell, 1967; J. P. Keeves, 'Approaches to the goal of educational equality', in J. V. D'Cruz and P. J. Sheehan, ed., *The Renewal of Australian Schools*, Richmond, Primary Education, 1975, 59–76, and 'The home, the school and achievement in mathematics and science', *Home Environment and School Study Report 1974:4*, Hawthorn, ACER, 1974.

5 P. Karmel *et al.*, *Education in South Australia*, Adelaide, Government Printer, 1971, chapter 14.

6 A. Everett, 'The anatomy of vocational preference and educational attainment in an industrial community', paper presented at ANZAAS conference, Perth, 1973.

7 D. K. Wheeler, 'Socio-economic status and the high school', *Australian Journal of Higher Education*, 1968, vol. 3, 119–25.

8 D. Toomey, 'Parents' preferences in secondary education: an Australian case', *Educational Sciences*, 1968, vol. 2, 141–9; F. J. Hunt, 'Father's occupation and the secondary school', *ANZ Journal of Sociology*, 1972, vol. 8, 174–83.

9 J. R. Prince, 'Religious and social attitudes in church and state schools in Western Australia', *Journal of Christian Education*, 1972, vol. 15, 34–55; R. Blandy and T. Goldsworthy, *Educational Opportunity in South Australia*, Adelaide, Flinders University, 1975, 82–4.

10 B. Choppin, 'Social class and educational achievement', *Educational Research*, 1967, vol. 10, 213–17. P. Hughes, 'The value of the IEA mathematics study', *International Review of Education*, 1969, vol. 15, 204–10, indicates differences between states in the sharpness of this selection.

11 W. C. Radford, *School Leavers in Australia, 1959–60*, Melbourne, ACER, 1962.

12 C. H. Fisher, J. S. Hagan, and P. R. de Lacey, 'High school retention rates and social class', *Australian Journal of Social Issues*, 1973, vol. 8, 221–6. K. R. McKinnon *et al.*, *Girls, School and Society*, Canberra, Schools Commission, 1975, 36.

13 W. E. Moore *et al.*, *In Loco Parentis*, quoted in P. Karmel *et al.*, *Schools in Australia*, Canberra, AGPS, 1973, 18.

14 R. Taft, 'Secondary scholarship holders in Victoria and their background', in D. E. Edgar, ed., *Sociology of Australian Education*, Sydney, McGraw-Hill, 1975, 14–25; F. J. Hunt, 'CSSE – and all that', *Education News*, 1973, vol. 14 (5 and 6), 30–4.

15 *Tertiary Education in Australia*, Report of the Commonwealth Committee on the Future of Tertiary Education in Australia, Canberra, Government Printer, 1964, vol. 1, 43.

16 W. C. Radford and R. E. Wilkes, *School Leavers in Australia 1971–1972*, Melbourne, ACER, 1975, 71–2.
17 K. L. Dow, L. D. Jones, and L. M. Osman, 'The social composition of students entering the University of Melbourne in 1969 and 1970', in R. J. W. Selleck, ed., *Melbourne Studies in Education 1972*, Melbourne, MUP, 1972, 92; M. B. Gilchrist and S. B. Hammond, 'University entrants and their non-entrant intellectual peers: A follow-up study of primary school boys', *Australian Journal of Psychology*, 1971, vol. 23, 317–33; N. F. Dufty, 'Entrance to tertiary education in Western Australia', *Australian Journal of Higher Education*, 1972, vol. 4, 235–52.
18 J. Champness and V. Taylor, 'Attitudes and motivation of students in an institute of technology', *Australian Journal of Advanced Education*, 1972, vol. 2 no. 5, 6–8.
19 J. I. Martin, 'Marriage, the family, and class', in A. P. Elkin, ed., *Marriage and the Family in Australia*, Sydney, Angus and Robertson, 1957, 24–53.
20 L. Broom and F. L. Jones, 'Father-to-son mobility: Australia in comparative perspective', *American Journal of Sociology*, 1969, vol. 74, 333–42. Compare the mobility table in Radford and Wilkes, *School Leavers*, 67.
21 G. W. Bassett, 'Doctors and their families', *Medical Journal of Australia*, 1961 vol. 1, 222–4; 'Some comparative aspects of the medical profession and teaching', *Australian Journal of Education*, 1963, vol. 7, 54–60.
22 J. D. Allingham, 'Class regression: an aspect of the social stratification process', *American Sociological Review*, 1967, vol. 32, 442–9, who studied birth and marriage records in the NSW Registrar-General's office. For the international comparisons, see F. L. Jones, 'Social stratification in Australia', *Social Science Information*, 1974, vol. 13, 99–118 and studies referred to there.
23 As is neatly shown in a little survey by P. Chopra, 'The drop-out phenomenon', in *Opportunity in Education*, Melbourne, Australian College of Education, 1968, 107–20.
24 See for instance *Recent Research on the I.Q. in New South Wales*, NSW Department of Education Division of Research and Planning, Research Bulletin No. 27.
25 The studies listed in Table 5 which have not yet been cited are: R. F. Porcheron, 'An investigation into the question of a social class bias in intelligence tests', *Forum of Education*, 1955, vol. 13, 117–28; T. G. Collins, 'An intelligence survey of Tasmanian school children', *Tasmanian Education*, 1950, vol. 5, 220–5; M. R. Middleton, 'Class and family (Part II)' in O. A. Oeser and S. B. Hammond, ed., *Social Structure and Personality in a City*, London, Routledge and Kegan Paul, 1954, 249–60; S. B. Hammond and F. N. Cox, 'Some antecedents of educational attainment', *Australian Journal of Psychology*, 1967, vol. 19, 231–40.
26 L. J. Kamin, *The Science and Politics of I.Q.*, Potomac, Lawrence Erlbaum, 1974, 1.
27 K. I. Lemercier and G. R. Teasdale, '"Sesame Street". Some effects of a television programme on the cognitive skills of young children from lower SES backgrounds', *Australian Psychologist*, 1973, vol. 8, 47–51.
28 B. Bernstein, *Class, Codes and Control*, vol. 1, London, Routledge and Kegan Paul, 1971.

29 E.g. A. T. Hird, 'Social vulnerability: the effect of cultural deprivation on the education of children', *Early Years*, 1974, vol. 1, 8–11.

30 J. Gunn, 'A study of pre-school language', *Australian Journal of Education*, 1963, vol. 7, 41–53; G. R. Teasdale and F. N. Katz, 'Psycholinguistic abilities of children from different ethnic and socio-economic backgrounds', *Australian Journal of Psychology*, 1968, vol. 20, 155–9; G. R. Teasdale, 'Environmental correlates of language retardation. Part II: an Australian study', *Australian Journal of Mental Retardation*, 1974 no. 4, 107–9; M. E. Poole, 'Social class differences in language predictability: written', *Australian Journal of Education*, 1973, vol. 17, 300–13, and 'Social class differences in code elaboration: a study of written communication at the tertiary level', *ANZ Journal of Sociology*, 1972, vol. 8, 46–55.

31 L. Owens, 'Syntax in children's written composition: relationships to socio-economic status and cognitive development', *English in Australia*, 1974, no. 29, 49–50. See the fuller report, 'Syntax in children's written composition, socio-economic status, and cognitive development', *Australian Journal of Education*, forthcoming.

32 Connell *et al.*, *12 to 20*, 131–3; P. R. de Lacey, 'A cross-cultural study of classificatory ability in Australia', *Journal of Cross-Cultural Psychology*, 1970, vol. 1, 293–304.

33 R. Taft, 'Predicting school examination results by tests of intelligence and creativity', *Australian Journal of Education*, 1967, vol. 11, 126–33; K. Dewing, 'Some correlates of creativity test performance in seventh grade children', *Australian Journal of Psychology*, 1970, vol. 22, 269–76. Dewing finds an apparent connection (unfortunately she only reports an ecological correlation) between creativity and class status, a result that should certainly be pursued.

34 See e.g. Hird, 'Social vulnerability'; P. Musgrave, 'The family', in F. J. Hunt, ed., *Socialisation in Australia*, Sydney, Angus and Robertson, 1972, 151–2; P. Musgrave, 'Socialisation in Australian schools', *Quarterly Review of Australian Education*, 1973, vol. 6 no. 2.

35 D. Toomey, 'What causes educational disadvantage?', *ANZ Journal of Sociology*, 1974, vol. 10, 31–7.

36 The studies listed in these tables which have not yet been cited are: F. N. Cox, 'An assessment of the achievement behaviour system in children', *Child Development*, 1962, vol. 33, 907–16; F. M. Katz, 'The meaning of success: some differences in value systems of social classes', *Journal of Social Psychology*, 1964, vol. 62, 141–8; J. P. Keeves, *Educational Environment and Student Achievement*, Melbourne, ACER, 1972; J. Maddock, 'Orientation to learning: a study of organisational differentiation in attitudes', *ANZ Journal of Sociology*, 1975, vol. 11, 62–4; A. Vinson and A. Robinson, 'Educational opportunities and social mobility', *Australian Quarterly*, 1968, vol. 40 no. 4, 29–43; N. T. Feather, 'Values and income level', *Australian Journal of Psychology*, 1975, vol. 27, 23–9.

37 See M. Goot and R. W. Connell, *Social Patterns in Public Opinion*, forthcoming.

38 As is shown by the correlations, in surveys of adults, between level of education on the one hand and occupation and income on the

other. See Broom, Jones and Zubrzycki, *op. cit.*, and their 'Social stratification in Australia', in J. A. Jackson, ed., *Social Stratification*, Sociological Studies No. 1, CUP, 1968, 212–33.

39 J. O'Neill and J. Paterson, *The Cost of Free Education: Schools and Low Income Families*, Melbourne, Cheshire, 1968; T. Roper, *The Myth of Equality*, Melbourne, NUAUS, 1970, an excellent survey of the situation which covers many of the points raised in this chapter. See also the excellent short descriptions of inner-city schools by M. Knittel *et al.*, 'The way we live now', *Current Affairs Bulletin*, 1973, vol. 50 no. 4, 4–9.

40 J. J. Smolicz, 'On educational equality, Part II', *South Australian Education*, 1970 no. 7, 27–45.

41 R. Taft, 'The social grading of occupations in Australia', *British Journal of Sociology*, 1953, vol. 4, 181–7; N. F. Dufty, 'Occupational status, job satisfaction and levels of aspiration', *British Journal of Sociology*, 1960, vol. 11, 348–55; and on adults, A. A. Congalton, *Status and Prestige in Australia*, Melbourne, Cheshire, 1969. Dufty's findings throw a shadow of doubt on Congalton's.

42 S. D'Urso, 'Hidden realities within schooling', *Australian Journal of Social Issues*, 1974, vol. 9, 114.

43 See especially the findings in Connell *et al.*, *12 to 20*.

44 *Ibid.*, 277, 281.

45 Australian Sales Research Bureau, *Understanding Young People – 1966*, vol. 3, 19–20; D. K. Wheeler, 'Expressed wishes of adolescents still at school', *Australian Journal of Education*, 1961, vol. 5, 84–90; Little, *The University Experience* – the agreement is noted in J. I. Martin, 'Suburbia: community and network', in A. F. Davies and S. Encel, ed., *Australian Society*, 2nd ed., Melbourne, Cheshire, 1970, 331–2; E. Scott and K. Orr, 'Values in the secondary school – a Queensland enquiry. III. Research findings', *Journal of Christian Education*, 1967, vol. 10, 148.

46 Connell *et al.*, *12 to 20*, chapter 4.

47 *Ibid.*, 236; compare ASRB, *Understanding Young People*, 21–6. For a comprehensive recent survey of counter-cultural life in Australia see M. Smith and D. Crossley, *The Way Out*, Melbourne, Lansdowne, 1975.

48 For example, two generally careful sociologists, Broom and Jones, make this error in their article on 'Father-to-son mobility'. The interpretation can only be valid if one defines class in terms of families, as for instance Parsons and Schumpeter do. But this is hardly satisfactory as it rules out by definition the kind of question Cole asked in his *Studies in Class Structure* about changes in the link between class position and family membership, i.e. it rules out historical questions of real importance.

49 This point was suggested in a criticism of the earlier version of this chapter, for which I am obliged to D. Ashenden and B. Abbey.

50 See Gallup Polls 189 and 197 (ages 15–20, 14–21); Australian Sales Research Bureau, *Understanding Young People – 1966*, vol. 1, 5–6 (ages 16–25); A. F. Davies, 'The child's discovery of social class', *ANZ Journal of Sociology*, 1965, vol. 1, 21–37 (age 13); R. W. Connell, *Construction* (ages 5–16), and 'Patterns of social and political opinion among Sydney youth', *Australian Journal of Politics and History*, 1974, vol. 20, 176–85 (ages c. 12–20).

51 Connell *et al.*, *12 to 20*, 277: the question was specifically framed to

investigate this point. Here I disagree somewhat with Davies, who is
impressed with the fact that young adolescents can class themselves.
(Further evidence of adolescent self-classing, though for an older and
partially employed group, is given in the Department of
Immigration's *Survey of Youth in Victoria*, Canberra, Good
Neighbour Council and Department of Immigration, 1967, 152–62.)
Part of the trouble is the technique of measurement. When
adolescents are given a list of class names and asked to pick one,
they certainly do so. But when 'none' and 'can't tell' options are
offered, these are also popular. And when open-ended questions are
asked giving an opportunity for the expression of class-conscious
interpretations of politics, very little is found. Thus Middleton's
point that a class *frame of reference* is not present (or at least, is not
common) among school children, is still valid.

CHAPTER 9

1 The Public Library of NSW is bringing out a handsome series of
  reprints of the *Sydney Gazette*, with a useful historical introduction.
  The quotation is from the front page of the first issue, 5 March 1803.
2 For an account of some of these conflicts from the viewpoint of the
  most influential of nineteenth-century pressmen, see C. E. Sayers,
  David Syme, Melbourne, Cheshire, 1965.
3 For notes on the radical press of these various periods see G. Nadel,
  Australia's Colonial Culture, Cambridge Mass., Harvard UP, 1957;
  A. Summers, *Damned Whores and God's Police*, Ringwood, Penguin,
  1975, 349ff. and the sources cited there; D. J. Murphy, 'Henry
  Boote's papers', *Labor History*, 1968, no. 15, 71–3. An interesting
  exception to the general decline of labour papers is Jack Lang's
  Century. On the whole question now see H. J. Gibbney, *Labor
  in Print*, Canberra, ANU, 1975.
4 H. Mayer, *The Press in Australia*, Melbourne, Lansdowne, 1964,
  esp. chapters 9 and 10.
5 For the background of this survey, see W. F. Connell *et al.*, *12 to 20*,
  Sydney, Hicks Smith, 1975. Other sections of the paper were also
  asked about; these ones are selected only for purposes of
  comparison.
6 See e.g. J. Power, ed., *Politics in a Suburban Community*, Sydney,
  SUP, 1968, 144–8.
7 A. E. Mander, *Public Enemy the Press*, Melbourne, International
  Book Shop, 1944, 64.
8 B. Irving, 'The Nationalist Party, 1919–1930', unpublished thesis,
  Sydney, 1972; D. Aitkin, *The Country Party in New South Wales*,
  Canberra, ANU Press, 1972; K. West, *Power in the Liberal Party*,
  Melbourne, Cheshire, 1965.
9 A. Grenfell Price, 'The Emergency Committee of South Australia
  and the Origin of the Premiers' Plan 1931–2', manuscript in State
  Library of South Australia, 1483, 11–13 and 17.
10 Price, Address to Liberal Federation, 16 July 1931, SLSA, *loc. cit.*
11 This point is laboured because I want to stress the difference
  between this argument and those left-wing critiques of the press that
  make deliberate bias their main accusation: one easily demolished, as
  Mayer has shown, by pluralist arguments about the other fellow's
  bias. Deliberate bias does occur, but is not as basic and pervasive as
  these processes.

12 D. W. Rawson, 'Political violence in Australia', *Dissent*, nos. 22 and 23, surveys violence connected with formal politics, concluding it is all fairly peaceful. A useful counter to this line of argument has now been developed by G. Lewis, 'Violence in Australian history: the Queensland experience', *Meanjin*, 1974, vol. 33, 313–19.

13 A useful compilation of this line of criticism is R. J. Thomson, 'The effects of mass media on mental health in the community', *Mental Health in Australia*, 1965, vol. 1 no. 3, 33–40.

14 The classification derives from L. Broom, F. L. Jones and J. Zubrzycki, 'Social stratification in Australia', in J. A. Jackson, ed., *Social Stratification*, Cambridge, CUP, 1968, 212–33; the census figures are from F. L. Jones, 'Occupational change in Australia, 1911–66', *Indian Journal of Sociology*, 1971, vol. 11, 123–36.

15 See the NSW Bureau of Crime Statistics and Research *Statistical Reports* in 1973 and 1974.

16 These headings are all taken from one issue of *Daytime TV*, vol. 2 no. 2, July 1971.

17 R. Barthes, *Mythologies*, St Albans, Paladin, 1973, esp. the concluding essay 'Myth today'.

18 On this point I depart from Barthes, who stresses the multiplicity of signifiers. The marked stylization and restriction of them – of course connected to the pressure of work in media organizations – seems to me a typical feature and an important clue to what is going on.

19 H. Mayer and R. Curnow, 'Hunting the P.M.: 33 traits in search of a man', *Australian Quarterly*, 1968, vol. 40 no. 1, 7–32.

20 H. Marcuse, *One Dimensional Man*, Boston, Beacon Press, 1964.

21 Or romanticizes them, as in the celebrated radio serial 'Blue Hills' which deals sentimentally with the contingencies of farming.

CHAPTER 10

1 A. Gramsci, 'The southern question', in *The Modern Prince and Other Writings*, NY, International Publishers, 1957, 28–51.

2 From a substantial literature, see especially W. Reich, *The Mass Psychology of Fascism*, the current edition being NY, Simon and Schuster, 1970; and H. Marcuse, *One Dimensional Man*, Boston, Beacon, 1964.

3 L. Althusser, 'Ideology and ideological state apparatuses', in *Lenin and Philosophy*, London, NLB, 1971, 121–73.

4 For a useful summary of this debate see D. Rawson, *Labor in Vain?*, Melbourne, Longmans, 1966.

5 For the comparison of Hammond's and Davies' surveys see A. F. Davies, *Images of Class*, Sydney, SUP, 1967, 90–2. On the occupational polarization of the vote see D. Kemp, 'Social change and the future of political parties: the Australian case', in L. Maisel and P. M. Sacks, ed., *The Future of Political Parties*, Beverly Hills, Sage, 1975, 124–64; and of opinion, M. Goot and R. W. Connell, *Social Patterns in Public Opinion*, forthcoming.

6 But for an argument that they really did believe this, see G. Clark, *In Fear of China*, Melbourne, Lansdowne, 1967. There is a useful outline of the political struggle over the Vietnam commitment in H. S. Albinski, *Politics and Foreign Policy in Australia*, Durham, North Carolina, Duke UP, 1970.

7 Material on anti-communism in this critical period, discussed from markedly different perspectives, can be found in L. C. Webb,

Communism and Democracy in Australia, Melbourne, Cheshire, 1954; A. Davidson, *The Communist Party of Australia*, Stanford, Hoover Institution Press, 1969; R. Murray, *The Split*, Melbourne, Cheshire, 1970; B. A. Santamaria, *The Price of Freedom*, Melbourne, Campion Press, 1964.

8 An indication of their penetration (if the word can be used here) is that it was widespread among children in the 1960s. See R. W. Connell, *The Child's Construction of Politics*, Melbourne, MUP, 1971, chapter 5.

9 For illustration see the rape imagery in anti-Chinese cartoons such as the 1888 example (from a radical periodical) reprinted in J. Harris, *The Bitter Fight*, Brisbane, University of Queensland Press, 1970, 59. For a good, though now somewhat dated, illustration of how this kind of thing can be done with clinical histories see R. E. Renneker, 'Some psychodynamic aspects of voting behavior', in E. Burdick and A. J. Brodbeck, ed., *American Voting Behavior*, New York, Free Press, 1959, 399–413.

10 As is wittily shown by K. S. Inglis, 'Religious behaviour' in A. F. Davies and S. Encel, ed., *Australian Society*, Melbourne, Cheshire, 1965, 73f. For the White Cross League, see the Towns Papers, ML 1279/24 Item 1.

11 W. F. Connell, R. E. Stroobant, K. E. Sinclair, R. W. Connell, and K. W. Rogers, *12 to 20*, Sydney, Hicks Smith, 1975, 145.

12 This is not to imply that it is peculiar to capitalism, which would be absurd, but that it is important in it.

13 See the MA thesis by T. Rowse, Flinders University, 1976; P. White, 'The Season at Sarsaparilla', in *Four Plays*, Melbourne, Sun, 1967, 75–177. The argument is summed up in a well-known cartoon by Bruce Petty showing a suburbanite crying from his TV chair 'O life, where is thy sting?': see *The Best of Petty*, London, Horwitz, 1968.

14 For an interesting account of this cycle in Sydney, see M. Neutze, *People and Property in Redfern*, Canberra, ANU Urban Research Unit, 1973.

15 For the friend, see the episode in *Australian Home Beautiful*, April 1946, 8–11. The magazine was published by Herald and Weekly Times, the Melbourne-based newspaper chain, and served both as an advertising vehicle and general purpose booster for real estate, building, furnishing and related trades.

16 R. G. Menzies, *The Forgotten People*, Sydney, Angus and Robertson, 1943.

17 K. Hancock and K. Moore, 'The occupational wage structure in Australia since 1914', *British Journal of Industrial Relations*, 1972, vol. 10, 107–22 (compare H. Lydall, *The Structure of Earnings*, OUP, 1968, 190–1); S. Encel, 'Social implications of the Engineers' cases', *Journal of Industrial Relations*, 1964, vol. 6, 61–6; the employment of women is generally surveyed in S. Encel, N. MacKenzie and M. Tebbutt, *Women and Society*, Melbourne, Cheshire, 1974.

18 H. Wolfsohn, 'The ideology makers', *Dissent*, 1964, vol. 4 no. 2, 3–8.

19 S. G. Firth, 'Social values in the New South Wales primary school 1880–1914', in *Melbourne Studies in Education 1970*, Melbourne, MUP, 1970, 123–59; and for some samples of newspaper nationalism, L. L. Robson, *The First A.I.F.*, Melbourne, MUP, 1970.

20 For illustration of emergent changes, and some further analysis along these lines, see *Inside Welfare*, Revolutionary Welfare Workers Working Papers No. 1, Brisbane, 1975.

21 A. Barcan, *The Socialist Left in Australia 1949–1959*, Sydney, APSA Monograph no. 2, 1960; R. J. Cahill, *Notes on the New Left in Australia*, Sydney, Australian Marxist Research Foundation, n.d. (1969); R. Gordon, ed., *The Australian New Left*, Melbourne, Heinemann, 1970.

22 The most comprehensive guide to this movement is M. Smith and D. Crossley, ed., *The Way Out*, Melbourne, Lansdowne, 1975.